PLACE AND PROGRESS IN THE WORKS OF ELIZABETH GASKELL

Critical assessments of Elizabeth Gaskell have tended to emphasize the regional and provincial aspects of her writing, but the scope of her influence extended across the globe. Building on theories of space and place, the contributors to this collection bring a variety of geographical, industrial, psychological, and spatial perspectives to bear on the vast range of Gaskell's literary output and on her place within the narrative of British letters and national identity. The advent of the railway and the increasing predominance of manufactory machinery reoriented the nation's physical and social countenance, but alongside the excitement of progress and industry was a sense of fear and loss manifested through an idealization of the country home, the pastoral retreat, and the agricultural south. In keeping with the theme of progress and change, the essays follow parallel narratives that acknowledge both the angst and nostalgia produced by industrial progress and the excitement and awe occasioned by the potential of the empire. Finally, the volume engages with adaptation and cultural performance, in keeping with the continuing importance of Gaskell in contemporary popular culture far beyond the historical and cultural environs of nineteenth-century Manchester.

This collection is dedicated to the British Women Writers Association.

Place and Progress in the Works of Elizabeth Gaskell

Edited by

LESA SCHOLL
Emmanuel College, University of Queensland

EMILY MORRIS
St. Thomas More College, University of Saskatchewan

and

SARINA GRUVER MOORE
Calvin College, Grand Rapids, Michigan

ASHGATE

Published by
Ashgate Publishing Limited
Wey Court East
Union Road
Farnham
Surrey, GU9 7PT
England

Ashgate Publishing Company
110 Cherry Street
Suite 3-1
Burlington, VT 05401-3818
USA

www.ashgate.com

British Library Cataloguing in Publication Data
A catalogue record for this book is available from the British Library

The Library of Congress has cataloged the printed edition as follows:
Place and progress in the works of Elizabeth Gaskell / edited by Lesa Scholl, Emily
    Morris, and Sarina Gruver Moore.
    pages cm
  Includes bibliographical references and index.
  ISBN 978-1-4724-2963-6 (hardcover: alk. paper) — ISBN 978-1-4724-2964-3 (ebook)
  — ISBN 978-1-4724-2965-0 (epub)
  1. Gaskell, Elizabeth Cleghorn, 1810–1865—Criticism and interpretation. 2. Place
(Philosophy) in literature. 3. Progress in literature. I. Scholl, Lesa, editor. II. Morris, Emily,
1979– editor. III. Moore, Sarina Gruver, editor.
  PR4711.P57 2015
  823'.8—dc23

                                                                        2014039124

ISBN: 9781472429636 (hbk)
ISBN: 9781472429643 (ebk – PDF)
ISBN: 9781472429650 (ebk – ePUB)

Printed in the United Kingdom by Henry Ling Limited,
at the Dorset Press, Dorchester, DT1 1HD

Contents

List of Figures

Notes on Contributors

Sophia Andres is Professor of English, Kathlyn Cosper Dunagan Professor in the Humanities, and Chair of the Department of Literature and Languages at the University of Texas of the Permian Basin where she teaches Romantic literature, Victorian literature and art, Literature and Mythology, as well as modern and postmodern British fiction. Her work has appeared in several journals and books including the following: *ELH, Journal of Narrative Technique, Journal of Narrative Theory, Victorians Institute Journal, Victorian Newsletter, Clio, George Eliot—George Henry Lewes Studies, Journal of Pre-Raphaelite Studies*. Her recent book, *The Pre-Raphaelite Art of the Victorian Novel: Narrative Challenges to Visual Gendered Boundaries* (2005), was published by Ohio State University Press and was awarded the 2006 South Central Modern Language Association Book Award. She is currently working on a book tentatively entitled *Poetry in Painting*.

Divya Athmanathan obtained her Master of Studies degree from the University of Oxford, the U.K. She completed her PhD at Nanyang Technological University (NTU) in Singapore. Her doctoral dissertation is titled *Courtship and Spatiality in Nineteenth-Century English Novels*. She is currently a postdoctoral teaching fellow in the faculty of the humanities, arts, and social sciences at Singapore University of Technology and Design (SUTD).

Josie Billington is a specialist in Victorian Literature in the School of English and Deputy Director of the Centre for Reading Research (CRILS) at University of Liverpool. She has published widely on nineteenth-century realism (Gaskell, George Eliot, Tolstoy) and on Victorian poetry. Publications include: *Faithful Realism* (2002), *Eliot's Middlemarch* (2008), *Elizabeth Barrett Browning and Shakespeare* (2012) and she was editor of Elizabeth Gaskell's *Wives and Daughters*, Vol. 10 of *The Complete Works of Elizabeth Gaskell* (2006). She is currently preparing an edition of Elizabeth Barrett Browning's poetry for Oxford University Press, a volume of Margaret Oliphant's novellas for Pickering & Chatto and the Connell Guide to *Jane Eyre*. She is a member of the academic board of The Gaskell Society.

Robert Burroughs is a Senior Lecturer at Leeds Metropolitan University. He received his PhD from Nottingham Trent University in 2007, and his research focuses on travel narratives, colonialism and ideas of slavery. He has published widely on naval narratives in nineteenth-century literature, including "Sailors and Slaves: 'The Poor Enslaved Tar' in Naval Reform and Nautical Melodrama" (*JVC* 16.3, 2011) and his monograph, *Travel Writing and Atrocities: Eyewitness Accounts of Colonialism in the Congo, Angola, and the Putumayo* (Routledge, 2010).

Julia McCord Chavez is an Assistant Professor at Saint Martin's University, Washington. She received her PhD from the University of Wisconsin-Madison in 2008, and her research interests include nineteenth-century British literature, novel studies, transatlantic literature, gender studies, and print culture. She has published several peer-reviewed articles and book chapters, and is currently working on a monograph, *Victorian Wanderers and the Serial Form*.

Emily K. Cody is a PhD candidate at the Ohio State University–Columbus, being supervised by Robyn R. Warhol. She has presented conference and colloquium papers on Charles Dickens and Elizabeth Gaskell.

Katherine Inglis is a Chancellor's Fellow in Medical Humanities at the University of Edinburgh. She received her PhD from Birkbeck College, University of London, in 2009. Her research interests lie in fiction of the long nineteenth century, the development of medical humanities, and cultural perceptions of book destruction and censorship. Inglis's doctoral research examined the operation of the material culture of science and medicine in the fiction of James Hogg, Charlotte Brontë and Charles Dickens. Her current research project explores the medical rhetoric of book destruction, with a particular focus on the discourse of contagion, sanitary reform, and eugenics.

Anna Koustinoudi received a BA, MA and PhD in English Literature and Culture from Aristotle University (School of English), where, as an adjunct faculty member, she has taught a number of literary courses and Computer Literacy and Research Methods. Her research interests and publications focus on nineteenth-century prose, especially on Victorian women's novelistic production, as well as on gender theory in combination with psychoanalytic and narrative theory. Her work has appeared in *Gramma: Journal of Theory and Criticism*, *College Literature*, *The Gaskell Journal* and *Gothic Studies*. Her monograph titled *The Split Subject of Narration in Elizabeth Gaskell's First-Person Fiction* was published in 2011 by Lexington Books.

Kathryn Levitan is an Assistant Professor of History at the College of William and Mary. She specializes in modern British and European history, with an emphasis on nineteenth-century Britain and the British empire. Her monograph *A Cultural History of the British Census: Envisioning the Multitude in the Nineteenth Century* has recently been published in the *Palgrave Studies in Cultural and Intellectual History* series (Palgrave Macmillan, 2011). She holds a PhD from the University of Chicago (2006).

Amy L. Montz is an Assistant Professor of English at the University of Southern Indiana. Her research interests centre on ideas of materiality, the body and hunger in literature, and she has published several peer-reviewed articles across Victorian and Neo-Victorian contexts.

Sarina Gruver Moore is a Visiting Assistant Professor of English at Calvin College, where she teaches British literature of the long nineteenth century and advanced academic and professional writing. Her research interests include the relationship of architecture and texts, Victorian urban lived experience, and pedagogical theory. She has published on Gaskell and is currently at work on a monograph entitled *Gaskell's Urban Imagination*. She holds a PhD in English Literature from the University of Virginia (2011).

Emily Morris teaches literature and composition at St. Thomas More College at the University of Saskatchewan, as well as acting as an editorial assistant for *Women's Writing* journal. Her doctoral dissertation (Saskatchewan, 2010) examines issues of gender and agency in the works of Elizabeth Gaskell. She has published in *The Gaskell Journal* on "Lizzie Leigh" and in *Brontë Studies* on Gaskell's *The Life of Charlotte Brontë*, and is currently working on Gaskell's negotiations of violence and humor in *Cranford* for an anthology compiled by Mitsuharu Matsuoka of Nagoya University, Japan.

Mary Mullen received her PhD from the University of Wisconsin-Madison in 2011. Her doctoral research examined narrative and history in nineteenth-century English and Irish novels. She has derived several peer-reviewed publications from this work, and is currently revising her thesis into a monograph.

Charalampos Passalis (Aristotle University) is a folklorist, currently employed as a teacher of Ancient and Modern Greek Language and Literature at the Intercultural School of Evosmos–Thessaloniki (Greece) and as a Researcher at the Centre for the Greek Language – Department of Greek Medieval Lexicography (Thessaloniki) since 1998. He is a member of the compiling team for the Dictionary of Medieval Vulgar Greek Literature 1100–1669, vols 15 (2003) and 16 (2006), 17 (2011), 18 (in press) published by the Centre for the Greek Language, Thessaloniki. Personal research interests mainly focus on vernacular folk literature and tradition as well as on the magico-religious system of Greek traditional culture.

Lesa Scholl is Dean of Academic Studies at Emmanuel College, University of Queensland. She has a PhD from Birkbeck College, University of London. Her research interests include roles of translation and adaptation in literature and cultural history, and her current project looks at representations of hunger in the long nineteenth century. She has published mainly on mid-nineteenth-century writers, including her monograph, *Translation, Authorship and the Victorian Professional Woman: Charlotte Brontë, Harriet Martineau and George Eliot* (Ashgate, 2011).

Nóra Séllei is an Associate Professor at the Department of British Studies, University of Debrecen, Hungary. Her publications include *Katherine Mansfield and Virginia Woolf: A Personal and Professional Bond* (Peter Lang, 1996) and four monographs in Hungarian, published by the University of Debrecen Press:

one on nineteenth-century women writers (1999); one on twentieth-century women's autobiographies (2001); one on Hungarian feminist theory and criticism (2007); and one on the cultural (self-)reflexivity in Virginia Woolf's writings of the 1930s (2012). She has also edited and translated several books on feminism, as well as Jean Rhys's *Smile Please*, and Virginia Woolf's *Moments of Being* and *Three Guineas*. With June Waudby, she co-edited *She's Leaving Home: Women's Writing in English in a European Context* (Peter Lang, 2011).

Fariha Shaikh is a PhD candidate at King's College London. Her research focuses on material cultures of migration in nineteenth-century literature and art. She has presented papers at several international conferences relating to emigration, as well as papers on Elizabeth Gaskell.

Frances Twinn holds a PhD from Durham University on the landscapes in Elizabeth Gaskell's writing, having studied physical geography for her first degree at the University of Wales, Aberystwyth. Now retired, she taught geography at the secondary level and remains a Senior Examiner for the subject. She has edited the *Gaskell Journal*, has published several articles on Elizabeth Gaskell, and chairs the London meetings of the Gaskell Society. Her current research interest focuses on meteorology in Gaskell's writings and she is also interested in pursuing research into the commodity culture in both Gaskell's life and writing.

Acknowledgements

This collection was birthed out of a timely encounter at an international conference. *Landmarks*, the 2012 British Women's Writers Conference in Boulder, Colorado, was the 20th anniversary of the BWWC, and it attracted, as always, colleagues from across the globe. In that spirit, when we planned this project, we deliberately sought contributors from across the world. We are excited to see the diversity of work being produced on Gaskell, even within the scope of the concerns that tie this work together: the importance of place and progress in Gaskell's outward social vision.

Also in the spirit of an anniversary conference, we chose to plan this volume to coincide with the 150th anniversary of Gaskell's death. These markers of time are noteworthy in our rapidly changing world, the pace of which resembles more than a little that Victorian whirl in which Gaskell herself lived. Many of the essays in this collection express at least implicitly the need for measured time and reflection within the changing landscape. We feel privileged to have had the time to work with such dedicated scholars on this project.

We are grateful for the support we have received from our institutions and colleagues in completing this work—Emmanuel College, St. Thomas More College, and Calvin College—and that of our colleagues and friends in the Gaskell Society and the BWWA. In particular, we thank Professor Jill Heydt-Stevenson, Kelli Towers Jasper, and Kirsty Leuner, who organized the conference in Boulder that inspired us. We have received ongoing encouragement and support from Professor Lisa Vargo and Professor Jennifer Holberg, and technical assistance with graphics from Emma Muller. Special thanks, too, to Professor Pamela Corpron Parker for her involvement in this project and her ongoing support.

We are indebted to Ann Donahue and the team at Ashgate for their commitment to this project and making the process so smooth-sailing. Our readers have been generous and supportive throughout, and we have truly enjoyed working with Ashgate.

Thanks to the Royal Collection Trust, the Birmingham Museums, the Minneapolis Institute of Arts, Tate Images, Bridgeman Images, and the Bridgeman Art Library International for granting permission to reproduce images in this volume.

Introduction
Placing Gaskell

Sarina Moore, Emily Morris, and Lesa Scholl

Elizabeth Gaskell's life was shaped by the places in which she lived and loved—places for which she longed, but also sometimes longed to leave. From her childhood in the pastoral idyll of Knutsford, to her busy life as wife, mother, and writer in the sooty world of industrial Manchester, to her various escapes to the seaside, the country, and the Continent, Gaskell understood her identity in relation to the places she experienced. Her letters reveal curiosity about the emotional tenor of a location, or its potential as a site of authorship, or its folkloric traditions and oral history. But Gaskell's interest in place is not limited to those of which she had first-hand experience; she expanded her world, for example, through questioning American friends about the differences between the new and old world, and reading everything she could on colonial India when her daughter's fiancé was posted there. Moreover, Gaskell worked to shape her own spaces and places. Her great plan of buying a retirement home in the country away from Manchester, carried out just before she died and without the knowledge of her husband, speaks to her insistence on finally determining her own place, her own physical home. The house at Alton was also meant as a permanent home for Gaskell's two unmarried daughters, underscoring the importance of providing a place for the traditionally out-of-place spinster.

In one of Gaskell's most quoted letters, she speaks of her many "mes"—the different roles and priorities she has as "a true Christian (only people call her a socialist and communist)," a "wife and mother," and another "self with a full taste for beauty & convenience," wondering how she will "reconcile all these warring members" (*Letters* 69). The categories that Gaskell herself identified—religion, domesticity, and localized aesthetics—became the categories through which critics viewed her literary output as similarly split. After her death in 1865, Gaskell was for a long time ignored by the kind of critical scrutiny that contemporaries like Dickens, Eliot, and the Brontës enjoyed; rather, her works were often brushed aside or damned with the faint praise of being perfect examples of either "feminine" or "provincial" writing. In his *Early Victorian Novelists* (1934), David Cecil's evaluation of "Mrs. Gaskell" epitomizes this kind of reading: "Gladly forgetful of weakness and imperfection, we linger for hours in the lavender-scented atmosphere of her quiet, artless, narrow world" (208). In the 1950s and 1960s, however, 100 years after her death, Gaskell's work finally began to receive serious critical attention from socialist critics.[1] This recognition blossomed into further examination over the next few decades, most of which focused on feminist readings of Gaskell. Coral Lansbury's *Elizabeth Gaskell* (1984), Patsy Stoneman's *Elizabeth Gaskell* (1987), and Deirdre d'Albertis's *Dissembling Fictions* (1999) began to suggest an overall coherence in Gaskell's work that had hitherto been ignored. This wave of feminist scholarship was quickly followed by materialist expositions such as Hilary Schor's *Scheherazade in the Marketplace* (1992) and Linda Hughes and Michael Lund's *Victorian Publishing and Mrs. Gaskell's Work* (1999). These readings of Gaskell in her domestic, professional, artistic, and intellectual worlds sought to expand understandings of Gaskell's accomplishments, artistic and otherwise, and reconcile those many "mes" as useful components in her creative vision and production. Building on these readings, recent academic work on Gaskell has been able to move beyond the resurrection of her reputation to explore, analyze, and theorize from an established sense of Gaskell's importance.[2]

Our organizing principle in this volume of place as central to understanding Gaskell's work is in some respects not a new one. It might in fact be seen as one of the culprits of the previous critical fracturing of Gaskell's work into categories such as "industrial" (versus "rural"), or "provincial" (versus "cosmopolitan"). Yet it is also arguably one of the first means by which Gaskell's work was taken seriously as a coherent whole; studies such as Edgar Wright's *Mrs. Gaskell: The Basis for Reassessment* (1965), W.A. Craik's *Elizabeth Gaskell and the English Provincial Novel* (1975), and John Lucas's *The Literature of Change: Studies in the Nineteenth-Century Provincial Novel* (1977) argue that the provincial settings and perspectives of Gaskell's works provide a critical counterpoint against the impulse to regard London as the central and only vantage point from which to view Britain. More significantly, while Gaskell's novels are set in different places—the industrial North, the pastoral village, the working seaside town—together they are about the importance of place itself and, specifically, they are about the phenomenon of moving between places as a means to progress—culturally, intellectually, and often economically. Far from being solely concerned with the parochial, Gaskell is a writer with global concerns—moving from place to place within narratives as fluidly as in her own life.

The interdisciplinary approach of our collection reinvigorates the longstanding discussion of place in Gaskell's work. With its focus on a variety of geographical, industrial, psychological, and spatial perspectives, *Place and Progress* expands our vision of Gaskell's work and Gaskell's position within the narrative of

---

[1]   Kathleen Tillotson in *Novels of the Eighteen-Forties* (1952), Arnold Kettle in "The Early Victorian Social Problem Novel" (1958), and Raymond Williams in *Culture and Society, 1780–1950* (1983) included her industrial or condition-of-England novels in their studies of the genre.

[2]   See Jill Matus, ed., *The Cambridge Companion to Elizabeth Gaskell* (2007); Sandro Jung, ed. *Elizabeth Gaskell, Victorian Culture and the Art of Fiction* (2010); and Francesco Marroni, Renzo D'Agnillo, and Massimo Verzella, eds, *Elizabeth Gaskell and the Art of the Short Story* (2011).

British letters and national identity. The various theoretical and methodological lenses of the essays stand against a purely parochial construction of place that has sometimes dominated Gaskell scholarship, emphasizing instead Benedict Anderson's "imagined communities" and experiential perspectives on space and place in human geography. While not ignoring the "homes and haunts" or regional literature tradition, these essays explore Gaskell's understanding and creation of space and place through postcolonial, topographic, phenomenological, ethnographic, and materialist readings, enlarging previous understandings of Gaskell's worldview, her position as a literary figure, and broader cultural constructions of place and space. We link these concepts of place with Victorian ideas of progress and personhood. In doing so, we acknowledge the reality of technological changes occurring during Gaskell's era as central to contemporary understandings of place and identity—the effect of the burgeoning rail industry and the consequent ease with which people became geographically mobile being one obvious example. This collection also recognizes how closely place is associated with constructions of identity and intertwined with ideas of profession, class, gender, colonization, and other categories by which people negotiate values. These essays make connections between technological progress and social progress and their influence on geographical, imaginative, psychological, and emotional spaces, suggesting the importance of rereading place in Gaskell and in reevaluating the category itself, from local to global, from static, nostalgic and narrow, to fluid, complex, and open. We take seriously Lefebvre's fundamental insight that space is always a production of social forces, a confluence of the perceived, the conceived, and the lived. This multifaceted nature of Gaskell's narrative spaces, in no small measure, makes her work and her life worthy of our attention.

Home Geographies

Concepts of home in the mid-Victorian period ranged from the private domestic space to the identity of the nation and, by extension, the empire. Within the empire, oceanic borders simultaneously created disruption and connection. With reference primarily to *Sylvia's Lovers* (1863) and *Ruth* (1853), Rob Burroughs identifies the waterfront as a neglected place in Victorian studies, one in which local, national, and international encounters were makers of culture and identity. Burroughs situates the disruptions and connections created on the coast within the broader social and cultural history of England's littoral regions in the mid-nineteenth century, while his discussion of the ways in which women attained some degree of remedial distance from the strictures of domesticity at the shore can also be read in relation to the changing domestic spaces that Gaskell explores in her more pastoral works. Nóra Séllei's chapter, "The Humanizing Transformations of the Space of the Home in Gaskell's *Cranford*," takes up the possibility of self-contemplation with a similar sense of fluidity and change. Séllei argues that progression is made possible through the transformation of home spaces by opening up previously heavily regulated spaces, to a place of communication and encounter with the foreign Other. The repression and nostalgia that Séllei identifies are echoed in Divya Athmanathan's examination of the ideological hybridity of the Thornton home in *North and South* (1854–1855). Athmanathan theorizes the reconstruction of the home and nation in terms of overlapping spaces and interrelated cultural identities—a reconstruction that ultimately allows for individual, personal transformation. The spacial momentum and social innovation that Emily Cody identifies in *Mary Barton* (1848) further builds into a fluid notion of identity, and the inability to find concrete, stable, and constant foundations. Specifically, Cody challenges the notion that the Victorian ideal home was a concrete space, instead offering a text defined through the mobile, embodied space of the characters—the transient and fluid, yet still distinct shoreline of the self defining the contours of "home."

Mobility and Boundaries

By opening our collection with a focus on the waterfront, we extend the international scope for transportation, trauma, and progress beyond discussions of the advent and expansion of the railway in the mid-nineteenth century. Katherine Inglis's discussions of maritime language and the potential dangers of trade routes in "Unimagined Community and Disease in *Ruth*" builds on the anxiety of increased mobility, especially as that anxiety relates to the destruction of the heroine and the diseased social body. Fears of cultural contamination were prevalent in the era, and Inglis provocatively asserts that it is only through immobility and isolation that Ruth can achieve moral redemption in the novel. Ships might carry disease, but they also carried people, and, as Fariha Shaikh points out, emigration is a neglected aspect of Gaskell's writing. Shaikh's chapter shifts our focus from the possibility of importing and transmitting disease to the perils of emigrating—more specifically, the danger of the threat of exile and of not being able to return home.

Yet while Inglis and Shaikh focus on these perils of mobility, the possibility for cultural evolution and social adaptation through mobility cannot be ignored. Lesa Scholl's chapter, "Moving Between *North and South*," acknowledges Margaret Hale's personal sense of homelessness and displacement, but also positions the disruptive fluidity of the geographical spaces and the dislocation of the female body as indicative of the necessity of cultural hybridity for social progress, arrived at by adapting to the new industrial order. Scholl's reading is complemented by Mary Mullen's examination of the same text, focusing on the instrumentality of time: the speed with which characters move and social change takes place in *North and South* reflects the incessant, unforgiving pace of Victorian progress.

Literary and Imagined Spaces

Victorian social progress necessarily goes beyond technology and industry, as the changing physical and geographical world played a significant role in reshaping the ideological framework of the nation and empire. As national borders opened up—better transport leading to more trade, more travel—so too did conceptual pathways open to access other cultural perspectives that might challenge established understandings of the world. Gaskell was a self-conscious traveler who sought influence and inspiration abroad, but with a clear understanding of her home location. Kathrin Levitan notes that communication with home was central to travel, and as such, the postal services were key. Such services could be experienced as an extreme inconvenience when waiting for news, but they could also be experienced as a nostalgic return to a pre-industrial rural society, responses that illustrate shifting notions of leisure, geography, communication, and tourism in the age of cosmopolitan industrialization. Levitan's chapter reads Gaskell's letters as illuminating the ways in which she experienced her own geographic mobility and connection to community, with the speed of the railway being relevant not just to the transportation of people, but also the transportation of their missives home.

Gaskell's desire to explore and incorporate the foreign in her work also can be seen in "Modern Greek Songs" (1854). Through their ethnographic reading, Anna Koustinoudi and Charalampos Passalis provide a Greek perspective on the influence of Greek folklore on Gaskell's work, examining the amalgamation of national cultures in Gaskell's imagined space of Greece. Yet within her imaginative spaces, Gaskell also sought to convey the details of everyday life, creating the social realism for which she has been justly praised. Julia McCord Chavez argues that a "bifocal" reading strategy is needed in addressing Gaskell's realism: like the shifting borders of the waterfront, the shifting foci of realism—at once domestic and international—that Chavez identifies in *Wives and Daughters* (1865–1866) destabilizes the construction of social and imagined borders. Gaskell's rootedness in everyday life is also the focus of Josie Billington's chapter on realism, memory, and authorial agency. Billington argues that it is this very rootedness in the spatial-social world of provincial domesticity that allows Gaskell to achieve her masterworks. Extending her analysis to Gaskell's life-writing, Billington makes useful comparison to George Eliot's and Charlotte Brontë's representations of their own authorial activity.

Visual Spaces and Cultural Performance

Both geographical and ideological mobility radically affected the construction of Gaskell's literary world and her cultural legacy. The final section of the collection brings Gaskell's literary influence more broadly into cultural history through narratives of visual observation, connecting science, aesthetics, and what it means to perform within a given space. It therefore looks forward to contemporary adaptations of Gaskell's work and her continuing influence on cultural construction. By exploring the role of landscape meteorology in "Cousin Phyllis" (1864) and *Wives and Daughters*, Frances Twinn delivers a fresh reading of realism that brings together visual aesthetics and science. From a consciously aesthetic perspective, Sophia Andres examines the role of the temporal and spatial arts in *Ruth* and *Sylvia's Lovers*, providing a history of the painterly influences that formed Gaskell's artistic vision. Finally, epitomizing the overarching vision of this collection with regard to space and progress, Amy Montz's chapter on visual performativity juxtaposes the visual and the technological in her critique of the BBC film adaptation of *North and South* (2004). Montz argues that the conscious recognition of traveling into the Victorian past in this adaptation not only draws the audience into the narrative, but also speaks to the continued mobility of Gaskell's work. The past and present, both changing through acts of performance and adaptation, reveal Gaskell's ongoing yet evolving legacy.

New Popularity and Place

One hundred and fifty years after Gaskell's death her works are at the peak of their popularity, both in terms of the scholarly activity devoted to them and their appeal to the mass market. BBC adaptations of *Wives and Daughters* (1999), *North and South* (2004), and *Cranford* (2007) have brought new readers into the Gaskellian universe. The predominance of work on *North and South* in this volume speaks to the pervasive cultural impact of the 2004 mini-series. This timely sexification of Gaskell introduced her work into popular culture in an extraordinary way, but perhaps even more extraordinary is the way in which it has reinvigorated the scholarly imagination.

While the BBC has thus arguably established Gaskell's position in the popular imagination, the commemoration of the 200th anniversary of her birth with the dedication of a window in Poet's Corner in Westminster Abbey marked her official canonization in British literary history. In addition, with the Gaskell Society's acquisition of the Gaskells' Georgian home in Manchester—Plymouth Grove—the restoration of the home with funding from English Heritage (2009–2014), and the public re-opening of the home in spectacular, restored form just in time for the 150th anniversary of her death, the opportunity exists for Gaskell to become the focus of literary tourism to the same extent as Dickens, Austen, and the Brontës.

As Susan Hamilton points out in her essay "Gaskell Then and Now" (2007), the recent popularity of Gaskell's work in film adaptations and the corresponding renewed interest in her novels and her biography have meant that specific places, particularly Manchester, Knutsford, and Lancashire, have sought to claim her and her allegiances as a tourist attraction. Hamilton argues that through these jealous attachments of particular places to Gaskell, she has once again become "as divided a figure as ever she was in 1865" (189). By acknowledging the complexity and expansiveness of Gaskell's understanding of and interest in place, and its relationship to progress and identity, this collection recognizes Hamilton's claims, but suggests that rather than dividing her, the complexities of place create a new understanding of the coherence of Gaskell's life and work.

Works Cited

Anderson, Benedict. *Imagined Communities: Reflections on the Origin and Spread of Nationalism*. London: Verso, 2006. Print.

Cecil, David. *Early Victorian Novelists: Essays in Revaluation*. 1934. London: Collins, 1964. Print.

Craik, W.A. *Elizabeth Gaskell and the English Provincial Novel*. London: Methuen, 1975. Print.

d'Albertis, Deirdre. *Dissembling Fictions: Elizabeth Gaskell and the Victorian Social Text*. London: Palgrave, 1999. Print.

Gaskell, Elizabeth. *Letters of Mrs. Gaskell*. Ed. J.A.V. Chapple and Arthur Pollard. Cambridge, MA: Harvard UP, 1967. Print.

———. *The Works of Elizabeth Gaskell*. 10 vols. Ed. Joanne Shattock. London: Pickering & Chatto, 2005. Print.

Hamilton, Susan. "Gaskell Then and Now." *The Cambridge Companion to Elizabeth Gaskell*. Ed. Jill Matus. Cambridge: Cambridge UP, 2007. 178–91. Print.

Hughes, Linda, and Michael Lund. *Victorian Publishing and Mrs. Gaskell's Work*. Virginia: U of Virginia P, 1999. Print.

Jung, Sandro, ed. *Elizabeth Gaskell, Victorian Culture and the Art of Fiction: Essays for the Bicentenary*. Ghent: Academia Scientific, 2010. Print.

Kettle, Arnold. "The Early Victorian Social Problem Novel." *The Pelican Guide to English Literature* 6 (1958): 169–87.

Lansbury, Coral. *Elizabeth Gaskell*. Woodbridge, CT: Twayne, 1984. Print.

Lefebvre, Henri. *The Production of Urban Space*. Oxford: Blackwell, 1991. Print.

Lucas, John. *The Literature of Change: Studies in the Nineteenth-Century Provincial Novel*. Brighton: Harvester Press, 1977. Print.

Marroni, Francesco, Renzo D'Agnillo, and Massimo Verzella. *Elizabeth Gaskell and the Art of the Short Story*. Bern: Peter Lang, 2011. Print.

Matus, Jill, ed. *The Cambridge Companion to Elizabeth Gaskell*. Cambridge: Cambridge UP, 2007. Print.

———. "Trauma, Memory and the Railway Disaster." *Victorian Studies* 43.3 (2001): 413–36. Print.

Schor, Hilary. *Scheherazade in the Marketplace*. Oxford: Oxford UP, 1992. Print.

Stoneman, Patsy. *Elizabeth Gaskell*. Brighton: Harvester P, 1987. Print.

Tillotson, Kathleen. *Novels of the Eighteen-Forties*. Oxford: Oxford UP, 1952. Print.

Tuan, Yi-Fu. *Space and Place: The Perspective of Experience*. Minneapolis: U of Minnesota P, 1977. Print.

Wright, Edgar. *Mrs. Gaskell: The Basis for Reassessment*. London: Oxford UP, 1965. Print.

PART I
Home Geographies

Chapter 1
Gaskell on the Waterfront:
Leisure, Labor, and Maritime Space in the Mid-Nineteenth Century

Robert Burroughs

As a writer of place, Elizabeth Gaskell's critical and popular reputation is based on her fictions of the city, provincial town, and countryside. Coastal settings and seafaring characters nonetheless recur, albeit often in the margins, in both her novels and shorter fiction, and in *Sylvia's Lovers* (1863) the maritime sphere is central. Recent studies have examined *Sylvia's Lovers* and the mutiny subplot of *North and South* (1854–1855) in the context of eighteenth- and nineteenth-century naval history (d'Albertis, *Dissembling Fictions* 103–36; Peck 131–9; Morse; Lewis). On the whole, though, when critics note Gaskell's interest in sailors and the sea, they tend to do so in biographical terms of the nautical careers of male members of her immediate family—above all her elder brother, John Stevenson, a merchant seaman apparently lost at sea when she was 18. Whereas Gaskell is routinely credited with deliberate and conscientious examination of urban society and history, critics associate her writing of the maritime sphere with the realm of the personal, even the unconscious. Deirdre d'Albertis, for instance, writes that through the mysterious disappearance and remarkable return of sea voyagers "Gaskell sought to repair imaginatively a rupture in her own family that could never be healed, or—if the letters we possess are any indication—directly spoken of again" ("Life and Letters" 18; see also Bonaparte 29–30, 195–6; Hyde; Uglow 54).

The biographical line of criticism is helpful in identifying some of the personal reasons for Gaskell's literary preoccupation with mariners and their environs. It furthermore begins to detect Gaskell's understanding of the sea as liminal space, enabling deep, reflective thought away from the material transience of industrialized places. Even the sailor, as a figure of disappearance and return, is transitory in contrast to the waters on which he travels. Of course, such an understanding of the sea was not Gaskell's alone. Nor did it stem purely from her private, intuitive grief. It was rather informed by various long-standing cultural constructions of the sea, as well as more recent cultural and material developments. In this chapter I situate Gaskell's writing on the waterfront in the cultural history of seaside tourism in the mid-nineteenth century, of which Gaskell's own holiday experiences provide valuable illumination. I recall the social debates that attended the rise of the beach holiday and examine their particular significance for women.

Turning the spotlight away from the sailor-heroes, and onto the waterfront peoples and individuals they leave behind, I argue that in Gaskell's writing the waterfront shapes not only men's but also women's lives, its construction as liminal space enabling the latter to experience to some extent moments of self-contemplation, and even self-assertion, which are limited in other locales.

Gaskell's Sailors

Sailors abound in Gaskell's fiction. Yet whether it is Will Wilson in *Mary Barton* (1848), "Poor Peter" in *Cranford* (1853), Frederick Hale in *North and South*, Frank Wilson in "The Manchester Marriage" (1858), or Charley Kinraid in *Sylvia's Lovers*, they make sudden exits. They furthermore often make ill-fated or incomplete returns: Peter comes home late in life; Hale must live in exile; Frank and Kinraid return to find their lovers have seemingly abandoned them, and their former homes are alien to them. Suicide proves the only release for Frank. Seamen's romantic dispositions and melodramatic forms of self-expression push them to the margins of narratives in which more cerebral characterization takes precedence: Wilson's yarn-spinning and salt-water colloquialisms leave him humorously at odds with Job Legh (but give melodramatic eloquence to his testimony at his cousin's trial); the Byronic portrait of the mutineer Hale contrasts with his sober, pragmatic sister; Kinraid's melodramatic heroism is pitched against the tragic, self-abnegating emergence of Philip Hepburn as the hero in the final volume of *Sylvia's Lovers*. Seafaring exploits, moreover, are generally described in sailors' yarns or in textual fragments that lack the authority attributable to other characters' reported speeches, or the words of a narrator: Hale's mutiny, for example, recorded in biased newspaper reports that are glossed by his grieving mother, or Frank's account of his shipwreck. For all their magnetism, then, Gaskell's sailors are illusory heroes. Painted in romantic and melodramatic hues, they feel "unrealistic and outmoded," as Stefanie Markovits has said of Hale (480). If, as Patsy Stoneman argues, the domestic sphere is crucial to the formation of positive, nurturing masculine identity in Gaskell (esp. 50–53), then the mobility and consequent lack of belonging of these characters explains their peripheral status, stalling characterization, and fragmented narratives. The sailor returns home and experiences the uncanny, only to become an embodiment of the uncanny.

   The focus of Gaskell's maritime writing is the coastal society from which the traveler departs. As sailors disappear beyond the representational horizon, their communities and loved ones remain in narrative focus. It is significant, for example, that in a novel so concerned with labor exploitation as *Mary Barton* the reader learns almost nothing about maritime work. Rather, the emotional travails of seafarers' mothers such as Alice Wilson and Mrs. Sturgis receive attention. To some degree the absent mariner finds his way into the home and the main plot through the reminiscences of loved ones, but his function there is to highlight a lack or absence in the domestic realm. The upshot is that Gaskell, especially in her "condition-of-England" fictions, contributes to what Allan Sekula describes as "the forgetting of the sea" as a space of ongoing capitalist exchange in mid-nineteenth-century literature and art as the "condition of England" was defined in terrestrial terms (45–54).

Perhaps this concern with sailors' families and waterfront communities, rather than sailors' deep-sea journeys, explains why, with the exception of John Peck's *Maritime Fiction: Sailors and the Sea in British and American Novels, 1719–1917* (2001), studies of maritime literature and culture have said next to nothing about Gaskell. Research in this field continues to overlook cultural production at the water's edge. Indeed, in her efforts to read maritime literature on its own terms, not as allegories of society on dry-land, Margaret Cohen arguably under-emphasizes the importance of the littoral in many of the texts examined in *The Novel and the Sea* (2010). Concentrating upon the representation of seafaring "craft," Cohen's work and other new Oceanic studies of literature tend to recycle and expand upon long-established definitions and canons of "maritime literature," in which firsthand experiences of deep-sea voyaging are privileged. Inevitably the focus of this field is upon masculine perspectives, traditions, and societies. To comprehend what Gaskell offers to this field entails drawing upon the work of cultural historians such as Isaac Land and Paul A. Gilje that highlights the primacy of the waterfront as a space in which not only men but also women lived and worked with, and wrote about, the sea.

To the Seaside

In the years that Gaskell wrote, many of the British waterfront spaces to which she traveled were undergoing economic, social, and cultural change, as parts of the coast were transformed into places of recreation *par excellence.*[1] In the late eighteenth and early nineteenth centuries the main reason, besides work, for travel to the seaside had been curative, but while the health benefits of a beach holiday continued to be claimed in resort advertising in the middle of the 1800s, increasingly the coast was identified as a place for pleasure. The spread of the railways made the shore accessible to the growing number of urban dwellers, enabling the increase in middle-class tourism from around the 1840s.[2] The beach then promised release and refreshment to self-consciously industrious Victorians jaded by urban living. This recreational mobility was conceived of as an antidote to bounded, responsible, sometimes even dreary, existence in the home, yet the extent to which it genuinely afforded such a release is debatable. That the railway allowed holidaymakers to travel in greater numbers, more often, and for shorter

---

[1] See Walton; Hassan (31–42); Payne.

[2] This chapter confines its discussion to the middle-class demand that drove the expansion of seaside tourism in the mid-nineteenth century. For discussion of the increasing mid- to late-nineteenth-century demand for coastal recreation among the working classes, and anxious middle-class responses thereto, see Walton (25–40, 188–90). On the broader impact of the railways on British society, see the chapter in this volume by Lesa Scholl.

14   *Place and Progress in the Works of Elizabeth Gaskell*

spells—even day trips—is a clue that the coastal "getaway" was not immune to those forces of industrialization (massification, acceleration, standardization, routinization) that it was intended to evade. Moreover, the kinds of recreational escape that the beach offered were carefully delimited. Mid-nineteenth-century writings about coastal recreation warn against indolence by promoting amateur-scientific, antiquarian, and sporting activities alongside aesthetic appreciation of the sublime natural environment. Such pastimes were envisaged not only to keep middle-class minds healthily busy, but also to enable continuing spiritual development: beach-combing guides by Charles Kingsley and Phillip H. Gosse promoted "themes dear to contemporaries, such as the way the natural world revealed close connections between religion, science and art" (Hassan 32). They maintained the identification of the sea as a profound space, "as close an approximation of the infinite as the visible, physical world can provide," which Christopher Connery traces back to ancient times (508). Religious and aesthetic contemplation allowed for restfulness while nonetheless meeting the demand for self-improving activity.

John K. Walton finds, however, that while "improving" commentators stressed the need for robust and educative activity, "[m]ost middle-class holidaymakers in most mid-Victorian resorts spent their time on the beach, promenade and pier, surrounded by their children ... [M]ost of the time was devoted to the idleness which was deplored by the serious-minded" (166–7). On the typical middle-class family seaside holiday of the mid-nineteenth century, the mother and children would take extended leave at the coast with the paterfamilias joining them at weekends. Children would spend much of their time in the company of nannies (Walton 24). Domestic arrangements tended to be upheld. Walton comments that "perhaps the most important function of the seaside holiday was to display the stability and affluence of the Victorian middle-class family" (41). Even so, if Gaskell's experiences are at all representative, holidaying at the seaside afforded middle-class women some degree of remedial distance from the strictures of domesticity and thus a space for contemplation. Gaskell's personal correspondence offers glimpses of her particular balance of responsibilities, work, and amusement at the seaside. The Gaskells took several family holidays on the British coast, above all at Morecambe Bay on England's North-West shores. Gaskell writes anxiously on occasion of the need for a coastal holiday to replenish the health of her husband or one of her daughters. Of one trip, Gaskell states to her daughter, Marianne: "one object of our summer change is *health*."[3] Elsewhere, she writes of her forthcoming holiday with her daughters: "we shall remain for six weeks, and all get as strong as horses."[4] But the beach also was sought for pleasure. In personal correspondence she describes the fishing village of Silverdale—"a little dale running down to Morecambe Bay, with grey limestone rocks on all sides, which in the sun or moonlight, glisten like silver,"[5] which became the Gaskells'

[3]   Gaskell to Marianne Gaskell [? Late April 1852], in *Letters*, L120.
[4]   Gaskell to Charles Eliot Norton 10 [and 14] May 1858, in *Letters*, L394.
[5]   Gaskell to Lady Kay-Shuttleworth, 16 July [?1850], in *Letters*, L120.

"regular holiday home" (Uglow 146)—fondly, if condescendingly, as a primitive departure from modernity. Silverdale is described as "so wild a place" and "a charming primitive desert" that catered only for "the rudest and most primitive life you ever met with."[6] It provided chances for the children "to learn country interests, and ways of living and thinking."[7] It was furthermore a place in which her straight-laced husband was able to unwind.[8]

The Gaskells partook of typical Victorian seaside pastimes such as sightseeing, sketching, and walking. The company of one or more of her children, and sometimes their nannies, her husband, extended family, or friends, not to mention correspondence with absent loved ones and acquaintances, meant that for Elizabeth Gaskell domestic obligations were always in tow. Correspondence by Gaskell and her circle suggests the writer experienced similar struggles to find free time on holiday as at home (see Uglow, 164, 301–2). Nevertheless, the waterfront proved highly productive for Gaskell's writing. The early works "The Sexton's Hero" (1847) and "The Moorland Cottage" (1850) took inspiration from Silverdale. As its coastal settings and sea symbolism testify, much of *Ruth* was written, in the summer of 1852, in a Silverdale top-level drawing room with "views all round, of the coast and bays to the south, the open sea to the west and the hazy Lakeland mountains to the north and east" (Uglow 302). Famously, Gaskell undertook primary research in Whitby in late 1859 while conceiving of the work that would become *Sylvia's Lovers*. With the holiday-making industriousness often advised in Victorian guidebooks, she combined pleasure with work, taking her daughters on fact-finding and sight-seeing trips. When Gaskell faltered two-thirds of the way into writing *Sylvia's Lovers*, a trip to Silverdale got the book back on course (Uglow 481–5; 498).

The fiction itself most eloquently testifies to the importance of the sea and seaside in developing Gaskell's ideas about not only place, but also character, fate and circumstance, history, and indeed the novel form. As Hughes and Lund argue, the narrative structure of *Sylvia's Lovers* observes the rhythms of nature, including those of the sea. Kinraid's movements between presence and absence, life and death, reflect the ebb and flow of existence, the sea's cruelty as well as its power to renew (51–2; 64). I will proceed to demonstrate that besides upholding

---

[6]   Gaskell to Norton, 10 [and 14] May 1858, p. 504; Gaskell to F.J. Furnivall, 17 June 1858, in *Letters*, L399; Gaskell to Harriett Bright, June 22 [?1858], in *Further Letters*, 294–5. Silverdale was nonetheless always enjoyed, in contrast to one trying holiday at Sea Scale, West Cumbria, where severe weather made the rented accommodation feel rather too rickety. See Gaskell to Marianne Gaskell [?9 October 1857], in *Letters*, L376a.

[7]   Gaskell to Lady Kay-Shuttleworth, 16 July [?1850].

[8]   "Papa does not like the idea of having a *stranger* in the house in holiday time when you know he likes to play pranks, go cockling etc etc. and feel at liberty to say or do what he likes." Gaskell to Marianne Gaskell, 4 May 1852, in *Letters*, L122a. The fullest descriptions of the Gaskell holidays at Silverdale are in letters to Charles Eliot Norton, 10 [and 14] May 1858, and 25 July [1858], in *Letters*, L394 and L401 respectively; and to Harriett Bright, June 22 [?1858], in *Further Letters*.

the Victorian view of the sea as contemplative space, *Sylvia's Lovers* and other novels further resonate with the Victorian debates on appropriately industrious and self-improving forms of seaside leisure, and with notions of respite from city living. They do so in part by reflecting Gaskell's regard of coastal settlements such as Silverdale as rustic throwbacks to bygone days (a view that continues to inform tourist advertising of seaside holidays in northern England).

Besides representing the coast as a place apart from industrial development, this rustic depiction of the maritime sphere is also determined by, or perhaps informs, the historical setting of *Sylvia's Lovers*. The novel is set in the 1790s. Its historical perspective is made apparent throughout by the narrator's interjections, often to comment on cultural and social differences between the present from which the tale is narrated and the past that it describes. Finally, in the epilogue, the narrator is identified as a holidaymaker with antiquarian interests in the present-day Monkshaven, a fictional substitute for Whitby. *Sylvia's Lovers* thus revisits a narrative form first adopted by Gaskell in one of her earliest short stories, "The Sexton's Hero," in which a tale of Christian self-sacrifice on "the Sands" of Morecambe Bay is heard by two male tourists. In contrast to the narrator of *Sylvia's Lovers*, the framing interlocutors of "The Sexton's Hero" seem unmoved by the sexton's memories. The story ends abruptly as the tourists, "having rested sufficiently, rose up, and came away" (110). The reader learns little about the narrator of *Sylvia's Lovers* other than that her time on vacation has been spent (in comparable fashion to Gaskell's spell in Whitby) learning from locals the story of Sylvia, Philip and Kinraid. The narrator notes Sylvia's tale has been warped by "popular feeling" in such a way as to misrepresent the former as the typically unfaithful sailor's wife of melodramatic lore (502). As Marion Shaw argues in her authoritative studies of this novel, the narrator thus identifies her role as the realist chronicler of an otherwise forgotten woman's history ("Elizabeth Gaskell, Tennyson and the Fatal Return" 52–3; "*Sylvia's Lovers*").

While the novel seeks to recover the truth about Sylvia beyond "popular feeling," part of the complexity of *Sylvia's Lovers* arises from Gaskell's, or the narrator's, refusal simply to discredit the songs and chanteys, yarns, supernatural beliefs, dreams, and other cultural fabric through which Sylvia's story has been transformed. Instead, lore is understood as the means by which the people of Monkshaven reassert their values in spite of the broader imperialist and capitalist forces that endanger them, namely the Napoleonic Wars and the transformation of the Monkshaven economy. As a holiday-maker, the narrator of *Sylvia's Lovers* would appear to exist at an end-point in the economic developments that have transformed Monkshaven into "a rising bath place" (502). She potentially encapsulates the modernity that threatens to sever these coastal peoples from their history and culture. This narrator, however, embodies the conscientious mid-Victorian tourist, and this informs her narrative style. Rather than simply correcting the historical record, she converses with the locals, recovers fragments of the local culture, and weaves them into the narrative. Famously, in the refrain, "And the waves kept lapping on the shelving shore," which repeats (with small variations) throughout the final chapter, Gaskell knowingly returns the fiction of Phillip, Sylvia, and Kinraid to its roots in the psalms, hymns, and songs that once had roused the people.[9] The realism of *Sylvia's Lovers* is a fidelity to the Monkshaven people's understanding of reality, not a disinterested attempt to record observable reality.

The culture that Gaskell seeks to preserve in *Sylvia's Lovers* is one formed through its close and profound relation to the sea. As a sign of her closeness to and comprehension of Monkshaven society, the narrator too hears "the waves come lapping on the shelving shore" (502), a sound that is "the only enduring connexion" between the past and the present, but, as J.M. Rignall observes, "one that remains inscrutable, revealing nothing but the mutability and transience of mankind" (27). The unfathomable immensity of "the great deep" (14) is a perpetual reminder to Monkshaven society of the transience of the rise of modern trade in the town, and even of war—"that buying and selling, eating and marrying, even life and death, were not all the realities of existence" (64; see also 75, 213; Rignall 26). As her chosen husband and her father are taken from her in the fall-out of war, leaving her prey to the advances of her prosperous, shopkeeper cousin, Sylvia's fate is defined by historical circumstance. Communion with the sea provides her with sanctuary—to the point that her husband Philip develops a kind of hydrophobia, growing "jealous of [Sylvia's] love for the inanimate ocean" (360), which she associates with the lost Kinraid. While Sylvia's romantic understanding of Kinraid proves to be illusory, the novel does not undermine her or other characters' emotional investment in the sublime element with which he is associated. Rather, the sea is a powerful medium through which spiritual and other forms of restoration of the self are possible.

The Sea and the Self

After the final repetition of "the waves come lapping on the shelving shore," the narrator continues by quoting *Revelation*: "And so it will be until 'there shall be no more sea'" (502). In doing so, she recalls one of the key texts in the discursive construction of "the ocean as an antithetical element or object," as charted by Connery (494). The biblical text speaks prophetically of the new heaven and the new Earth, in which "there shall be no more sea." Gaskell's allusion to it is a reminder of the religious underpinnings of nineteenth-century travel to the sea for bodily and psychic reparation. Its vision of a new, or re-formed, physical realm—a space without boundaries—perhaps resonates with Gaskell because of her conception of the waterfront as a space for personal renewal, including women's discovery, or rediscovery, of their inner resources. Non-residents of the coast such as Mary Barton, Ruth Hilton, and Margaret Hale all join Sylvia in experiencing it as a site of personal reckoning, where past and present are brought into some kind of focus. "[T]he hard, echoing sands" and "the ceaseless murmur

---

[9]   For further analysis see Uglow 505–28, esp. 512–13.

of the salt sea waves" reflect Ruth Hilton's turmoil in her waterfront confrontation with Bellingham in *Ruth* (243). As with Mary Barton, whose turmoil regarding Jem's murder charge forces her to venture to Liverpool, culminating in a boat voyage up the Mersey, which leads to her physical and mental collapse, Ruth's very sanity will be tested by her foray to the coast. Ruth travels to the fictional Abermouth in her capacity as governess to the ailing Emma Bradshaw. There, she has an ill-starred reunion with Bellingham.[10] Both characters at this time assume false identities: to escape the stigma of her fallenness, Ruth passes as the widow Mrs. Denbigh, while Bellingham reinvents himself as Mr. Donne. The timeless, changeless sea stands in contrast to two social chameleons. Yet Ruth proves herself to be uncorrupted, rejecting Bellingham's proposal of marriage upon recognising that "to go back into sin" by returning to Bellingham would be a more "awful corruption" than "[t]he errors of my youth" (247). At this moment of self-understanding she is granted what Angus Easson identifies as a "Wordsworthian epiphany" (xx–xxi): a glorious sunset which renews her strength (250–51). The sea, the sun, and the God with which they enable closeness, are on Ruth's side.

Overseeing all on the earthly plain is the fisherman, Stephen Bromley, who watches Ruth and Bellingham from afar while tending to his nets. Ruth feels that despite his reputation as "a very desperate, violent man" (247), Bromley, who is known to her by name, will protect her from Bellingham's passion. As a minor character, Bromley is figured in appreciative if belittling terms as a representative of the briny but steadfast peoples that provided local color for visitors to the seaside. But he offers more to Ruth than mere color because of their implied kinship, which is established by the parallel between the fisherman's geographical marginality and Ruth's mental liminality. Bromley's minorness and his uncanny characterization (we learn almost nothing about him other than that he is knowable, predictable) is paradoxically the indicator of these unspoken bonds: as with Ruth, he has uncharted depths.

Time spent by the sea again leads to personal resolution in *North and South*. Throughout this novel, Margaret Hale plays a complex mediatory role in the transmission of ideas between ship and shore. She learns from her brother's mutiny on HMS *Russell* that "[l]oyalty and obedience to wisdom and justice are fine; but it is finer to defy arbitrary power, unjustly and cruelly used—not on behalf of ourselves, but on behalf of others more helpless" (127; see also 307). Margaret then applies this moral in lying to the police to protect the "helpless" Frederick, and in urging Thornton to become a wise and just master to end the conflict that threatens to embroil Milton-Northern. Yet it would be possible to overstate Frederick's influence upon Margaret. It is the latter, after all, who provides the most eloquent interpretations of the mutiny, including the above quotation. She is more evidently the author of Frederick's Byronic image than he is the inspiration for her actions. Moreover, Margaret reaches her key decision to return to Milton and work alongside Thornton during one of her own firsthand encounters with the sea.

---

[10] For further discussion of this journey see the chapter in this volume by Katherine Inglis.

In *North and South,* observes Hilary M. Schor, "the heroine need not leave England to attain her wider vision" (124). The vision that marks Margaret as a heroine is indeed reflected in her decisions not to travel—to Corfu, for instance, to visit Edith, as her father suggests (341)—and to remain ultimately committed to life in Milton. In these ways she contrasts positively with the decadent émigré Edith. And yet as Scholl explores in detail in this volume, Margaret does travel. Among her various journeys are two to England's coasts. Early in the novel, prior to arriving in Milton, she ventures to Heston with her parents; toward its conclusion she joins Aunt Shaw and the Lennoxes at Cromer. The positioning of these two journeys at opposite ends of the narrative is important to understanding their meanings for Margaret's character development. At Heston, Margaret feels and thinks little more than Mrs. Hale when the latter looks toward "the pleasure and delight of going to the seaside" (57). Heston provides her with little more than rest:

> There was a dreaminess in the rest, too, which made it still more perfect and luxurious to repose in. The distant sea, lapping the sandy shore with measured sound; the nearer cries of the donkey-boys; the unusual scenes moving before her like pictures, which she cared not in her laziness to have fully explained before they passed away; ... the white sail of a distant boat turning silver in some pale sunbeam:– it seemed as if she could dream her life away in such luxury of pensiveness, in which she made her present all in all, from not daring to think of the past, or wishing the contemplate the future. (65–6)

Historically, the waterfront had been the space in which maritime labor became visible to non-seafarers. It was then transformed by tourism into the space of recreational diversions from labor for the middle and working classes (Lencek and Bosker 129). Margaret's experience of Heston is testament to the modern tourist beach's ability to de-materialize experience and erase history, be it personal or social, in the promotion of indolent pleasure. Margaret joins "the ignoble army of idlers" whose (in)activities at the beach were but "the life-in-death in which thousands spend the golden weeks of summer," to the disdain of Kingsley (1, 2). The passage, then, records the difficulty for middle-class women restricted to tourist experience of the waterfront in perceiving such problems of labor at sea as Frederick encounters. As Rosemarie Bodenheimer writes, "Margaret's struggle to define her life is ... a battle against forms of idleness," to which women in this novel, more than men, are prey (63).

The passage describing Margaret's time at Heston contrasts with that at Cromer. Here, Margaret joins other heroines such as Ruth and Sylvia in reflecting upon the past, and deciding on the future, in the mental space she finds at the waterfront. Markovits likens the passage's romantic description of the sea's "eternal psalm" to Matthew Arnold's "Dover Beach" (1867), suggesting that the poem's retreat from a world-gone-mad into the security of interpersonal relations shares the direction of Gaskell's thought in *North and South* (490). This comparison helps establish the world-weariness of Margaret at this juncture in the narrative. As the passage develops, however, her agency is rekindled. While her relatives indulge in seaside pastimes, her time at Cromer "enabled Margaret to put events in their right places, as to origin and significance, both as regarded her past life and her future. Those hours by the sea-side were not lost, as any one might have seen who had the perception to read, or the care to understand, the look that Margaret's face was gradually acquiring" (*NS* 495). Edith is no such reader: she attributes the improvement in her cousin's appearance to the new bonnet that she has bought for her. The real reason for Margaret's awakening is that in her time by the sea she determines to reject Henry Lennox and the life of luxury that he offers in order to return to Milton. This spell leads Margaret to her much-quoted attempt "to settle that most difficult problem for women, how much was to be utterly merged in obedience to authority, and how much might be set apart for freedom in working" (497). In its concern with obedience and authority, Margaret's problem echoes the moral dilemma that she extracts from her brother's mutiny and extends to the Milton strike. And yet, especially in its suggestion of "freedom in working," this passage is illustrative of the tension between leisure and labor that concerned Victorian writing about the beach holiday, Gaskell's correspondence included. The novel moreover reveals a paradox at the heart of this tension, which is that pleasurable diversion from everyday responsibilities of work and status could lead to earnest contemplation of these very same aspects of social identity—a point which seems to be not far from the surface of each of the novels by Gaskell discussed above.

In her interpretation of *Sylvia's Lovers*, Shaw identifies the importance of the sea as the liminal space in which Sylvia comes to terms with her existence. In her own communion with the sea, an appreciation of its endlessly destructive and restorative motions, the narrator of *Sylvia's Lovers* comes to regard Sylvia's place—or absence—in history. In *Ruth* and *North and South* the water's edge is again a crucial space in which scrutiny of the self, nature, and questions of society and morality are brought productively to bear upon one another. These representations of the littoral might be seen to anticipate explorations in twentieth-century women's writing. Examples in fiction alone range from the modernism of Kate Chopin in *The Awakening* (1899), Katherine Mansfield in "At the Bay" (1922), Virginia Woolf (especially in *To the Lighthouse*, 1927), and Jean Rhys in *Wide Sargasso Sea* (1966), to the gothic melodrama of Daphne du Maurier, not least *Jamaica Inn* (1936) and *Rebecca* (1938). This relationship between Gaskell and later writers is complicated, however, for as I have shown, in Gaskell's time such deep, impressionistic thinking about the waterfront was closely tied to Christian constructions of the seaside as a space, which, in its sublime power, might aid contemplation of God's plan and the role of the individual within it. Gaskell moreover shares in the mid-Victorian association of sublime seaside experience with morally improving activity: for Ruth, Sylvia, and Margaret to gaze at what Joseph Conrad would later call "the mirror of the sea" provides but brief respite for lives lived in dutiful industriousness. "[F]reedom in working": Margaret's wish must have struck a chord with Gaskell, who wrote so productively while holidaying on the coast.

Works Cited

Arnold, Matthew. "Dover Beach." 1867. *The Poems of Matthew Arnold*. Ed. Kenneth Allott. London: Longman, 1965. Print.

Bodenheimer, Rosemarie. *The Politics of Story in Victorian Social Fiction*. Ithaca, London: Cornell UP, 1988. Print.

Bonaparte, Felicia. *The Gypsy-Bachelor of Manchester: The Life of Mrs. Gaskell's Demon*. Charlottesville: UP of Virginia, 1992. Print.

Chopin, Kate. *The Awakening*. Chicago: H.S. Stone, 1899. Print.

Cohen, Margaret. *The Novel and the Sea*. Princeton, NJ: Princeton UP, 2010. Print.

Connery, Christopher. "There was No More Sea: The Supersession of the Ocean, from the Bible to Cyberspace." *Journal of Historical Geography* 32 (2006): 494–511. Print.

Conrad, Joseph. *The Mirror of the Sea: Memories and Impressions*. London: Methuen, 1906. Print.

d'Albertis, Deirdre. *Dissembling Fictions: Elizabeth Gaskell and the Victorian Social Text*. New York: St. Martin's P, 1997. Print.

———. "The Life and Letters of E.C. Gaskell." *The Cambridge Companion to Elizabeth Gaskell*. Ed. Jill L. Matus. Cambridge: Cambridge UP, 2007. 10–26. Print.

du Maurier, Daphne. *Jamaica Inn*. 1936. London: Arrow, 1992. Print.

———. *Rebecca*. 1938. London: Arrow, 1992. Print.

Easson, Angus. Introduction. 1997. *Ruth*. Ed. Angus Easson. London: Penguin, 2004. vii–xxvi. Print.

Gaskell, Elizabeth. "Cranford." 1853. *Cranford and Other Stories*. Ed. John Chapple. Ware, Hertfordshire: Wordsworth, 2006. 23–184. Print.

———. *Further Letters of Mrs. Gaskell*. 2000. Ed. John Chapple and Alan Shelston. Manchester: Manchester UP, 2003. Print.

———. *The Letters of Mrs. Gaskell*. Ed. J.A.V. Chapple and Arthur Pollard. Manchester: Manchester UP, 1966. Print.

———. "The Manchester Marriage." 1858. *The Moorland Cottage and Other Stories*. Ed. Suzanne Lewis. Oxford: Oxford UP, 1995. 227–53. Print.

———. *Mary Barton*. 1848. Ed. Thomas Recchio. New York: Norton Critical Editions, 2008. Print.

———. "The Moorland Cottage." 1850. *The Moorland Cottage and Other Stories*. Ed. Suzanne Lewis. Oxford: Oxford UP, 1995. Print.

———. *North and South*. 1854–1855. London: Penguin, 1994. Print.

———. *Ruth*. 1853. Ed. Angus Easson. London: Penguin, 2004. Print.

———. "The Sexton's Hero." 1847. *The Moorland Cottage and Other Stories*. Ed. Suzanne Lewis. Oxford: Oxford UP, 1995. 101–10. Print.

———. *Sylvia's Lovers*. 1863. Ed. Andrew Sanders. Oxford: Oxford World's Classics, 1982. Print.

Gilje, Paul A. *Liberty on the Waterfront: American Maritime Culture in the Age of Revolution*. Philadelphia: U of Pennsylvania P, 2004. Print.

Gosse, Phillip H. *Tenby: A Sea-side Holiday*. London: John Van Voorst, 1856. Print.

Hassan, John. *The Seaside, Health and the Environment in England and Wales since 1800*. Aldershot: Ashgate, 2003. Print.

Hughes, Linda K., and Michael Lund. *Victorian Publishing and Mrs. Gaskell's Work*. Charlottesville: UP of Virginia, 1999. Print.

Hyde, William J. "'Poor Frederick' and 'Poor Peter': Elizabeth Gaskell's Fraternal Deviants." *GSJ* 9 (1995): 21–6. Print.

Kingsley, Charles. *Glaucus; or, The Wonders of the Shore*. 1855. Cambridge: Macmillan, 1859. Print.

Land, Isaac. "Review Essay: Tidal Waves: The New Coastal History." *Journal of Social History* 40.3 (2007): 731–43. Print.

Lencek, Lena, and Gideon Bosker. *The Beach: The History of Paradise on Earth*. New York: Viking, 1998. Print.

Lewis, Michael D. "Mutiny in the Public Sphere: Debating Naval Power in Parliament, the Press, and Gaskell's *North and South*." *Victorian Review* 36.1 (2010): 89–113. Print.

Mansfield, Katherine. "At the Bay." *The Garden Party, and Other Stories*. New York: Alfred A. Knopf, 1922. 1–58. Print.

Markovits, Stefanie. "*North and South*, East and West: Elizabeth Gaskell, the Crimean War, and the Condition of England." *Nineteenth-Century Literature* 59.4 (2005): 463–93. Print.

Morse, Deborah Denenholz. "Mutiny on the *Orion*: The Legacy of the *Hermione* Mutiny and the Politics of Nonviolent Protest in Elizabeth Gaskell's *North and South*." *Pirates and Mutineers of the Nineteenth Century: Swashbucklers and Swindlers*. Ed. Grace Moore. Farnham: Ashgate, 2001. 117–31. Print.

Payne, Christiana. "Seaside Visitors: Idlers, Thinkers and Patriots in Mid-nineteenth-century Britain." *Water, Leisure and Culture: European Historical Perspectives*. Ed. Susan C. Anderson and Bruce H. Tabb. Oxford: Berg, 2002. 87–104. Print.

Peck, John. *Maritime Fiction: Sailors and the Sea in British and American Novels, 1719–1917*. Basingstoke, Hampshire: Palgrave Macmillan, 2001. Print.

Rhys, Jean. *Wide Sargasso Sea*. 1966. Harmondsworth: Penguin, 1968. Print.

Rignall, J.M. "The Historical Double: *Waverley, Sylvia's Lovers, The Trumpet-Major*." *Essays in Criticism* 34.1 (1984): 14–32. Print.

Schor, Hilary M. *Scheherazade in the Marketplace: Elizabeth Gaskell and the Victorian Novel*. Oxford: Oxford UP, 1992. Print.

Shaw, Marion. "Elizabeth Gaskell, Tennyson, and the Fatal Return: *Sylvia's Lovers* and *Enoch Arden*." *GSJ* 9 (1995): 43–54. Print.

———. "*Sylvia's Lovers*, then and now." *GSJ* 18 (2004): 37–49. Print.

Stoneman, Patsy. *Elizabeth Gaskell*. Brighton: Harvester, 1987. Print.

Uglow, Jenny. *Elizabeth Gaskell: A Habit of Stories*. 1993. London: Faber and Faber, 1999. Print.

Walton, John K. *The English Seaside Resort: A Social History, 1750–1914*. Leicester: Leicester UP, 1983. Print.

Woolf, Virginia. *To the Lighthouse*. 1927. London: Hogarth, 1990. Print.

Chapter 2
The Humanizing Transformations of the Space of the Home in Gaskell's *Cranford*

Nóra Séllei

Elizabeth Gaskell was for a long time known as Charlotte Brontë's first biographer, but as feminist literary criticism recovered marginalized texts, Gaskell has become more and more acknowledged as a novelist in her own right. According to one of her first critics, Ellen Moers, Gaskell was "a careful student of Jane Austen's realism" (20). The question remains, though, as to how her realism is to be understood, and how a major component of (realist) fiction—space—functions in her work, particularly in *Cranford* (1851). Just as Austen was interpreted on the basis of the marriage-plot-based romance stories, utterly disregarding the ironic distance created by the narrator, which, in turn, disrupts the seamless surface of the narrative, in Gaskell's case, there are aspects in the mode of narration that disrupt the apparently self-contained and unproblematic fictional world.

A major means of this disruptive aspect of *Cranford* is how space functions in the text. *Cranford* is a text dominated and defined by its spaces, the focus of which is the home of the old maids living in the town, particularly that of Miss Matty. This space, however, undergoes a transformation: the apparent homeliness of the home is destabilized as a result of the appearance of memories and experiences that are uncontainable within given frames. The uncanny psychic content erupting from several characters breaks the seemingly seamless surfaces, and opens gaps and cracks in the structures. By encountering their own repressed otherness, sometimes as a result of meeting foreignness, and articulating their long-repressed desires and traumatic memories, Miss Matty and the other inhabitants of Cranford can break out of their restrictive narrative and social spaces and push their boundaries beyond a limited definition of femininity. What looks at first sight an Amazonian utopia, turns out to be a patriarchal dystopia, only to get transformed into an almost impossible (and as such, again utopistic) space of feminine empowerment.

The opening of the text makes the link between space, gender and subjectivity explicit by claiming that "[i]n the first place, Cranford is in possession of the Amazons" because "all the holders of houses above a certain rent are women" (1). This first sentence, however, with its apparently victorious overtone, is deceptive, and can be compared to the first sentence of Austen's *Pride and Prejudice* (1813). Whereas in Austen's case the famous opening covers the unadmittable logic of the marriage market where it is the young women who are in need of rich, marriageable men for a proper social survival, what the reader has to realize when reading *Cranford* is that the apparent self-possession and the homeliness of the home as stated in the opening sentence cannot be taken for granted; they are undermined by experiences that are uncontainable within the given linguistic, narrative, and social frames. Furthermore, the reader also realizes that homeliness and self-possession as indicated by the first sentences have never been characteristic of this fictional world: they are created only by a special linguistic code, "the phraseology of Cranford" (Gaskell 3), which is not dissimilar from the language of the Austenian novel of manners inasmuch as it tries to hide unutterable contents. The revelation of the psychic contents hidden by the code, however, does not simply disrupt the deceptive surface, but also helps the characters and the community to develop a more habitable and humane (narrative) space.

No matter how assertive and affirmative both Austen's and Gaskell's first sentences are, hiding and covering up by a special linguistic code is close to impossible. Classic realism, a category applied to Gaskell's texts, is characterized by Catherine Belsey as a mode of "ideological practice" in the sense that it "smooth[s] over contradiction in the construction of a position for the reader which is unified and knowing" (90). Belsey goes on to claim explicitly that "[c]lassic realism clearly conforms to the modality Benveniste calls *declarative*, imparting 'knowledge' to a reader whose position is thereby stabilized, through a privileged discourse which is to varying degrees invisible" (91). Based on this idea, one could easily assume that classic realism appeals to the reader in the way that it invites identification with the unified subject of the enunciation. Belsey, however, modifies this far too simple pattern, adding that the declarative and the interrogative texts "are in no sense self-contained and mutually exclusive, nor are their characteristics timelessly sealed within specific texts. More important, a different way of reading, a different critical approach can transfer a text from one modality to another" (91–2).

My interpretation in this chapter will transfer *Cranford* from a classic realist—and as such declarative—text to the interrogative modality, and point out that *Cranford* does not offer a unified subject position to the reader, due to both its narrative technique and to the construction of fictional spaces. I will argue this using primarily the Freudian notion of the uncanny that is present in the text—not only thematically inasmuch as the Cranford ladies are haunted by the memory of the long-repressed knowledge of what their lives could have been like, but also because the uncanny is present in the textual structure of *Cranford*. Whereas it looks a seamless text, I claim that the homeliness and security suggested by realism is regularly opened up by miraculous events that verge on the fantastic, or by elements of the crime story, revealing the hidden aspects of middle-class stability and propriety in a psychoanalytical way. The intrusion of the textual otherness of the fantastic, the miraculous and of the crime story opens up cracks and gaps both in the realist text and in the psychic spaces that, as a result, reveal their repressed otherness and, thus, provide a language, a literary code to represent what is unrepresentable within a seamless realist text.

A Self-Regulating Amazonia

Patsy Stoneman finds the space of *Cranford* problematic. Disagreeing with Nina Auerbach's celebratory claim that "the cooperative female community defeat the warrior world" (qtd. in Stoneman 91), Stoneman argues that although this community is "admirable, it is not triumphant. All it can do is to make the best of the *little space allowed it*" because "Miss Matty and the others have been diminished as human beings by the constraints of femininity," and in general she characterizes the state of these women as "stasis" (91, emphasis added). Although I fully agree with Stoneman that space is a key aspect of the text, and that the limited space functions both as an indicator of social and economic position and as a means of psychic repression, I can see a dynamism in the text, from stasis to opening up. As a consequence, the novel can be read as a process of psychoanalytical therapy for the characters. By encountering and articulating their long-repressed desires and traumatic memories (obviously related to Victorian sexual politics), Miss Matty and the other inhabitants of Cranford can break out of their dehumanized and dehumanizing repetitiveness in which the key word is "elegant economy," a state of deprivation, which is even celebrated by this community of spinsters as a desirable state. Thus, the text seems to proceed from repression through disruption and opening up towards an articulation and acceptance of desires, that is, towards the possibility of a more humane life story, which is also present in, and represented by, the transformation of the spaces of the home by opening it up from a heavily regulated space to a place of communication.

Cranford consists of a series of episodes and lacks linearity and a tightly woven, coherent plot, which originates in its inception. As Martin Dodsworth explains, the text began on the basis of two short stories published in Dickens's *Household Words* in 1851, and it was on Dickens's advice that Gaskell developed the stories into a novel (Dodsworth 132–3, 135).[1] Instead of being a narrative failure, however, in my reading the episodic quality is rather the source of the textual dynamism, with each episode following the same course: an extra-ordinary incident disrupts and endangers the repetitive routine in which these elderly ladies are entangled, but each incident functions as a step in their psychoanalytic healing process, a recovery from the trauma that is defined by Eileen Gillooly as an anxiety rooted in and "provoked by the conflict between self-denial and desire, between the internalized cultural demand to submit oneself to the role of daughter and a psychological resistance to that demand," which in itself is the source of humor in *Cranford* (890). The anxiety that is present at the beginning of the text, in spite of the apparently victorious opening sentence, gradually abates as a result of either formalized repetitive rituals to revisit the past and as such to come to terms with it, or one-time acts that help to alleviate the pain of irrecoverable loss and thus to restructure the psyche and the psychic spaces.

---

[1]   Hilary M. Schor points out an interesting aspect of the publication history of *Cranford*, first appearing in Dickens's magazine *Household Words*: it "began with an argument about his presence as author in the text. … at issue is a writer's presentation of self: Dickens thought it inappropriate that he appear by name in his own publication" (289).

Whether old letters, read in utmost privacy and intimacy; the visit to an old-time lover's home (or that lover's fatal trip to Paris); a kiss-like sound heard under the roof of the home; the performance of a foreign-looking conjuror; or the appearance of a brother long thought lost: all of the episodes, in their own sometimes tearfully humorous way, contribute to the emergence of a new sense of the space of the home, which can also be understood as a new sense of the self. All of these disturbing and at first sight disruptive elements, however, are rooted in the repressive emotional economy of this micro-community, embodied by Miss Matty's father, an avid reader and imitator of Dr. Johnson's stilted style, which serves as a repressive mechanism, excluding any form of impropriety ranging from simple (but slightly lower-class) marriage proposals, through letter writing formalities, to parodistic, sexually loaded, and as such transgressive, pantomimes in the front garden. The father's style—or rather Law—is continued by Deborah, the elder sister, who walks in the footsteps of the patriarchs, following their behavioral and linguistic code, which makes her both threatening and pathetic at the same time, because, as Hilary M. Schor argues:

> Part of what is so absurd about Deborah Jenkyns's writing is simply that it is in the wrong place: if she were an archdeacon and writing up charges, if she were, as her sister imagines, writing advice books, the Johnsonian sentences she can toss off so easily would not seem inappropriate or pompous. Women have no room for the grand style in their writing, for they never write anything grand. Literary daughters are not given the language they need: rather, they are given languages, often dead languages, which mediate their experience for them. (294)

The "dead language" that cannot mediate women's experiences functions in multiple ways in Cranford: literally as a linguistic code and, in a broader sense of the word, as behavioral code, too. At the beginning of the novel, space and time are more than limited as there are strict social rules and regulations concerning where, when, how, and for how long certain activities, especially social visiting, can take place, which is all the more paradoxical as visiting is the only socially acceptable pleasure allowed in this community. Nevertheless, there are set and intransgressable periods of time for calling hours ("from twelve to three"), for the time allowed between receiving and returning a call ("never let more than three days elapse") and for how long a visit may last ("you are never to stay longer than a quarter of an hour"); to the question of how to keep track of this quarter of an hour, Matty instructively responds to the narrator: "You must keep thinking about the time, my dear, and not allow yourself to forget it in conversation" and, as a result, "no absorbing subject was ever spoken about" (2), that is, nothing that would really engage any of the characters. These visits, of course, take place in the drawing room, the space of propriety, where even oranges become unseemly:

> When oranges came in, a curious proceeding was gone through. Miss Jenkyns did not like to cut the fruit; for, as she observed, the juice all ran out nobody knew where; sucking (only I think she used some more recondite word) was in fact the only way of enjoying oranges; but then there was the unpleasant

association with a ceremony frequently gone through by little babies; and so, after dessert, in orange season, Miss Jenkyns and Miss Matty used to rise up, possess themselves each of an orange in silence, and withdraw to the privacy of their own rooms to indulge in sucking oranges. (Gaskell 26)

The passage resonates with connotations of enjoyment and potentially sexual pleasure (evoking the first phase of sexual pleasure as defined by Freud: the oral pleasures of breastfeeding related to sucking), but the relegation of pleasure to the most private space of the house, together with the internalized self-control concerning the social visits, indicates the impossibility of relaxation and self-fulfillment in the social spaces of the text. Not coincidentally, on visiting her old-time suitor whom she could not marry due to her father's prohibition, Matty observes succinctly: "It is very pleasant dining with a bachelor ... I only hope it is not improper; so many pleasant things are!" (34). The text thus proceeds from prohibition, repression, and self-regulating inhibition toward a construction of a homely and habitable space that makes a less repressed subjectivity possible.

Public Spaces

Paradoxically, the decisive impetus for restructuring this psychic space comes not from the internal structure of the home, but from a public space, as if the traumas caused by paternal repression could not be worked through by the characters from the inside and by themselves only. What they have to go through is work indeed, in the psychoanalytical sense of the word. So as to restructure their own psyche—or psychic space—they have to encounter all those deeply buried, apparently obliterated and as such, non-existing and dead memories from which they have been trying to hide all their lives, but which are the cause of their "elegant economy," and a reason why they cannot "spend" their (sexual) energies. All of these memories are lurking in their unconscious, waiting to surface, as if rising from the dead, in the way of the uncanny. There is a crucial episode which can be associated with the Freudian notion of the uncanny: indeed, this incident seems to be a focal point of gaining a new mode of articulation. This uncanny incident is the performance of a conjurer in Cranford, a performance all the spinsters attend, and a performance which is in close association with a marriage on the one hand (even the possibility of marriage is a long-forgotten and repressed experience for all these old women), and subsequently, with a series of fantasies related to breaking into their houses at night.

   Chronologically, the marriage of Lady Glenmire and Hoggins comes first, an experience that absolutely breaks down "the phraseology of Cranford," including all the routine-like habits that give shape to the life of Cranford society. As the narrator remarks, "I must recover myself; the contemplation of it, even at this distance of time, has taken away my breath and my grammar, and unless I subdue my emotion, my spelling will go too" (113). Everything becomes confused because marriage seems to be an unnameable taboo (as it is the unutterable desire of all the Cranford spinsters) that can only be referred to as "that thing"—at the most: "we felt that it would be better to consider the engagement in the same light as the Queen of Spain's legs—facts which certainly existed, but the less said about the better" (117). At this point, the function of repressed speech is taken over by the language of clothing:

> I don't know if it is a fancy of mine, or a real fact, but I have noticed that, just after the announcement of an engagement in any set, the unmarried ladies in that set flutter out in unusual gaiety and newness of dress, as much as to say, in a tacit and unconscious manner, "We are also spinsters." Miss Matty and Miss Pole talked and thought more about bonnets, gowns, caps, and shawls, during the fortnight that succeeded this call, than I had known them do for years before … I was thankful that I was on the spot now, to counteract the dazzling fascination of any yellow or scarlet silk. (116–17)

This is the moment when the phrase "elegant economy" is transformed. As the narrator's description indicates, whereas before the emphasis is on "economy," covering up a limited and limiting psychic and social economy with the attribute "elegance" (with the implication that spending of any kind is vulgar and improper), at this stage "elegance" takes the upper hand over "economy," and spending on colorfulness and on fashion, evoking images of birds in a "flutter," replaces the thriftiness of the previous psychic economy. This new economy of spending and showing off, at the same time, creates a new system of communication: they communicate not via linguistic codes (the "phraseology of Cranford" breaks down), but via their body language—even if, paradoxically, only by covering their bodies with signs of different semiotic meanings.

Similarly, the wish for a new—fashionable—piece of clothing is closely associated with how language becomes fragmented and confused, and with the invitation to the performance of Signor Brunoni, the magician. Miss Matty's letter, including the invitation and also a request for a sea-green turban is characterized by the narrator in the following way: "a very mysterious letter it was. She began many sentences without ending them, running them into one another, in much the same confused sort of way in which written words run together on blotting-paper" (81). To make the interrelation of linguistic fragmentation and body language even more conspicuous, Signor Brunoni, the Grand Turk, also wears a turban (quite like Major Jenkyns's body-servant, who reminds Miss Matty of Bluebeard), and Signor Brunoni's English comes quite close to the quality of the fragmented language of the Cranfordians in panic: "in very broken English, so broken that there was no cohesion between the parts of his sentences; a fact which he himself perceived at last, and so let off speaking and proceeded to action" (Gaskell 87).

The question is how the engagement of Mr. Hoggins and Lady Glenmire, and the magician's performance are connected in a way that, as a result, the life—and linguistic and other codes—of Cranford ladies will fall apart, get merged and confused. Reading Signor Brunoni's performance and the subsequent panic in Cranford in terms of the Freudian notion of the uncanny (*unheimlich*), one can discover the connection between these events and the disintegration of a conscious—and very consciously created—system of signs of the old maids.

Signor Brunoni's public performance, in my reading, is the final step in the process needed by Miss Matty (and the other Cranford spinsters) to bring their traumatic experiences to the surface, to integrate them into their personality, to make them part of their everyday life. To do so, however, they must face what they seem to have overcome, though it has been haunting them all their lives.

Signor Brunoni's performance has the very same impact on Cranford ladies as the effect of the uncanny as it is defined by Freud:

> an uncanny effect is often and easily produced when the distinction between imagination and reality is effaced, as when something that we have hitherto regarded as imaginary appears before us in reality … It is this factor which contributes not a little to the uncanny effect attaching to magical practices. (367)

Freud also emphasizes that one of the most significant elements in achieving the effect of the uncanny is "the belief in the omnipotence of thoughts and the technique of magic based on that belief" (363).

What the Cranford ladies need, indeed, is magic, but even more: their suspension of disbelief—or rather, their belief in the potentially therapeutic function of magic which here functions as a communal and public healing of the most private wounds and traumas. For this reason, it is telling that the text does not betray too much of Signor Brunoni's dazzling performance, only how it affected the ladies present as the communal and public experience is translated into the terms of the individual psyche:

> Miss Matty and Mrs. Forrester were mystified and perplexed to the highest degree. Mrs. Jamieson kept taking her spectacles off and wiping them, as if she thought it was something defective in them which made the legerdemain; and Lady Glenmire, who had seen many curious sights in Edinburgh, was very much struck with the tricks. (87)

Affected by Signor Brunoni's tricks, the boundaries between reality and fantasy become blurred for the ladies of Cranford, and they enter a world which is part of the prohibited, the taboo, the uncanny. Simply watching the magician's performance is an act of transgression, because as its effect, fantasies repressed and supposedly overcome will once again be part of reality. This experience is quite close to how Freud explains the uncanny: "the uncanny [*unheimlich*] is something which is secretly familiar [*heimlich-heimisch*], which has undergone repression and then returned from it" or "when primitive beliefs which have been surmounted seem once more to be confirmed" (368, 372). Not accidentally, Miss Matty and Mrs. Forrester feel uneasy after a time:

> Miss Matty asked Mrs. Forrester, "if she thought it was quite right to have come to see such things? She could not help fearing they were lending encouragement to something that was not quite—" a little shake of the head filled up the blank. Mrs. Forrester replied, that the same thought had crossed her mind; she, too, was feeling very uncomfortable; it was so very strange. (Gaskell 88)

The broken sentence, the shaking head, the blank space in the communication indicate not only both the breaking down of the linguistic codes and the replacement of verbal language by body language, but also the psychic and social vacuum that is the basic experience of these elderly ladies. Filling in this vacuum itself is what makes these well-disciplined spinsters all of a sudden feel that they transgress the boundaries of decency. This is why simply by watching the magician's performance, "his wonderful magic [exhibited] in the Cranford Assembly Rooms" (Gaskell 81), they feel uneasy; and this is why external help—the rector—has to be called for to decide the question whether they can stay on or not. Certainly, if the rector, "this wonderful man is sanctioned by the Church" (88) is there, they can stay on. The question is what kind of psychic content, what kind of belief—even though, perhaps, not a primitive one, but one related to the fulfilment of desires—is brought to the surface in them by the magician, a belief that suddenly merges reality and fantasy, and why this public experience (or why experiencing it in public) is so disturbing and destabilizing. In Freud's opinion, by blurring the boundaries between reality and fantasy (and he himself categorizes magicians' performances among the practices that bring about this effect), "we do not feel quite sure of our new beliefs, and the old ones still exist within us ready to seize upon any confirmation. As soon as something *actually happens* in our lives which seems to confirm the old, discarded beliefs we get a feeling of the uncanny" (370–71).

The feeling of the uncanny is, actually, not *directly* evoked by the magician and his tricks in the ladies; he rather functions as the means by which they can bring something to the surface in themselves; and this is their lost youth and unfulfilled desires represented by entries in the space of the first column in their diaries. The place where Signor Brunoni's performance takes place is the scene of the ladies' balls when they were young, when there were "beaut[ies] blushed and dimpled along the lines of the Cranford Assembly Room," but now, instead, "Miss Matty gave a sigh or two to her departed youth, and the remembrance of the last time she had been there, as she adjusted her pretty new cap before the strange, quaint old mirror in the cloakroom" (85). The ladies' thoughts and associations that give a frame to Signor Brunoni's performance suggest that it is not really the tricks that they feel uneasy about and regard as indecent, as something that entices them to impropriety; by way of the performance everything they have been trying to repress in themselves for years returns irresistibly: the desires and fantasies of their girlhood, and thus the artificial and repressive boundary between fantasy and reality dissolves. It is quite necessary that they should engage in thoughts of their former balls (the social opportunity for marriage), and it is just as necessary that, the end of the performance approaching, a story is revealed about the rector (whose presence legitimates the ladies' participation) that could never before be told: the story is that Mr. Hayter the rector "was an old bachelor, but as afraid of matrimonial reports getting abroad about him as any girl of eighteen," and, at this stage, even the suspicion arises that Miss Pole "g[ave] very rigorous chase to Mr. Hayter when he first came to Cranford" (88). Signor Brunoni's magic, then, gains its importance not because of the tricks themselves, but by way of his strangeness (*unhomeliness, unheimlich*)—he is considered a stranger, he does not seem to speak their code, the English language, he wears Hindu clothes and has a name that sounds Italian, crosses his legs when sitting, which is an absolute breach of code in Cranford—the ladies of Cranford can integrate into their personality and make homely (*heimlich*) what used to be a traumatic, alien body in themselves.

Apart from the magical performance, the space of this performance—or the performative space—is just as significant as the act itself. Because the almost paralyzing and dehumanizing extent of repression as caused by regulations that limit the articulation of desires in the broadest sense of the word are imposed by social codes, the partial relief should also be offered in a public space so that even the private can be transformed. This is what happens in the public space of the Cranford Assembly Room, where due to the alienness of Signor Brunoni's body, all of a sudden the bodies of all the ladies are situated differently, and are willing to perform in a transformed and transformative *fashion*, both literally and in an abstract sense of the word. This is another reason why Signor Brunoni's magic is not described in detail: what is more important is how he is responded to. This process emphatically takes *place*: as Linda McDowell argues:

> [t]he body is the place, the location or site, if you like, of the individual, with more or less impermeable boundaries between one body and another. While bodies are undoubtedly material, possessing a range of characteristics such as shape and size and so inevitably taking up space, the ways in which bodies are presented and seen by others vary according to the spaces and places in which they find themselves … contrary to common sense and first impressions, our bodies are more fluid and flexible than we often realize. (34)

What happens in this public space is this very opening up of the bodies, of psychic spaces. The result is a fluidity which is both communal and individual, both private and public, both social and psychical at the same time. In the communal space of the first ball, the Cranford spinsters can relive and come to terms with the traumatic effects that this very public space has imposed on them psychically, and as a result of this public healing they can position themselves slightly differently even after leaving this heterotopic and carnivalesque space of transformation.

Only two of the ladies insist, during the performance, by all means, to keep off the impact of the magician's performance from themselves, and to interpret it in the framework of a conscious and institutionalized system of codes, to remain in canonized reality. One of them is Miss Pole, who comes to the performance armed with the knowledge of an encyclopedia, and recurrently makes an attempt to expose the tricks saying that she could do them any time, it is just the techniques that have to be known (Gaskell 87). She has her notes with her, and keeps rationalizing everything with such success that at one point even Signor Brunoni verges on losing his control. The other person in the audience who comes to see the show is the very person about whom matrimonial reports with Miss Pole got abroad: Mr. Hayter. He does surrender himself to the magic, but he is careful enough to surround himself with a wall of young boys. He can enjoy the performance only because he feels free from what has been opened up for the ladies:

he had treated the National School boys this very night to the performance; and virtue was for once its own reward, for they guarded him left and right, and clung round him as if he had been the queen bee, and they the swarm. He felt so safe in their environment, that he could even afford to give our party as we filed out. (Gaskell 88–9)

Significantly, both Miss Pole and Mr. Hayter need defense mechanisms. Miss Pole uses the very means that function to keep the unconscious desires at bay—reason, rationality, a faculty of consciousness—whereas Mr. Hayter can only be saved by the swarm of the boys of an age still unthreatened from the "magic" that could penetrate his own defense mechanisms. While a rector by definition is supposed to be "safe" from the trauma of the old maids (being a bachelor does not carry a social stigma with it), his need of surrounding himself with the boys, building a defensive fortress around himself indicates that even the impermeability of his ego boundaries can only be maintained by force. The old maids, however, at this stage do not even wish to maintain their own artificially constructed boundaries, they give in to the "magic" they cannot—and do not even want to—resist, and crack their shells of identity that both limited and in some sense protected them before.

A Spatial Restructuring

The impact of Signor Brunoni's performance, however, is not over with the show. Real panic comes next (evidenced by the title of the next chapter, "The Panic"). The state of the genteel society of Cranford can best be described at this stage in terms of the Freudian anxiety hysteria, once we accept that these symptoms are most frequently produced by repression, and manifest themselves in diverse phobias (Laplanche and Pontalis 218, 455) as the most conspicuous feature of Cranford panic is the absolutely irrational fear of invasion and breaking in—breaking into those closely and rigorously constructed and defended (psychic) spaces—that provide the spatial framework for their subjectivities. Their symptomatic space-related phobias, in turn, betray the deeply hidden sources of their anxieties.

The associations related to the so-called burglars are identical with the notions Signor Brunoni is associated with: they are dark, they are men, strangers, they are foreigners by all means (French or Indian), and they approach their victims unnoticeably (unrecognized by *conscious* observation), and are "in search of some unwatched house or some unfastened door" (Gaskell 89). Miss Matty could not really be persuaded that all this is not manipulated by Signor Brunoni from the background. And she seems to be quite right: in a psychological sense this is all Signor Brunoni's making. Miss Matty even gives up constructing defense mechanisms, and argues: "'What was the use,' said she, 'of locks and bolts, and bells to the windows, and going round the house every night? That last trick was fit for a conjuror. Now she did believe that Signor Brunoni was at the bottom of it'" (91).

In a psychologically consistent way, it is Miss Pole who spreads the wildest stories about the burglaries just as she is not willing to surrender to the impact of the magic. As she has a lot to make up for in the psychological process, she experiences more intensively the penetrating fear of the uncanny feeling that their houses (which are closely related to their carefully built system of defense) are vulnerable, that they are exposed to threatening external powers, that their inhabitants are incapable of protecting them, that they can be entered and penetrated, that something uncontrollable can come up, something that resists Cranford codes: "Cranford had so long piqued itself on being an honest and moral town, that it had grown to fancy itself too genteel and well-bred to be otherwise, and felt the stain upon its character at this time doubly" (Gaskell 90). At this moment, the psychic construction of Miss Pole and the old structure of the space of the Cranford ladies are in correlation, and the result is a paranoiac fear of anything, something entering and disturbing a well-known psychic and social space.

The threat *at night*, however, urges the company to follow Mr. Hayter's model of creating a fortress around them: they strengthen their houses, go to bed as soon as possible so that they can be through with the night, and carefully go round the house before going to bed. Miss Pole is the most hysterical: in fear of burglary (which, being a forceful penetration into the private space, connotes sexuality, even rape), she even leaves her house, yet next day she is the one eager to hear the story about her burgled house, and she is the one who makes up the most unbelievable stories (for example, Mr. Hoggins's cat stole a bit of a meat, and this incident is transformed in her imagination into the story that Mr. Hoggins was knocked down right in front of his door and his house was burgled). The major constitutive elements of her stories are the fear of strangers breaking into houses, and that they invade the buildings in the most fearful way, by making holes in the wall. In another character, Miss Matty's case, girlhood anxieties come to the surface:

> I saw Miss Matty nerving herself up into a confession; and at last out it came. She owned that, ever since she had been a girl, she had dreaded being caught by her last leg, just as she was getting into bed, by some one concealed under it. She said, when she was younger and more active, she used to take a flying leap from a distance, and so bring up both her legs up safely into bed at once, but that this had always annoyed Deborah, who piqued herself upon getting into bed gracefully, and she had given it up in consequence. (Gaskell 98)

It is not very difficult to interpret these fears as the Cranford ladies' Achilles heels, almost caught, and by all means wounded, their problematic, as their feared and desired sexuality. Signor Brunoni's magic has evoked in them, thus, not only the (lost) chance of getting married, but the experience of the uncanny that has made their genuinely "primitive," ancient, and unconscious desire return, the desire they long thought overcome and repressed. In their fantasies of burglary they merge reality and fantasy, and encode their unconscious desires in the elements of Gothic fiction. One cannot help supporting Dennis W. Allen's view: in Cranford, "paradoxically, sexuality must but cannot be spoken about" (80).

It is a significant feature—in harmony with how Freud describes the uncanny—that they want to keep off the sources of threat, the "harmful and secret powers" (Freud 370) by all means: this is why they consider them foreigners, more precisely the most "dangerous" foreigners, the French. They argue, with the most illogical twists, that Signor Brunoni (and the burglars) can only be French:

> therefore, we must believe that the robbers were strangers—if strangers, why not foreigners?—if foreigners, who so likely as the French? Signor Brunoni spoke broken English like a Frenchman, and, though he wore a turban like a Turk. Mrs. Forrester saw a print of Madame de Staël with a turban on, and another of Mr. Denon in just such a dress as that in which the conjuror had had made his appearance; showing clearly that the French, as well as the Turks, wore turbans: there could be no doubt Signor Brunoni was a Frenchman—a French spy, come to discover the weak and undefended places of England; and, doubtless, he had his accomplices. (90)

Signor Brunoni's (and the burglars') supposed French nationality is significant for these elderly ladies. In this respect, a clear parallel can be drawn between them and a male character, Mr. Holbrook (Matty's old suitor), for whom Paris and France signify his unfulfilled and destructively returning repressed desires. Holbrook goes to Paris, faces the disparity between his fantasy world and reality, comes back home to Britain and gradually pines away. The ladies go through a very similar process: their phobias and fantasies of desire threaten them to an extent that everyday routine becomes impossible, all the normal frames of living disintegrate, and are taken over by the defense mechanisms against the "invasion," and all this threatens them with the ultimate disintegration of their self.

Disintegration, however, is not the final phase in the case of the ladies. They can manage what Holbrook could not: they can make their uncanny (*unheimlich*) experience homely (*heimlich*), they can integrate the "alien body" of their trauma into their personality. Signor Brunoni, as it turns out, is a man called Samuel Brown, a discharged soldier, who, in fact, has just come back from India, but is in no way different from an average Englishman. As a result of this discovery,

> [s]omehow, we all forgot to be afraid. I dare say it was, that finding out that he, who had first excited out love of the marvellous by his unprecedented arts, had not sufficient every-day gifts to manage a shying horse, made us feel as if we were ourselves again. (104)

Regaining themselves means, on the plot level, that they take good care of Samuel Brown and his family—this is how they make him known and part of their home (homely). They nurse him in his illness, and Miss Matty covers with rainbow-colored thread the small ball which, in time of the panic, she rolled across under her bed to check whether anybody was hiding there, and she gives this ball to Phoebe Brown, Samuel Brown's daughter, to play with. A genuine female heritage, the ball embodies the original fear, its defeat; transformed, it is passed on to Phoebe to amuse herself with, and, perhaps, to protect and empower her. As a result of all these actions, the phobias cease to exist and get integrated, in a transformed way, into the everyday life of the Cranford ladies, and into the structure of their (psychic) spaces. This is the moment when Miss Matty has the courage to admit "by the flickering fire-light" that "she remember[s] the time when she looked forward to being married as much as any one" (106).

Samuel Brown, also on account of his name, is the direct continuation of the process initiated by Captain Brown at the beginning of the text, and what is more, the link between the names works both ways: Captain Brown's excessive, huge meals are called "Brunoni meals" (13). It is on *S*ignor/*amuel B*runoni/*r*own's impact that the repressive system of codes, "the phraseology of Cranford" collapses. Not only language but all kinds of sign systems will disintegrate because as a result of these experiences, the unutterable, the taboo can be *somehow* spoken about, and a deeper layer of the personality, including desires, no matter how faint by that time, can be revealed. That this process, by way of its nature, can never be complete; that there always remains some residues of repression, no matter how intensive the therapy; that the uncanny will never cease to exist entirely, and can at any time be evoked by another magician is signified by S.B.'s twin brother, who disappears at the moment when Signor Brunoni is transformed into Samuel Brown. He and his disappearance are almost as magical, incomprehensible, and unexplainable as Signor Brunoni's tricks were: he is gone, but nobody notices it. The Cranfordians have never seen him, or, rather, they do not know whether they have seen him or not. He replaces Signor Brunoni, and goes around "the weak and undefended places of England," so there is always a chance for his return.

His haunting presence (or rather, absence), however, does not mean that whatever Samuel Brown alias Signor Brunoni has brought into this female community is eradicated. Quite the contrary, as a result of his magic, Miss Matty is capable of accommodating desires—even if by this time mostly those of her servant—under her roof, and can restructure her (psychic) space in a way that she is both able to admit that even her "elegant economy" has collapsed, and is able to engage in what looks the most degrading activity: trade. In her case, though, this is also a form of psychic exchange: giving pleasure to little children by giving away some comfits whenever they come to her teashop. Characteristically, to create the teashop, a window—an opening—has to be made in the parlor wall, what is more, the space is called the shop-parlor, indicating that this is no longer a unified, homogeneous, self-contained and closed space but a heterogeneous space of (psychic) exchange with a crack, a gap that under the rector Mr. Jenkyns's rule would have been inconceivable, and which creates an opening that turns the space into a habitable structure.

Works Cited

Allen, Dennis W. *Sexuality in Victorian Fiction*. Norman, OK: U of Oklahoma P, 1993. Print.

Belsey, Catherine. *Critical Practice*. New Accents. London: Methuen, 1980. Print.

Dodsworth, Martin. "Women Without Men in Cranford." *Essays in Criticism* 13 (1963): 132–45. Print.

Freud, Sigmund. "The 'Uncanny.'" *14. Art and Literature.* Ed. Albert Dickson. Trans. James Strachey. Harmondsworth: Penguin, 1990. 335–76. Print.

Gaskell, Elizabeth. *Cranford.* Ed. and intr. by Elizabeth Porges Watson. Oxford: Oxford UP, 1972. Print.

Gillooly, Eileen. "Humor as Daughterly Defense in *Cranford.*" *ELH* 59.4 (1992): 883–910. Print.

Laplanche, J., J.-B. Pontalis. *A pszichoanalízis szótára.* Budapest: Akadémiai, 1994. Print.

McDowell, Linda. *Gender, Identity and Place: Understanding Feminist Geographies.* Cambridge: Polity Press, 1999. Print.

Moers, Ellen. *Literary Women.* London: Women's Press, 1978. Print.

Schor, Hilary M. "Affairs of the Alphabet: Reading, Writing and Narrating in *Cranford.*" *NOVEL: A Forum on Fiction.* 22.3 (1989): 288–304. Print.

Stoneman, Patsy. *Elizabeth Gaskell.* Key Women Writers. Brighton: Harvester, 1987. Print.

Chapter 3

"You might pioneer a little at home": Hybrid Spaces, Identities, and Homes in Elizabeth Gaskell's *North and South*

Divya Athmanathan

Elizabeth Gaskell's *North and South* (1854–1855) is a narrative that juxtaposes the domesticities in the North and the South, the country and the town, the country and the forest, and the town and the suburbs. Gaskell would have titled her novel after its heroine Margaret Hale—the only figure to experience the "homes" in all these places and spaces—thus plotting the traversal of the romantic love plot over the narrative's multiple spatialities by her progress, if Charles Dickens had not intervened with his alternative title that invokes the English regional binary of the industrial North and the agrarian South (Bodenheimer 281).[1] The novel was serialized between September 1854 and January 1855 in Dickens's *Household Words*. The spatial politics of the London home, the New Forest in Helstone, and the homes in Milton Northern are thematically and structurally important to the narrative development of *North and South*. In fact, there is a dynamic relationship between the novel's spatiality and its courtship or romantic love plot. The heterogeneous interests of Margaret in the outdoors or the public sphere and Thornton's complementary interests in the private sphere have functional implications for the progression of the plot. In this chapter I analyze the interplay between the novel's spaces and its courtship plot in order to map a trajectory of spatiality that orients and is reoriented by the hybrid sensibilities of the central characters as they move towards the narrative's marital teleology.

The spatial politics of the novel have largely been read in terms of the Victorian private and public spheres ideology, especially in relation to the intertwining of its political/industrial and the domestic/marriage plots. Although Deirdre d'Albertis does not discuss the marriage plot in any depth, in her study of Gaskell's "social texts" she considers *North and South* as an "innovative narrative hybrid," comprising the "traditional marriage plot of Jane Austen," and an industrial plot (64). She characterizes Margaret's role in the crucial industrial strike as that of a "middle class woman's movement through public space," and underlines the heroine's sense of "sexual humiliation" that is the consequence of her spatial trespass (67). Hilary Schor, however, argues for the political nature of the novel's

---

[1] I am using the terms "space" and "place" interchangeably, following Doreen Massey's theory that places and spaces are produced through social relations ("Space Place" 151–5).

sexual plot, stating that "capitalism itself is eroticized in the novel—as … the moment of submission, which both characters act out at the close of the novel, as they end, practically kneeling on the floor, in each other's arms" (128).

Nevertheless, if approached from the context of the connection between the novel's spatiality and the romantic plot, Margaret's and Thornton's gestures convey a different set of implications. The intense spatial displacement that Margaret suffers in the novel, especially at the beginning when she is forced to relocate from her aunt's home in London to her parents' home in Helstone, and then to a rented suburban home in Milton, is a case in point. While her dislocation is the result of a combination of factors such as dysfunctional families, economic constraints, and the religious issue of her father's doubt about the authority of the Church, it is also, crucially, a deliberate decision by Gaskell to displace her onto spaces that are conducive to establishing an ideal domesticity for Margaret. Schor states that the "geographic movement" of the novel has generic implications as it shifts the novel "from a novel of marriage to a novel of religious doubt, from a society novel to a political novel, from family relations to industrial relations, from private to public and back" (125). Yet the one narrative thread that connects the London home of the opening scene, the Helstone home of the "religious doubt" novel and the Milton world of industrial politics, is Margaret's courtship trajectory that is unconventional in its aborted beginnings, and complex in its courtship rituals and resolution. *North and South* is narratively structured in such a way that its central romantic couple not only migrate towards spaces that will complicate and inevitably forward the cause of romance, but they also reorient the nature of spaces through their agency.

"Dismantled Places" and Aborted Beginnings

The Harley Street home in London performs significant narrative functions. It is the space in which Margaret's first suitor, Henry Lennox, a striving lawyer and brother-in-law of Margaret's cousin Edith is introduced. Despite being quickly rejected by Margaret, Lennox continues to provide narrative tension for the courtship plot as he embodies the tantalizing possibility that he might ultimately convince Margaret to accept him in marriage. His failure to win Margaret's affection can be linked to his perception of femininity in terms of the gendered spatial ideology. When Lennox sees Margaret acting as a model to display Edith's Indian shawls in the drawing room, he comments on the disjunction between the feminine and the masculine pursuits: "Well, I suppose you are all *in the depths of* business—ladies' business, I mean. Very different to my business, which is the real true law business. Playing with shawls is very different work to drawing up settlements" (*NS* 12; emphasis added). His disparagement of the feminine pursuits prompts Margaret, who is generally critical of materialism, to comment defensively that "Indian shawls are very perfect things of their kind" (12). Lennox's choice of the word "depths" indicates that he sees women and their activity as occupying, in a hierarchy of spaces, the bottom position, a level so deep that it will be impossible for women's intellect to reach high enough to comprehend the "real true" masculine business of law. Lennox's evaluation of Margaret's activity through a spatial metaphor reveals the spiritual chasm between the two.

The notion of unreality and insubstantiality that Lennox associates with femininity also informs his assumption that Margaret's description of Helstone belongs "in a tale rather than in real life" (14). His comment shows his refusal to grant legitimacy to the attributes of a space in which Margaret has her roots. Therefore, when Lennox offers his condescending perspective that gardening is "a proper employment for young ladies in the country," Margaret dismisses his opinion by flippantly stating: "I don't know. I am afraid I shan't like such hard work" (14). While Margaret again deliberately offers a misleading insight about her character to Lennox, her attitude to physical labor in this instance, her words are more significant in their critique of the ideology of the garden space, especially its association with traditional gender expectations. Elizabeth Watts in her book *Flowers and the Flower Garden* (1867) writes that "The Pleasure Garden, in all its various forms, can scarcely fail to be the delight, the occupation, the pride, the glory of the English gentlewoman" (1). Though the Hales maintain their garden in perfect condition during their stay at the parsonage, it is not a place of "delight" for Margaret as she uses it for the revelation of unhappy news. Margaret conveys to her mother the painful news of the family's migration to the North in the garden. Watts further comments that those "Englishmen" who have "wives or relatives" who are "so fond" of the garden are "blessed" (1). In the light of the aborted courtship narrative of Lennox, Margaret's rejection of Lennox's proposal in the garden, a space in which he expects Margaret to occupy herself "properly," is ironically befitting.

The Harley Street home also reveals the hybridity of Margaret's personality. By contrasting her with her decoratively feminine cousin Edith, Margaret is shown as being a lady without being "fearful, delicate and dainty" (*NS* 387). Unlike Edith, Margaret is practical and useful in the domestic realm, and also later takes an interest in public spaces such as London's poorer streets that Edith describes as "horrible," "wretched places," which are "not fit for ladies" (387). Further, in her aunt's home, she is treated simultaneously like a daughter of the house, and a poor relation who has to contribute physically to its management. Therefore, in contrast to Edith and her mother Mrs. Shaw, she suffers exhaustion from her involvement in her cousin's wedding arrangements. Margaret's labor within the home that brings her closer to the servant figure is a constant throughout the novel, thus attributing a dual class status to her.

Though Margaret has a strong emotional bond with the Harley Street home, she is also subtly critical of its domestic management. Her implicit criticism relates to the spatial segregation of its inmates and is conveyed through her recollection of her poignant childhood experience in the home's now "dismantled" nursery (10). She remembers that in Helstone, before she came to live with her aunt, "her mother's dressing-room had been her nursery; and as they kept early hours in the country parsonage, Margaret had always had her meals with her father and mother" (10). Though the Hales' poorer economic circumstances could be cited as the reason behind the absence of a proper nursery in the parsonage, the lack of a nursery does strike as an oddity in the middle-class household of the Hales. Andrea Kastan Tange argues that, in the context of the enormous emphasis on the nursery in "advice literature," the "household feature" of a nursery is "a given rather than an aspiration" for the middle class in the Victorian period (222). While the child Margaret enjoys the lack of spatial discrimination, along with its associated benefits of physical and emotional proximity to her family in the parsonage, she experiences an emotional disjunction when she is placed within the Harley Street nursery for the first time. She uses a stark spatial analogy that verges on the archetypal spiritual contraries of Heaven and Hell to describe the physical and emotional distance between her and rest of the occupants in the house on her first day there: "She recollected her first tea up there—*separate* from her father and aunt, who were dining somewhere down below an infinite depth of stairs; for unless she were up in the sky (the child thought), they must be deep down in the bowels of the earth" (*NS* 10; emphasis added). That nurseries are about establishing "order" within the home is also conveyed through the remark of Mrs. Hepworth, the wife of the new vicar in Helstone, who is building a nursery for her numerous children in the parsonage: "When the nursery is finished, I shall insist upon a little order. We are building a nursery out of your room, I believe" (*NS* 357). The fact that a nursery is being constructed out of Margaret's room in the parsonage is itself telling in the context of spatial demarcation, fluidity of movement and emotional connectivity between family members. Spatial segregation within domesticity in the name of discipline and order reflects a desire to demarcate homogeneity of behavior and function, one that can be emotionally confining for the occupants. If Lennox trivializes and therefore marginalizes the feminine pursuits by a spatial metaphor, Mrs. Shaw's apparently well-meaning domestic management contributes to a spatial restriction of the child Margaret who had hitherto experienced physical and therefore emotional proximity with her family. Hence, it is not without significance that the adult Margaret's room in the Harley Street home is the same as the "day nursery of her childhood" (373). This specific detail is added by Gaskell in the novel in the edition of 1855 to emphasize the incongruence of Margaret's continuing subordinate status in the Harley Street home to which she returns after her maturing experiences in Milton; it highlights a spatial aspect of the home that not only marginalizes but also refuses to acknowledge her adulthood.

The London home at the beginning of the novel functions according to middle-class etiquette premised on a strictly gendered division of duties in the domestic space and thus offers no scope for a romantic narrative that will suit the character of Margaret. Neither does the country space of Helstone contain the possibility of the development of Margaret's courtship narrative. With Margaret's rejection of the clumsy courtship of Lennox in Helstone, and with no further opportunity for romance in this space (at least, none that Margaret will actively pursue), the narrative is soon forced to relocate to Milton. If Margaret's early critical appraisal of the London home subtly highlights its spiritual curbing of her character, the country space serves the function of establishing Margaret's heterogeneous spatial interests through illustrating her love of, and relation to, the open, pastoral and wild spaces in the country. Her interest in the people of the New Forest certainly goes beyond paternalism as she assimilates into the community of the foresters:

> She took a pride in her forest. Its people were her people. She made hearty friends with them; *learned and delighted in using their peculiar words*; *took up her freedom amongst them*; nursed their babies; talked or read with slow distinctness to their old people; carried dainty messes to their sick" (*NS* 18; emphasis added).

Margaret simultaneously considers herself as a denizen of this sphere, and partakes in activities that can be classified as belonging to those of a clergyman's daughter. This forest space is simultaneously public, natural and pastoral, and a space "therefore of coexisting heterogeneity" (Massey, "Of Space" 9).

The same thematic and narrative parallel can be noticed in Margaret's adoption of the factory dialect of Milton-Northern. It is intriguing to note that both Margaret's beloved forest and the main thoroughfare in Milton where Thornton's mill is situated share similar first names, "New Forest" and "New Street," respectively. Despite a few initial hiccups brought about by the clashing social etiquette of the South and the North, Margaret adopts some of the mannerisms of the factory people. When her mother chastises her for her use of "factory slang," Margaret defends herself in terms that contain an unconscious pride in her knowledge of the industrial world: "And if I live in a factory town, I must speak factory language when I want it. Why, mamma, I could astonish you with a great many words you never heard in your life. I don't believe you know what a knobstick is" (*NS* 218). At this moment, the spatial context of an industrial town structures her identity: she perceives herself as its citizen, before considering herself as a "lady" or an ex-clergyman's daughter with wealthy and aristocratic connections. That it is not an automatic spatial bond created through the sharing of the same space is made clear when she explains the practicality and precision coded in the factory lingo. Her words further expresses a hidden glee in her newfound knowledge and discovery about the factory people, a joy that is not much different from the one that she experiences in the New Forest with all its natural wonders, falling cottages, and ailing cottagers. If the London of the novel's beginning confines Margaret with its domestic regulations and gender conventions, New Forest in Helstone, and Milton-Northern in varying degrees allow her to participate in interests outside her home. The relegation of the forest space to the margins of the novel's canvas, as Margaret leaves that space behind in her progress through the novel, is due to the fact that it contains no scope for the development of her romantic narrative. The industrial space of Milton, however, offers the heroine both the scope for participating in the life outside the home as well as an opportunity for her to exploit unwittingly the public sphere and ultimately construct a satisfying domestic life within the home.

"A Romantic" in Industrial Action

The climactic scene of the industrial strike is not only crucial because it captures the consequences of Margaret's involvement in the public sphere. By forcing her to step out of the sanctuary of Thornton's house to protect him from angry workers, the strike stages or brings to the fore her unconscious love for Thornton. Her behavior can be perceived as a distorted or implicit courtship ritual. Stoneman points out that Margaret's "desire to protect the man she is coming to love" is part of the "complex motivation" behind her intervention during the strike (138–9). Margaret's retrospective self-examination of her role in the episode is revealing: "I went down and must needs throw myself into the mêlée, like a romantic fool! … But what possessed me to defend that man as if he were a helpless child!" (*NS* 173). While she refuses to acknowledge her love for him, her interpretation of her behavior points to the romantic nature of her relationship to Thornton. Her choice of analogy of a protective mother safeguarding her child from harm to describe her attitude towards Thornton cannot be seen in non-romantic terms as it is a simile that has been used in the context of romantic love in nineteenth-century discourse. Sarah Stickney Ellis in her chapter on "Love and Courtship" invokes "the solicitude, the careful watching of the mother" amongst others to describe a woman in love: "for would she not suffer to preserve him from harm?" (176). The courtship aspect of the industrial strike scene is reiterated when Margaret re-enacts her embrace of Thornton in the novel's final scene that shows the successful conclusion of the courtship plot.

The space outside the Thornton house and within the factory compound thus becomes the stage on which Margaret is inexorably fashioned into "a girl in love" (*NS* 169). In fact, Margaret's mother's illness that sends Margaret to borrow a water bed from the Thorntons on the day of the strike, and indeed the strike itself, appear to be "plotted" in order to bring Margaret to the factory so that the romantic narrative between Margaret and Thornton can be at once established and complicated. While the industrial action fizzles out in the aftermath of her injury from her stoning by a worker, Thornton's proposal of marriage to Margaret and its rejection the next day intensify the tension in the courtship plot that begins to overtly dominate the narrative from this point forward.

Margaret's action in that space outside the Thornton home and in front of the factory changes the nature of that space itself. Her sheltering of Thornton with her body connotes and prefigures Margaret's offer of domestic sanctuary to her future husband; it simultaneously evokes courtship and domesticity, just as her final embrace assures love and marriage. Her action thus crucially turns the space of industrial violence into an intimate and domestic space. Referring to the wife's encircled arms around her injured soldier-husband in John Everett Millais's "Peace Concluded" (1856; see Figure 3.1), Tange describes domesticity as the "circle of protection" to be found within the woman's arms (223). The interlinked theme of romantic love and domestic protection is also shared by two other paintings of Millais, all of which are contemporary with the serialization of *North and South* between 1854 and 1855. Each of the three women in Millais's "A Huguenot on St. Bartholomew's Day" (1851–1852; see Figure 3.2), "The Order of Release 1746"

Fig. 3.1   John Everett Millais, "Peace Concluded," 1856. By permission of
             The Putnam Dana McMillan Fund and the Minneapolis Institute of
             Arts.

(1852–1853; see Figure 3.3) and "Peace Concluded" offers comfort and protection
(or attempts to, in the case of the first painting) to her man in a different historical
and spatial context. Though Tange reads resignation and "exhaustion" in the
expression of the "protector" in "Peace Concluded" (223), the wife's expression
fits in with the idea of angelic stoicism that is evident not only in the wife of

Fig. 3.2   John Everett Millais, "A Huguenot on St Bartholomew's Day,"
                  1851–1852. By permission of Bridgeman London Images, United
                  Kingdom.

Fig. 3.3   John Everett Millais, "The Order of Release 1746," 1852–1853. By permission of Tate Images, Tate Enterprises Ltd., England and Wales.

the man released from prison in the aftermath of the Jacobite rebellion in "The Order of Release" but is also indicated obliquely in the apparently dispassionate protection that Margaret offers to Thornton during the strike. Reading "The Order of Release 1746," Frances Fowle suggests that the wife "may have been forced to sacrifice her virtue in order to save her husband," a thematic of sexual taint that also attaches to Margaret when she attempts to save Thornton from the irate factory workers. It is to be noted that the Huguenot in Figure 3.1 refuses the protection offered by the scarf that will connote his allegiance to Roman Catholicism, just as Thornton struggles to accept Margaret's protection. Yet the tightening of the knot against the Huguenot's arm is figuratively evocative of Margaret's forceful embrace of Thornton.

If Margaret's action during the industrial strike is colored by romantic love, then Thornton's action can also be interpreted in a domestic context. When Thornton stands defiantly in front of his barred home—his confrontation of the workers is itself prompted by Margaret— that shelters his family, and initially Margaret too, he is not only facing the angry workers, but he is also protecting his hearth from the violence of the mob. It is to be remembered that, just as Thornton's family hides in their home, the Irish workers also take shelter within the mill from the wrath of the local striking workers. Margaret's exhortation to Thornton to face the rioters also appeals to his "paternalistic duty" of safeguarding the Irish who have taken over the jobs of the striking Milton workers. The factory in which the Irish workers stay and eat for a brief period of time therefore becomes a domestic space belonging to Thornton. When Margaret joins Thornton, the space, instead of connoting a conflict between masters and men, is reoriented to depict a struggle for the preservation of the home from the rioting workers in the mill yard. Thus Margaret and Thornton change the meaning of industrial space at a crucial moment in the novel through their agency.

Factory Homes

If Margaret actively rewrites the meaning of the industrial space, Thornton makes inroads into the female sphere through his appropriation of the kitchen space. When he pays a visit to Higgins's house, ostensibly to make some "trifling payment," his attention is caught by the poor dinner at the table: "I saw such a miserable black frizzle of a dinner—a greasy cinder of meat, as first set me a-thinking" (*NS* 328). Though Thornton likens himself to a "steward to a club" (329), he resembles more a housekeeper or the mistress of a household attempting to maximize benefits from limited resources: "I bethought me how, by buying things wholesale, and cooking a good quantity of provisions together, much money might be saved, and much *comfort* gained" (328; emphasis added). Mr. Bell's gentle mocking of Thornton—asking him if "in his new capacity" the manufacturer was "a good judge of onions and potatoes?" (329)—reveals that Thornton efficiently brings together both the domestic and the manufacturing spheres within his factory space towards the end of the novel. He liaises with the housekeeper in procuring provisions for the dining room (329), and his supervisory role reminds us of Isabella Beeton's advice to the mistress of a household "to make a round of the kitchen and other offices, to see that all are in order" (9). The harshness of the public space is reduced by the introduction of the attributes of domesticity in it. Dorice Williams Elliott calls the process a domestication of the factory (48). However, the construction of the dining room can also be seen as the culmination of Thornton's attempt to balance the inroads made by the public sphere in his life through his pursuit of a private intellectual life through classical studies, and an emotional life through a persistent and indirect courtship of Margaret. The fact that he is instrumental in getting the owner of the house to remove the offending wallpapers from the house that the Hales rent in Milton is a potent sign in the context of Thornton's relationship with the private sphere. Still, it is to be noted that in the Victorian period the dining room in a home has masculine connotations, despite the fact that "it was women who spent the most time in them" (Flanders 253). Tange writes that "the dining room was associated with masculinity in much the same way that the drawing room signified and defined femininity" (138). Though the space of the dining room is traditionally linked with the masculine, Thornton collapses the sexual division of labor and gendered spatial differences by appropriating the supervisory role of the mistress of a household in his enterprise of "the dinner-scheme" (*NS* 330).

Thornton's desire to destabilize the homogeneity of the industrial space stems from his inspiration by the Hales' domesticity and a subconscious desire to change the kind of the domesticity practiced in his own home. The Hales' drawing room in Milton does not "exclude the night-skies, and the outer darkness of air" of the town (73), and is symbolic of their embrace of plurality and hybridity, a feature which is also reflected in the objects culled from a variety of places, ranging from Helstone curtains to American apples, that decorate their drawing room. On the contrary, the single-minded philosophy that dictates Mrs. Thornton's view of life directs the rigid, functional and mechanical nature of her domesticity. Decrying the multiple pursuits of "characters who are full of this thing to-day, to be utterly forgetful of it in their new interest to-morrow," Mrs. Thornton describes, and advocates, the one homogenous pursuit in her son's life: "It is, or ought to be, enough for him to have one great desire, and to bring all purposes of his life … To hold and maintain a high, honorable place among the merchants of his country" (104). Her displeasure at her son's courtship of Margaret partly arises from this single-minded ideological perspective centered on the public functions of Thornton. Moreover, she disapproves of her son's interest in the study of classics with Mr. Hale, nor is she pleased with her son's desire to build a "dining-room—for the men" (328).

In the context of Mrs. Thornton's worldview, the location of their home within the factory compound is befitting as it functions to contribute to that "one great desire." Elliott writes that the Thornton home "sits on the same ground as the factory," and where the married "Margaret will presumably live blurs the boundaries between the public and private spheres" (48). However, mere spatial proximity of private and public structures does not imply a truly hybrid site, or a space with a genuine simultaneity of heterogeneous interests. It is evident from the explosive strike scene that the nature of a space is dependent on the practices of its occupants. Elliott herself adds a footnote referring to the fact that Gaskell toyed with the idea of burning down the mill and the house so that the married Margaret would not have to live in Thornton's home (48). Gaskell's consideration of the possibility of destroying the factory, especially the house of Thornton, confirms the notion that it is not yet an ideal home for Margaret.

The Thorntons' house is empty of domestic warmth and comfort, and is spiritually an extension of the public sphere of the factory. Massey reads space as a "network of interrelations" and "as the sphere in which distinct trajectories coexist" ("Of Space" 9). However, in the light of the philosophy of homogeneity practiced by Mrs. Thornton, and prior to Margaret's entry into the space during the strike, the factory has almost edged out the private life associated with the home. When Margaret asks to be directed to Thornton's home from a passer-by, she has the "factory lodge door pointed out to her" (*NS* 102). She is astonished by the fact that he has his house "in the continual whirl and din of the factory" instead of in the "country, even in some suburb" (103). It is worth quoting at length the description of the positioning of the house in relation to the factory, as it indicates the imbalance in the traffic between the domestic and the non-domestic and justifies Margaret's desire in this specific instance for the separation of home and work space:

> The lodge-door was like a common garden door; on one side of it were great closed gates for the ingress and egress of lurries and wagons. The lodge-keeper admitted them [Margaret and her father] into a great oblong yard, on one side of which were offices for the transaction of business; on the opposite, an immense many-windowed mill, whence proceeded the continual clank of machinery and the *long groaning roar* of the steam-engine, enough to *deafen those who lived within the enclosure*. Opposite to the wall, along which the street ran, on one of the narrow sides of the oblong, was a handsome stone-coped house—*blackened*, to be sure, by the smoke, but with paint windows, and steps kept scrupulously clean … The stone facings—the long, narrow windows and the number of them—the flights of steps up to the front door, ascending from either side, and guarded by railing-all witnessed to its age … *her unaccustomed ears could hardly catch her father's voice*, as they stood awaiting the opening of the door. (102–3; emphasis added)

The house is hemmed in by the mill and the offices attached to it, while the factory dominates the entire space: the animalistic roar of the steam-engine deafens every other sound inside the yard. The near drowning out of the private conversation between Margaret and her father when they visit the Thornton house literally demonstrates the overpowering of the private lives by the factory system. The blackened exterior of the house symbolizes the erasure of an ideal domesticity indoors, one with an emotional bond between family members who are open to pursue diverse interests in life. Thornton's comment on his drawing room, a space that can be a synecdoche for the entire interior of his home, is significant primarily because it points out the room's lack of domestic warmth and comfort by highlighting its functional and ornamental purpose: it is "handsome, ponderous, with no sign of feminine habitation, except in the one spot where his mother sate, and no convenience for any other employment than eating and drinking" (73).

The domesticity hinted at in the "sign" of his mother's presence ultimately remains only a sign because of her emotional limitations. Also, the noise of the factory outside the house which makes conversation difficult has a parallel indoors as the ambience of the drawing room forces Margaret and her father into speaking in "low" voices in order to avoid awakening the "the unused echoes" of the room (103). Nevertheless, the erasure of the private sphere is stopped by Margaret and Thornton whose actions assert and reclaim the private trajectory in the factory-home space. Thornton's inclusion of the dining room in the factory towards the end of the novel can be seen as the triumph of Margaret's belief that Thornton has a moral and a paternal obligation to care for his workers.

Back Drawing Rooms and Romantic Resolution

The narrative returns to the back drawing room of the Harley Street home, in which it began, to stage the romantic resolution, thus enacting a structural circularity. Yet there is also a crucial difference: the connotations of the back drawing room of the opening scene, where Margaret sits by the "Sleeping Beauty" Edith, has undergone a transformation when it makes its appearance in the final stages of the novel. The fact that it is the "back" drawing room has been emphasized in the first chapter of the novel to indicate not only the fact that there are two drawing rooms in this wealthy household, but also that the one at the "back" is a very feminine and therefore a more private space. In fact, the representation of Edith is so feminine that comparisons can only be drawn from fairy-tale characters such as Titania "dressed in white muslin and blue ribbons," and from inanimate material such as a "soft ball of muslin and ribbon" (*NS* 7), all of which accentuates her femininity by erasing her human identity and depth of character. This back drawing room of the opening scene is therefore suffused with the intense aura of femininity associated with Edith, the name with which the novel begins in an exclamatory mode.

During Margaret's second stay in the Harley Street home, after her estrangement from Thornton and the death of her parents, she subtly reorients the spatial functions of the back drawing room, thus opening up the space to spheres other than the decoratively feminine. Her agency proves David Harvey's notion that while space controls, it is also controlled and restructured by human practices (11). While Lennox happily advises Margaret on her business affairs, hoping that his financial and legal guidance also will give him control over her heart eventually, she subverts his philosophy that "real true business" belongs outside of the drawing room by compelling him to bring it even within the more private back drawing room. Lennox asks Edith to "have the back drawing-room undisturbed … In general, the children and servants are so in and out, that I can never get any business satisfactorily explained" (*NS* 393). His remarks illustrate the changes wrought onto the homogeneous nature of the back-drawing room of the opening scene. The space that had been permeated by femininity has been expanded to include the discourse of business affairs. Margaret can thus be seen as performing the task of pioneering "a little at home" in the way she realigns the meaning and function of a domestic space (113). The back drawing room in the

Fig. 3.4   Dante Gabriel Rossetti, "Kneeling Man and a Seated Girl,"
                1849–1852. © Birmingham Museums Trust.

final stages of the novel is transformed into a hybrid space, where domestic and non-domestic spheres operate simultaneously. The rigid compartmentalization of domestic life also witnesses alterations in certain respects: children who are supposed to be enclosed in nurseries are freely moving within the house. Unlike the space of a study or a library that is conventionally marked as masculine, this back drawing room gradually comes to accommodate plurality. Massey's argument that "space is always under construction" is thus exemplified as the spatial significance of the back drawing room is realigned by Margaret's actions ("Of Space" 9). The highlight of the final scene is in Margaret's assumption of full control over her business affairs. Hitherto, Lennox had been interpreting the world of her business affairs for her. However, when he fails to arrive for the proposed meeting with Margaret and Thornton, Margaret takes charge of the role of explaining the nature of her business offer to Thornton. Lennox's quiet withdrawal from Margaret's business affairs once he realizes that he cannot win her heart makes an interesting foil to Margaret's decision to initiate business negotiations with Thornton, despite her belief that she is forever estranged from him. Margaret's business proposal and Thornton's marriage proposal further establish the back drawing room as a space capable of allowing multiple interests to flourish.

Contrary to Schor's view, it is not the association of personal wealth intertwined with power that eroticizes the couple in each other's eyes (128). In fact, the accumulation of wealth earned through trade is what Margaret initially finds repulsive in her prospective lover. Nor is Margaret's economic status the most attractive of her attributes as a potential partner in Thornton's estimation. It is essentially the removal of an apparent rival for Margaret's affections that brings narrative resolution to the courtship plot. Thornton mistakes Margaret's brother for her lover, and it is the combination of sexual taint—produced through her presence in the public space of the "Outwood" railway station (the name plays on the meaning of its being outside the bounds of respectability) in the company of the unknown young male—and his erroneous belief that she loves another that estranges Thornton from Margaret for the latter half of the novel. That the factory worker Higgins is used to reveal the identity of the secret male friend of Margaret as her fugitive brother is also significant for the way in which industrial figures and conflicts are deployed to complicate and resolve the romantic narrative.

The final scene in which Margaret and Thornton are "practically kneeling on the floor" (Schor 128) is potent with signification, primarily because it shows the emotional and spatial culmination of their negotiation of spaces as they progressed towards romantic resolution. Moreover, the gesture of kneeling is a common ritual of courtship on the part of the man in front of his beloved. In Elizabeth Barrett Browning's poem "Lady Geraldine's Courtship" (1842), Bertram the poor poet and lover of the lady, on finally knowing that she reciprocates his love, falls to his knees before her. Dante Gabriel Rossetti's sketch of a pair of lovers titled "A kneeling man and a seated girl" (1849–1852; see Figure 3.4) depicts a spatial positioning that echoes that of Margaret and Thornton at the end of the novel. It is to be noted that it is Thornton who is on his knees in front of Margaret, who is seated at a table, and it is he who literally and figuratively (his financial fall) parallels, and balances, the literal and metaphorical "falls" that Margaret suffers in the course of the narrative.

North and South demonstrates the power of spatiality in structuring the romantic trajectory of Margaret and Thornton, while also simultaneously being restructured by the agency of the central characters' spatial practices. The hybrid sensibilities of the hero and the heroine make them migrate away from homogeneous spaces to spaces that allow the existence of heterogeneous pursuits. The extent to which Gaskell found homogeneity in a space anathema can be seen in her dallying with the idea of burning down Thornton's home in a fire.[2] The fact that she refrains from

---

[2] Jenny Uglow quotes Gaskell's question to Katie Winkworth, "What do you think of a fire burning down Mr Thornton's mills *and house* as a *help* to failure? Then Margaret

doing so perhaps suggests the possibility that even the factory-home can be changed for the better through the companionate domesticity of Margaret and Thornton.

Works Cited

Beeton, Isabella. *Mrs Beeton's Book of Household Management* (1859–1861). London: Cassell, 2000. Print.

Bodenheimer, Rosemarie. "A Permanent State of Change." *Nineteenth-Century Fiction* 34.3 (1979): 281–301. Print.

d'Albertis, Deirdre. *Dissembling Fictions: Elizabeth Gaskell and the Victorian Social Text*. New York: St. Martin's P, 1997. Print.

Elliott, Williams Dorice. "The Female Visitor and the Marriage of Classes in Gaskell's *North and South*." *Nineteenth-Century Literature* 49.1 (1994): 21–49. Print.

Ellis, Sarah Stickney. *The Daughters of England*. New York and Philadelphia: D. Appleton and George S. Appleton, 1843. Print.

Fowle, Frances. "The Order of Release 1746 (1852–1853)." *Tate* 2000. Web. 11 Feb. 2013.

Gaskell, Elizabeth. *North and South*. 1854–1855. Ed. Alan Shelston. New York and London: Norton, 2005. Print.

Harvey, David. *Social Justice and the City*. 1973. Athens, GA: U of Georgia P, 2009. Print.

Johnston, Susan. *Women and Domestic Experience in Victorian Political Fiction*. Westport, CT and London: Greenwood Press, 2001. Print.

Langland, Elizabeth. "Domestic Ideology and Middle-Class Women in the Victorian Novel" *PMLA* 107.2 (1992): 290–304.

Massey, Doreen. *For Space*. London: Sage, 2005. Print.

———. *Space, Place and Gender*. Minneapolis, MN: U of Minnesota P, 1994. Print.

Schor, Hilary. *Scheherazade in the Marketplace: Elizabeth Gaskell and the Victorian Novel*. New York: Oxford UP, 1992. Print.

Stoneman, Patsy. "Gaskell, gender, and the family." *The Cambridge Companion to Elizabeth Gaskell*. Ed. Jill L. Matus. Cambridge: Cambridge UP, 2007. Print.

Tange, Andrea Kastan. *Architectural Identities: Domesticity, Literature and the Victorian Middle Class*. Toronto, Buffalo and London: U of Toronto P, 2010. Print.

Uglow, Jenny. *Elizabeth Gaskell*. London and New York: Faber and Faber. 1999. Print.

Watts, Elizabeth. *Flowers and The Flower Garden*. London: Frederick Warne, 1867. Print.

---

would rebuild them larger & better & need not go & live there when she's married" (369; emphases in original).

Chapter 4
Grave Matters:
Gothic Places and Kinetic Spaces in Elizabeth Gaskell's *Mary Barton*

Emily K. Cody[1]

> Day by day he became aware that the space between the walls of his apartment was narrowing, and then he understood the end. Those painted walls would come into hideous nearness, and at last crush the life out of him.
>
> —Elizabeth Gaskell, *Mary Barton* (1848)

In this haunting scene from her 1848 social problem novel, *Mary Barton: A Tale of Manchester Life*, Elizabeth Gaskell alludes to a method of criminal punishment once popular in early modern Italy. She appropriates the ever-enclosing walls as a metaphor for the effects of John Barton's "diseased thoughts," ones rooted in difficulties with the Chartist movement and opium addiction, in order to bring his hardships to life for her readers (*MB* 225). But the moving walls also speak to the more literal characteristics of the physical spaces Barton inhabits: the kinetic and dynamic spatial forces of industrial Manchester that leave him "sinking under the pressures of want," threatening to "crush the life out of him" (225).

Gaskell's account of the moving walls of Barton's apartment is at once didactic and descriptive—a framework for how to interpret space in *Mary Barton* that can in turn guide how we formulate conceptions of both real and fictional nineteenth-century landscapes. Traditionally, the diegetic spaces of realist texts from this century have received less attention within narrative theory; scholars in the field tend to overgeneralize when considering the characteristics of these spaces—labeling them as fundamentally secure and stationary—which makes it easy to overlook more peculiar aspects of these diegetic layouts. Hilary Dannenberg's recent work aims to minimize this gap in scholarship, but even as her analysis endeavors to elevate the importance of space in studies of nineteenth-century texts, it continues to draw on more conventional facets of narrative theory, concluding that the spaces of nineteenth-century realist fiction function

---

[1]   I am grateful to Robyn R. Warhol, Mark Conroy, and David Herman for their comments and enthusiasm for this project. I am also indebted to Jack Downs and Julie Schoelles for their willingness to read drafts at various stages and for their continuing support. Finally, I owe special thanks for generous feedback to Linda K. Hughes, a fellow Gaskellian, whose fondness for Gaskell inspired my own; and to Jill Galvan and Alisa Clapp-Itnyre, sororal Victorianists and kindred spirits.

as "firm and concrete spatial scenario[s]" (Dannenberg 82). As the depiction of Barton's surroundings illustrates, spatial planes are decidedly more kinetic than Dannenberg implies, suggesting the need to reevaluate the spaces of realist fiction with a broader analytical eye.

The macabre, torture-chamber walls of Barton's home have equally important implications for genre in *Mary Barton*, speaking to the ways Gothic modes overlap with realist elements to form the diegetic layout of industrial Manchester.[2] Setting tales in urban environments is a standard characteristic of Gothic literature in the Victorian era, when the walls of the genre itself began to "close in" as the conventional trope of the rural, isolated setting gave way to anxieties about industrialization and the ever-growing population, thus relocating to constricted urban spaces.[3] Despite Gaskell's reputation as both a realist author of industrial fiction and a prolific writer of Gothic stories, the ways in which elements of these genres interact in *Mary Barton* have not been explored in depth. To this end, I will demonstrate how Gaskell's innovative use of diegetic space corresponds with her dual employment of realist and Gothic elements in the novel, a blending of genres that forms a crucial underpinning of her arguments for social reform in the text. Through specific use of scientific theories of pressure and the Gothic trope of entrapment, Gaskell fuses elements of the realist with the Gothic at the most spatially compressed points in the novel, creating a diegetic world shrouded in a veil of supernatural horror, but one informed by the actual terrifying realities of industrial Manchester that, ironically, turn the revered space of the Victorian home into a site of fear and dread. The ever-constricting urban environment transforms working-class domestic spaces into claustrophobic sites of torture, as members of the middle class maneuver the industrial system to their benefit, indifferent to the pressures to which they might subject members of the working class. However, by pressing spaces and compressing genres in *Mary Barton*, Gaskell ultimately complicates and collapses rather than reinforces nineteenth-century socioeconomic boundaries predicated on the values of bourgeois domestic ideology—ones that effectively punish the poor for their hardships by increasing the pressures to which they are exposed rather than providing outlets for relief. Recognizing the need to reverse these trends, Gaskell gradually recodes the relationship between pressure and punishment by situating grave space as a positive antithesis to more disagreeable domestic spaces; harnessing the momentum of moving diegetic spaces alongside Gothic elements reconfigures the grave as an alternative site of morality and self-transformation that encourages sympathy rather than judgment

---

    [2]   Harvey Peter Sucksmith argues that Gaskell's metaphor of closing walls is a direct allusion to William Mudford's *The Iron Shroud* (1830), a popular Gothic tale with which her readers would have been familiar. In the story, similar to John Barton, "the prisoner only gradually comes to understand his fate, the growing realization of impending doom arising out of his observation that the windows in his dungeon are disappearing one by one" (461). See "Elizabeth Gaskell's *Mary Barton* and William Mudford's *The Iron Shroud*."

    [3]   Robert Mighall outlines the fundamental characteristics of the "urban Gothic" subgenre in *A Geography of Victorian Gothic Fiction: Mapping History's Nightmares*.

between classes. Through these formal techniques, Gaskell, in effect, anticipates critics who maintain that authors of realist fiction claim that their works stand as "unmediated presentations of social reality" (Gallagher xii). Far from insisting that *Mary Barton* stands as an unfiltered source of truth, Gaskell consciously deploys and strategically manipulates the inevitable formal paradoxes of the realist novel, taking creative liberties to better envision solutions to the seemingly insurmountable social problems she presents in her work. If in the course of writing her first novel Gaskell was "searching for the appropriate stance and tone to do the work of bringing opposing classes together," looking at the merging realist and Gothic modes in *Mary Barton* allows us to see how she indeed began to do this work to great rhetorical effect (Hughes and Lund 47).

In *The Condition of the Working-Class in England in 1844* (1845), Friedrich Engels records his impressions of urban Manchester:

> Of the irregular cramming together of dwellings in ways which defy all rational plan, of the tangle in which they are crowded literally one upon the other, it is impossible to convey an idea … If any one wishes to see in how little space a human being can move … it is only necessary to travel hither … Everything which here arouses horror … belongs to the industrial epoch. (48–53)

The description of the city illustrates the extent to which issues surrounding industrialization were, quite literally, problems of space—a competition between bodies *of* space and bodies *for* space. The buildings of Manchester "are crowded one upon the other" (48) as new structures fight for space among the old, in turn compromising the mobility of a growing population constantly pushed to the threshold of "how little space" in which it can move (53). Perhaps even more attuned to these spatial pressures, Elizabeth Gaskell records their effects on the nineteenth-century landscape in both the structure and content of *Mary Barton*. She remarks in the preface: "Living in Manchester, but with a deep relish and fond admiration for the country, my first thought" in composing the novel "was to find a frame-work for [the] story in some rural scene" (*MB* 29). The congested urban atmosphere, combined with inspiration from "the lives of those who elbowed [her] daily in the busy streets of town," contributed to a desire to write, as if the pressures of the crowded city compelled—or rather propelled—her to write the novel (29). Indeed, once while visiting the home of a laborer in the city, "the head of the family took hold of [Gaskell's] arm, and grasping it tightly said, with tears in his eyes, 'Ay, ma'am, but have ye ever seen a child clemmed to death?'" (Hompes 131).[4] Through her philanthropic work among the poor in Manchester, Gaskell witnessed firsthand how the pressures of industrial poverty could eventually lead one to feel "it would be no sin to steal" in order to find relief from the crippling despair of watching a child slowly starve (56). These experiences inform the working-class sympathies that manifest so forcefully in *Mary Barton*, in which Gaskell attempts to relay her accounts of the "Faith [and hardships]" among the poor "such as

---

[4] Mat Hompes writes of Gaskell's experience in his article "Mrs. Gaskell," which appeared in the August 1895 issue of *The Gentleman's Magazine*.

the rich can never imagine on earth"—circumstances the average middle-class Victorian might only expect to encounter within the fantastical world of a Gothic tale (95).

With a shrewd eye for spatial frameworks and an acute understanding of the pressures surrounding the working class, Gaskell appropriates the Gothic trope of entrapment to illustrate how the spaces of an industrial city actively confine its inhabitants. *Mary Barton* begins in an open, rural setting in Manchester, Green Heys Fields, where the townspeople, "deafened with noises of tongues and engines, may come to listen awhile to the delicious sounds of rural life" (*MB* 34). The narrative immediately moves into an urban area in the following chapter, so that readers, akin to the Barton and Wilson families leaving the scene, might feel "the effect of contrast in these … thoroughly rural fields, with the busy, bustling manufacturing town" (33). Entering the city, the party proceeds "down this entry, cutting off that corner, until they turned out of one of these innumerable streets into a little paved court" (43), where "among the pent-up houses...various articles of linen [dangled] so low" that they nearly "flapped in their faces" as they passed (44). The spaces of the novel continue to compress, moving indoors to further demonstrate the effects of varying kinds of pressure on the most impoverished members of the working poor, most notably the typhus-stricken Ben Davenport. Pools of raw sewage "overflow and stagnate" outside the Davenport residence, where "a person standing would have his head about one foot below the level of the street, and might at the same time, without the least motion of his body, touch the window of the cellar and the damp muddy wall right opposite" (97). In moving the setting from open to increasingly narrower spaces in *Mary Barton*, Gaskell brings the "horrors" that "belong to the industrial epoch" (Engels 53) to life, effectively literalizing the "narrowing walls" of John Barton's apartment, slowly but steadily bringing the spaces of the diegetic world "into hideous nearness," threatening to "crush the life" out of her characters and readers alike *(MB* 225).

In compressing the spaces of her novel, Gaskell fashions a diegetic world that forces readers to confront the consequences of industrialization and the harsh realities of urban poverty. Akin to a closed system in experimental physics, the intratextual space of *Mary Barton* functions as a diegetic system to which Gaskell applies pressure, maneuvering the spatial structure of the narrative to better illuminate the forces and stresses that burden certain residents of urban Manchester. Indeed, the novel's structural and thematic focus on pressure and confined spaces enters a notably scientific—and by extension an especially realist—dimension in "The Mill on Fire—Jem Wilson to the Rescue," but in a way that also engages the Gothic trope of entrapment simultaneously. The chapter opens with a reference to the *Principia Mathematica*, or *Principia* (1686–1687), the work in which Sir Isaac Newton famously outlined his laws of motion and theories of gravitational pull.[5] The reference to the *Principia* is aptly placed at the

---

[5]   Gaskell's narrator insists on the intellectual competencies of members of the working class in Manchester, who "yet may claim kindred with all the noble names that science recognizes … Newton's *Principia* lies open on the loom" of weavers, "to be snatched at in work hours, but reveled over in meal times, or at night" (*MB* 72).

beginning of this particular chapter given the depictions of spatial behavior that unfold in the titular scene—behavior Gaskell portrays in a way that a physicist might describe the movement of particles during experiments, only in this case in relation to human bodies and their responses to the pressures of their surroundings. The content of *Mary Barton* indicates that Gaskell was well acquainted with both established and emerging scientific theories circulating during the first half of the nineteenth century. She had chances to begin honing this knowledge at an early age, as influential scientists often visited her childhood home of Knutsford as part of lecture circuits; Reverend William Gaskell's borrowing record at the Manchester Portico Library also indicates that he checked out, alongside numerous literary works, books on the latest scientific research and advancements.[6] Gaskell's innovative descriptions of the Carsons' mill fire suggest that she had a solid command of prominent scientific principles and ideas, even if, akin to "Political Economy" or "theories of trade," she did not openly purport to possess such knowledge (*MB* 30).

Indeed, in describing the mill fire scene Gaskell uses language similar to Newton's *Principia*, demonstrating how, as outlined in the Third Law of Motion, "whatever draws or presses another is as much drawn or pressed by that other" as the mill fire unfolds (*P* 83).[7] The crowd gathered to watch the burning spectacle bends to the whim of the fire's movement, the "raging flames ... driven by the wind" directing the motion of the "sea of upward-turned faces [that] moved with one accord ... struggl[ing] more and more to press into Dunham Street" (*MB* 86). The spontaneous ebb and flow of the mass gathered on the street creates repetitive surges of "pressure ... the front rows bearing back on those behind," until Mary Barton and Margaret Jennings are nearly "sick with the close cramming confinement" (88). The narrative execution of the mill fire seems to draw specifically on the fundamental principles of what would eventually become thermodynamics. Although more contemporary models of thermodynamics did not emerge until the mid-nineteenth century, early theoretical frameworks were well under way by the time Gaskell began writing *Mary Barton* in 1845.[8] After its rise to

---

[6]   Among these visitors to Knutsford was English scientist John Dalton (1766–1844), best known for his contributions to atomic theory and Law of Partial Pressures which helped pave the way for the advent of modern thermodynamics. Jenny Uglow provides a detailed account of Gaskell's education and intellectual influences in her biography *Elizabeth Gaskell: A Habit of Stories*. Uglow also attributes Gaskell's hesitancy to display scientific understanding to the more conservative facets of her early education that saw intellectual ambition as incompatible with "ideal" femininity; she explains, "warnings against displayed learning seem to have had their effect [on Gaskell], since for many years, as an adult, she hid her cleverness, claiming not to have read economics, not to understand science ... But she ... drew on her reading constantly ... for different visions of the world—and for ways of telling stories" (44).

[7]   Isaac Newton, *Principia Mathematica*, trans. Andrew Motte, 1729 (New York: Daniel Adee, 1846). *Principia* abbreviated as *P* and "A Scale of the Degrees of Heat" as "SDH" for Newton citations.

[8]   The Industrial Revolution provided much of the impetus for the development of thermodynamics in the late eighteenth and early nineteenth centuries, as more sophisticated

prominence in the 1850s, thermodynamics "very quickly ... was disseminated and applied to a range of social issues during the latter half of the century, including theories about work, waste, time, and history," which effectively "replace[d] the narrative of capitalist progress with an entropic narrative" (Alexander 100–101). The relationship between heat, temperature, and pressure forms the core concepts of thermodynamic theory, focusing on the ways heat moves from warmer to cooler bodies to achieve thermal equilibrium. Newton gestures toward the development of these theories in his essay "A Scale of the Degrees of Heat" (1701), in which he describes the way "Bodies heated in the Fire" gradually cool and return to temperatures close to that of their surroundings ("SDH," sec. 1). Here, of course, Newton uses the term "body" to mean "object" or "entity," but he also uses the temperature of the human body as a common point of reference in the same essay; both nuances of "body" are important to the mill fire scene. The mill fire, in effect, causes the pressure levels of the setting to elevate—that is, pressure brought on by the actual temperature of the flames *and* the ever-growing number of bodies in the street—which eventually stabilize once the crowd abates and the fire ceases. Mary further demonstrates this process in her own bodily responses to the increasing pressures of the space surrounding her. When "the heated air, the roaring flames, the dizzy light, and the agitated and murmuring crowd" prove too overwhelming, she faints and leaves Margaret "pale and almost sinking under the weight of Mary's body ... [Margaret then] gently let her down on the cold clean pavement ... The difference in temperature, [once] the people had withdrawn ... speedily restored her to consciousness" (*MB* 87–91). Mary, akin to a particle in a closed pressure system, experiences an increase in heat and temperature, and thus must return to cooler temperatures in order to achieve equilibrium—or rather to regain consciousness, which her contact with the "cold, hard bed" of the street quickly facilitates (91).

If Mary's experience in the mill fire crowd parallels the movement of bodies exposed to fluctuating pressures in a closed system, then her fainting spell can also read as equally problematic within a scientific framework. According to Blaise Pascal, seventeenth-century French physicist and early influence on Isaac Newton, pressure introduced to a closed system is distributed equally to all parts of that system.[9] The emphasis on *equal* pressure makes Mary's response seem rather

---

understandings of pressure and heat would help engineers design more energy-efficient machines. French physicist Joseph Fourier (1768–1830), for instance, expanded Newton's "law of cooling" in *The Analytic Theory of Heat* (1822), while French scientist Sadi Carnot (1796–1832) set some of the most crucial groundwork for the field of thermodynamics in his studies of steam engines. Allen MacDuffie argues that "thermodynamic science can be seen as [equally] central to the 19th-century cultural and literary imaginary," explaining that, "for the Victorians, the thermodynamic process of energy conservation, transformation, and waste were intimately tied to built environments, especially in urban centers and factory towns" (212). See "Victorian Thermodynamics and the Novel: Problems and Prospects."

9   This principle—known as "Pascal's Law" or "Pascal's Principle"—and other work by Blaise Pascal (1623–1662) also prefaced John Dalton's work on the Law of Partial Pressures.

peculiar, since fainting suggests that the pressure she faces on Dunham Street is somehow greater than that which other individuals in the crowd experience. If Mary indeed experiences greater pressure, then this would constitute a violation of the natural law Pascal articulates in his pressure principle, rendering the diegetic space of the narrative more "unnatural," less rooted in the physical realities that govern extratextual space. In these contexts, when read through the lens of physics, the Carson mill fire scene, ironically, underscores the unnatural qualities of the diegesis, more closely aligning the novel with the Gothic, as narratives in this genre often do not conform to—but rather actively contradict—the laws of science in portrayals of space.

The concept of uneven distribution of pressure represents a significant underpinning of both the formal structure of *Mary Barton* and Gaskell's rhetorical gestures toward social reform. Through this particular attention to pressure, Gaskell demonstrates that such an extreme disparity between the living conditions of members of certain classes is as morally unethical as scientifically puzzling (as in the case of Mary's experience in the mill fire crowd). Indeed, the after-effects of the mill fire result in an increase in the pressure of want on certain members of the working class, but one that benefits the Carson mill owners, who occupy a privileged position in the bourgeois-driven conditions of the industrial landscape:

> The mills were merely worked to keep the machinery, human and metal, in some kind of order and readiness for better times. So [the fire repairs were] an excellent opportunity ... for refitting their factory with first-rate improvements, for which the insurance-money would amply pay ... The weekly drain of wages given for labour, useless in the present state of the market, was stopped ... There were happy family evenings, now that the men of business had time for domestic enjoyments. There is another side to the picture. There were homes over which the Carsons' fire threw a deep, terrible gloom; the homes of those who would fain work, and no man gave unto them—the homes of those to whom leisure was a curse. (*MB* 95)

The reference to the "Carsons' fire," placed after the account of "domestic enjoyments," allows the phrase to simultaneously evoke the mill fire and the hearth that warms the family's home, establishing a significant link between the two. The mill fire prompted the layoffs that now allow the hearth to keep burning over extended scenes of domestic bliss—bourgeois comforts maintained at the expense of underpaid and unemployed members of the working class. Members of the working class are at the mercy of a fluctuating market economy and the capitalist-driven caprices of the middle-class mill owners, who actively intensify the pressures of want that push them into deeper states of poverty and destitution in failing to provide steady jobs. As a consequence of unemployment, the ever-escalating pressures that the working class experiences register as a form of "undeserved punishment" that renders any "leisure" time spent at home a burden.[10]

---

[10] Gaskell strengthens the connection between pressure and punishment as related to the hardships of the working class through Biblical allusion: "So long and so weary was the pressure of the terrible times ... The people had thought the poverty of the preceding

Thus, the Carsons' fires—from both mill and hearth—effectively "curse" the working class with leisure, throwing a "deep, terrible gloom" over their homes, that gradually transforms would-be spaces of domestic tranquility into confined spaces of pressure and torture (95).

The effects of the unevenly distributed pressures of want emerge with great force in depictions of the inhabitants of Ben Davenport's home. While visiting the home during Davenport's final days, John Barton and George Wilson attempt to soothe and console the "fainting, dead-like" Mrs. Davenport by "pull[ing] her feet to the fire, which [had begun] to emit some faint heat," but which ultimately fails to have any discernible effect on her disposition (*MB* 99). The heat of the fire, even that from the revered Victorian symbol of the domestic hearth, fails to bring comfort to the inhabitants of the Davenport household. In this vein, the fire in the Davenport home is peculiar and otherworldly—and thus more quintessentially Gothic—for it seems almost without heat, as if the compressing spaces have caused fire's natural properties to change. Mrs. Davenport also experiences feelings of Gothic entrapment via the pressures of other bodies in her environment, describing how she has "pinched" herself in attempts to provide for her unweaned two-year-old child, who continues to physically burden her by suckling from her "dry, withered breast" (*MB* 102). Even a loving touch from her dying husband, first felt with "a feeble pressure of endearment," becomes "a heavy stiff weight on [her] head" the moment he passes away (111). The demands of other dependent bodies bring those attempting to provide for them closer to death themselves. The novel is littered with the bodies of walking corpses, "lank, ragged, dispirited, and famine-stricken" members of the impoverished working poor overwhelmed by the pressures of other bodies (243). The fear of these "corpses" causes members of the working poor to actively avoid their homes, which they see as places of dread rather than places of refuge, akin to John Barton's fellow Chartist John Slater, who confesses that his children's "cries for food [ring] in his ears" without respite, "making [him] afeard of going home" (247).

Based on the effects registered in the domestic scenes of the middle- and working-class residents of Manchester, the pressures of the industrial landscape are decidedly uneven in distribution. Even though Mr. Carson assures George Wilson "during these bad times … th' masters suffer too," the domestic pleasantries that continue in his home indicate otherwise (*MB* 105). Quite the contrary, "hard times" for Carson provide *additional* opportunities to engage in "domestic enjoyments," while John Barton's home, akin to the dwellings of other ill-fated members of the working class, becomes merely a place to sit in front of a cold, empty hearth, as the walls of his abode continue to "come into hideous nearness," leaving him

---

years hard to bear … but this year added sorely to its weight. Former times had chastised them with whips, but this chastised them with scorpions" (*MB* 160–61). Here she evokes the callous response of King Solomon's son King Rehoboam to subjects seeking lighter (tax) burdens as detailed in I Kings 7:11: "And now whereas my father did lade you with a heavy yoke, I will add to your yoke: my father hath chastised you with whips, but I will chastise you with scorpions."

"suffering and sinking under the pressure of want" that gradually pushes him into a premature grave (225). The peculiar, unconventional ways spaces behave in these instances—both the unequal distribution of pressures and Barton's perception of the moving walls around him—effectively defy the natural laws of physics. As the diegetic landscape becomes increasingly constricted, realist elements give way to the Gothic, which results in an inversion of the conventional associations that accompany the Victorian domestic setting. As the spaces of *Mary Barton* become increasingly constricted, the parallel currents of the realist and Gothic modes begin to bend toward each other and intersect, fusing the real with the surreal, the natural with the supernatural, to create a sense of diegetic and ideological pandemonium. Thus, the home effectively becomes the quintessential site of Gothic horror completely devoid of any human comforts, where a roaring fire cannot provide relief from the cold, the walls of rooms close in on their inhabitants, and the dead seem to walk among the living.

The ironic inversion embodied in the Gothic industrial home sets the scene for Gaskell to forward broader critiques of bourgeois domestic ideology by recoding the relationship between pressure and punishment as related to members of the working class.[11] If the domestic transforms into a site of horror in *Mary Barton*, then reconfiguring the grave as a site of moral transformation is all the more logical. While the virtue of the domestic sphere is a decidedly important, often venerated, theme in the novel as well as in Gaskell's larger body of work, in *Mary Barton* she makes equally significant gestures toward social reform through unique depictions of the grave: a space that shares links with the domestic sphere, but one distant enough from it to offer a subtler space in which to root more controversial arguments about class.

To move the novel in this direction, Gaskell begins to release spatial tensions as she pushes the narrative toward its conclusion—and more specifically, toward the shared grave of John Barton and Esther—gradually ushering *Mary Barton* back into a rural setting. In the wake of an increasing number of publicly funded cemeteries and the infamous Victorian "cult of mourning," graves become a prevalent—nay, highly popular—way to express bourgeois success, an extension of that which the domestic setting offered.[12] The "wooden mockery of stone respectabilities" that temporarily covers Ben Davenport's pauper grave, in which

---

[11]   Rebecca Styler argues that one of Gaskell's signature Victorian Gothic flourishes is the depiction of home as a "source of horror," which allows her to challenge "the bourgeois idealization of home as the haven of virtue, a safe realm governed by tenderness and Christian kindness which the public world could not afford" (38). See "The Problem of 'Evil' in Elizabeth Gaskell's Gothic Tales."

[12]   Sarah Rutherford explains in her concise yet comprehensive study, *The Victorian Cemetery*, "The cemetery was segregated socially by price of plots, so ensuring that civic rank would be maintained forever, even in death, an idea enthusiastically taken up in British cemeteries. These social divisions were often expressed physically by impressive and expensive monuments. Those who could not afford perpetuity could purchase a five-year lease on a plot; paupers were buried in common graves that each contained seven corpses" (11).

"pauper bodies were piled until within a foot or two of the surface," is a cheap imitation of the more ornate, ostentatious middle-class memorials that adorned the landscapes of nineteenth-century cemeteries (*MB* 113). However, the resting place that John Barton and Esther eventually share does not seem to match the grave depicted at Davenport's funeral:

> They laid her [Esther] in one grave with John Barton. And there they lie without name, or initial, or date. Only this verse is inscribed upon the stone which covers the remains of these two wanderers. Psalm ciii. v.9. —"For He will not always chide, neither will He keep His anger for ever." (*MB* 481)

Mary Elizabeth Hotz reads Gaskell's particular representation of John Barton and Esther's resting place as a reflection of her anxiety about the possibility of a working-class challenge to middle-class authority, which "results in death and burial in an unmarked grave ... While Gaskell's Unitarian beliefs held that no one is punished forever in the afterlife ... her depiction of the material conditions of Barton and Esther's burial betrays an adversarial judgment of them" (Hotz 51–2).[13] But this burial space clearly departs from the standard pauper grave. For instance, the presence of an inscription of any sort—Bible verse or otherwise—on a pauper grave is especially peculiar. Pauper graves, with the exception of temporary wooden tombstones, were often completely unmarked; sometimes nothing at all was left to designate the presence of human remains. For this reason, the grave that Barton and Esther share instead seems closer to a "guinea grave," which offered "a solution to the shame of an unmarked pauper's grave ... One guinea purchased a place in the plot and up to thirty-six letters of inscription on a communal headstone" (Rutherford 41–2). Furthermore, the likelihood of in-laws being buried together in a pauper grave, or even a guinea grave, would have been considerably small; those who ended up in either were most often buried with strangers, who had died in close proximity, rather than with kin, the latter a privilege reserved for those who owned family plots.[14]

In these contexts, the grave that Barton and Esther occupy is an ambiguous space in terms of class signification—a cut above the typical lowly pauper grave (and to an extent even that of the guinea grave), but of course nothing compared to the more elaborate middle-class resting places. The presence of an inscription on

---

[13]   Hotz argues that although Gaskell criticizes the middle-class "commodity of ritual" surrounding mourning practices while praising the more subdued customs of the working class, she ultimately undercuts this progressive attitude in her representation of John Barton's and Esther's death. Amanda Anderson prefaces Hotz's criticism in *Tainted Souls and Painted Faces: The Rhetoric of Fallenness in Victorian Culture*, reading *Mary Barton* as a novel that displays an "ambivalent" attitude toward the issue of "agency" vs. "victimization" of John and Esther—that is, the extent to which they were or were not able to control the circumstances that led to their premature demise (125).

[14]   Esther and John Barton die roughly two weeks apart, which makes it unlikely that they might have shared a pauper grave merely as a result of expiring in close proximity (*MB* 477–81).

their grave marker and their interment with family members ultimately suggests a forgiving, hopeful attitude toward the fate of these "two wanderers" in the afterlife (*MB* 481). Rather than condemning Barton and Esther for their failure to adhere to bourgeois standards of morality, Gaskell emphasizes the inadequacy of bourgeois institutions to execute proper judgment and punishment. Neither Barton nor Esther undergo prosecution for their most severe violations of the law, as opposed to Jem Wilson, who faces a full criminal trial for a crime he did not commit. Gaskell recognizes the extent to which bourgeois normalcy informs Victorian moral codes, and thus renders authorities unfamiliar with the hardships of the working poor unqualified to assess their moral character. Members of the middle class are at best indifferent and at worst utterly insensitive to the pressures of poverty in industrial Manchester; the latter attitude manifests with great force in Harry Carson's caricature of the half-starved men at the Chartist meeting, about which John Slater pensively remarks, "It seems to make me sad that there is any as can make game on what they've never knowed" (247).

In directing attention to the grave in *Mary Barton*, Elizabeth Gaskell effectively turns Barton and Esther—and other ill-fated members of the impoverished working class by extension—over to the ultimate moral authority "where no policeman can step in between," and in doing so encourages understanding and compassion between classes (*MB* 237). As the narrator explains in detail, although "the vices of the poor sometimes astound us *here* ... when the secrets of all hearts shall be made known, their virtues will astound us in far greater degree. Of this I am certain" (96). The reversal of spatial signification at the end of the novel—reconfiguring the "confined" space of the grave as something more positive than the torture-chamber walls of the home—demonstrates the rigid nature of middle-class (domestic) morality that suggests members of the working class have earned the deplorable conditions to which they are subjected. Through her focus on pressure and compression of spaces via combined Gothic and realist modes, Gaskell transvalues the unusually compressed space of the home with the traditionally compressed space of the grave to argue against this conception of the working class. Gaskell reverses the compression of grave space, and by extension the ever-enclosing walls of Barton's abode, pointing to God as the ultimate moral judge instead of human systems of authority invested in maintaining class stratification. In transforming the physical space of the grave through blurred class signifiers, Gaskell, in turn, opens the possibility for the ideological transformation of the classed nature of domestic ideology, just as she eventually reopens the spatial layout of the diegetic world at the conclusion of *Mary Barton*, ending in an open field "with room enough to spare" (481).

Works Cited

Alexander, Sarah C. "The Residuum, Victorian Naturalism, and the Entropic Narrative." *Nineteenth-Century Contexts* 35.2 (2013): 99–120. Print.

Anderson, Amanda. *Tainted Souls and Painted Faces: The Rhetoric of Fallenness in Victorian Culture*. Ithaca, NY: Cornell UP, 1993. Print.

Dannenberg, Hilary. *Coincidence and Counterfactuality: Plotting Time and Space in Narrative Fiction*. Lincoln, NE: U of Nebraska P, 2008. Print.

Engels, Friedrich. *The Condition of the Working-Class in England in 1844*. London: Swan Sonnenschein, 1892. Print.

Gallagher, Catherine. *The Industrial Reformation of English Fiction: Social Discourse and Narrative Form, 1832–1867*. Chicago, IL: U of Chicago P, 1985. Print.

Gaskell, Elizabeth. *Mary Barton*. 1848. Toronto: Broadview, 2000. Print.

Hompes, Mat. "Mrs. Gaskell." *The Gentleman's Magazine* 279 (August 1895): 124–38. Print.

Hotz, Mary Elizabeth. *Literary Remains: Representations of Death and Burial in Victorian England*. Albany, NY: State U of New York P, 2009. Print.

Hughes, Linda K., and Michael Lund. *Victorian Publishing and Mrs. Gaskell's Work*. Charlottesville: U of Virginia P, 1999. Print.

MacDuffie, Allen. "Victorian Thermodynamics and the Novel: Problems and Prospects." *Literature Compass* 8.4 (2011): 206–13. Print.

Mighall, Robert. *A Geography of Victorian Gothic Fiction: Mapping History's Nightmares*. Oxford: Oxford UP, 1999. Print.

Newton, Isaac. *Principia Mathematica*. 1686–1687. Trans. Andrew Motte. 1729. New York: Daniel Adee, 1846. Print.

———. "A Scale of the Degrees of Heat." 1701. *The Philosophical Transactions of the Royal Society of London* (1749). Print.

Rutherford, Sarah. *The Victorian Cemetery*. Oxford: Shire Publications, 2008. Print.

Styler, Rebecca. "The Problem of 'Evil' in Elizabeth Gaskell's Gothic Tales." *Gothic Studies* 12.1 (2010): 33–50. Print.

Sucksmith, Harvey Peter. "Elizabeth Gaskell's *Mary Barton* and William Mudford's *The Iron Shroud*." *Nineteenth-Century Fiction* 29.4 (1975): 460–63. Print.

Uglow, Jenny. *Elizabeth Gaskell: A Habit of Stories*. London: Faber and Faber, 1993. Print.

PART II
Mobility and Boundaries

Chapter 5
Unimagined Community and Disease in *Ruth*[1]

Katherine Inglis

Ruth dies of typhus. Contrary to the assertions of otherwise perceptive scholarship, Ruth is *not* a victim of typhoid, cholera, or a sexually transmitted disease.[2] Although, as Heather Levy has noted, Gaskell omits some of typhus' symptoms, Ruth's condition is largely in line with typical presentation.[3] Ruth experiences an oppressive headache, fever, flushed cheeks, fatigue and disordered cognition, temporary lucidity, and delirium. Certain symptoms stressed by Gaskell—amnesia, choreic hand movements, lack of aggression, and ataxia—were also identified by mid-century fever specialists as characteristic of the last stages of typhus. William Jenner, for example, who established the non-identity of the two diseases, typhus and typhoid, in 1849, noted that typhus patients were generally inactive, sometimes sinking into a "coma-vigil" (rather like Ruth's waking unconsciousness) that was invariably fatal. The critical impulse to convert that which is clearly identified as typhus into a disease more readily explicable in terms of sexual transgression and punishment is understandable given the novel's principal subject, but this critical move does disservice to the novel's attention to contemporary medical theory and practice. If we insist on reading Ruth's death only as a consequence

---

[1]   This work was supported by the Wellcome Trust [101771/Z/13/Z].

[2]   Kate Flint names typhoid instead of typhus (21). Allan Conrad Christensen names typhus, but identifies it with venereal disease, noting a popular association between diseases of urban degradation, such as typhus, and "areas" where "sexual immorality also flourishes." He therefore reads Ruth's typhus as "a sort of venereal disease" (22). R.K. Webb sees Ruth's work as a nurse in a "cholera epidemic" as the last act in a "succession of penances" (166). Amanda Anderson's landmark reading of *Ruth* (to which this essay is indebted for its insights into Gaskell's depiction of radically intersubjective forms of consciousness) also misidentifies cholera as the cause of death (127). These minor misreadings may seem trivial, but the prevalence of such errors in criticism of this novel indicates a lack of critical interest in the pivotal typhus chapters. One aim of the present essay is to consider what a reading of *Ruth* that is attentive to the typhus epidemic—as the cause of Ruth's death, but also as a critical event in its own right—might reveal.

[3]   Like the present essay, Levy's reading is attentive to the etiology and symptomatology of typhus in *Ruth*, but in her depiction of typhus as a mechanism for the delivery of moral judgment, Levy differs significantly in her conclusions. For Levy, "typhus fever is the vehicle of castigation"; Ruth's death, therefore, "advances the conventional Victorian moral tone that the novel ultimately endorses" (86).

of her relationship with Bellingham/Donne, then we fail to acknowledge that which Florence Nightingale praised—Gaskell's depiction of the development of a hospital matron (qtd. in McDonald 785). Criticism that interprets Ruth's career as a paid nurse as a marker of her social degradation fails to acknowledge the professional identity that *Ruth* helps to create.

The critical tendency to reduce the meaning of the typhus epidemic to the intimate relation between Ruth and Bellingham also diverts attention from another of the novel's major achievements: its depiction of an *unimagined* networked community, traceable by the circulation of typhus, which extends beyond the known—or, rather, *imagined*—social and political limits of kinship, town, region, and nation. The "meanwhile ..." plot structure that Benedict Anderson proposes as a precise analogue for the idea of nation is at work in *Ruth*, but, crucially, it proceeds in advance of the understanding of the focalizing characters (22–33).[4] *Ruth* is concerned with the activity and movement of members of a community who fail to imagine each other's existence and their community's extent.

I borrow this idea of the unimagined community from Robert Thornton's recent anthropological study of sexual networks and HIV prevalence. The network through which HIV is transmitted can be made visible through the analysis of epidemiological data using network theory, but it is invisible to its constituents. Thornton explains that the constituents of sexual networks "do not represent the extent, size, pattern, or even existence of these networks either to themselves or to social scientists. Thus, unlike the explicit networks of friendship or kinship, the sexual network is an invisible community; it is *unimagined*" (Thornton xviii). The network through which typhus is transmitted in *Ruth* is perceived by the narrator and represented to the reader, but it is invisible to the constituents of the network. Its composition is in part determined by familiar, visible connections structured by kinship and shared urban space, but it is also influenced by less visible extended connections: trade networks, international military campaigns, and transport systems. The network's real density and extension are not fully visible until typhus brings it into view. At the same time that Dickens was using communicable disease to make visible the common society of aristocrats and crossing sweepers in *Bleak House* (1852–1853), Gaskell used typhus to reveal the real interconnectedness and broad scope of a fallen woman's community. Ruth, in her shame, and her accusers, in their anger, wish that she could be isolated from that community. Their desire might seem to be gratified in the closing chapters, when Ruth combats the typhus outbreak within the "lazar-house" (343). The designation of the Infirmary as a lazar-house, a term associated with quarantine, could be read as a marker of Ruth's isolation from the interconnected social body; however, far from being cut off from

---

4   Mary Mullen's essay in this collection also responds to Anderson, and introduces a productive distinction between the novel's ideological commitment to national unity and its representation of a "heterogeneous present." In *North and South*, Mullen argues, "national, temporal consensus is one of the *ends* of the novel rather than an organising principle within the narrative," and that end is not fully achieved within the diegesis. *Ruth*, however, does achieve a moment of unity in its closing pages, which I discuss in my essay.

the community, within the Infirmary Ruth is revealed to be at the center of a dense web of social and professional connections. Typhus, disclosing the community's form (that of a network) and scale (international), demonstrates the idea of moral quarantine to be an impossible fantasy.

Barriers

Ruth imagines the world as a system of boundaries and barriers that can (and should) separate her from those she loves. A horizon to Ruth marks not merely the limits of perception, but the limits of community. Abandoned by Bellingham, Ruth looks out onto the "immovable mountains" that separate her from her lover: they represent "the barrier horizon" that she has failed to traverse and will not attempt again (81). That horizon in Eccleston becomes a "hilly line" that bounds her world (114). Ruth's sense of her own boundedness shapes her response to the discovery of her son Leonard's illegitimacy. In a state of acute distress (figured as mental and physiological), Ruth comes to believe that that her removal is necessary to save Leonard from disgrace: "[i]f she were away, and gone no one knew where—lost in mystery, as if she were dead—perhaps the cruel hearts might reflect, and show pity on Leonard; while her perpetual presence would but call up the remembrance of his birth" (281). Ruth's spatial imagination leads her to confuse distance and memory: sufficient distance (being "away") is necessary to permit her offence to be expunged from the community's memory. As such, her instinctive response to remove herself from the community enacts the policy of Urania Cottage, the philanthropic project of Angela Burdett-Coutts and Charles Dickens. In 1850, Gaskell sought Dickens's advice in the case of a 16-year-old female prisoner named Pasley who had been seduced and abandoned by her doctor. Gaskell wished Pasley to emigrate "with as free and unbranded a character as she can; if possible, the very fact of having been in prison &c to be unknown" (*Letters* 61). She may not have shared Dickens's views on the dependence of the fallen woman's redemption on exile, but Gaskell did believe that Pasley was vulnerable to further exploitation. Emigration was necessary to preserve Pasley from real, present hazards; crucially, however, this solution is rejected for Ruth. Gaskell represents Ruth's fevered fantasy of self-isolation as an idea born of temporary mental derangement and reasoning from false principles. It would have separated her from her child and removed the best influence on his character.

Ruth's most vocal exponent of moral quarantine, Bradshaw, demonstrates the incompatibility of notions of ineradicable impurity and moral isolationism with Christian charity. Bradshaw imagines morality in terms of disease geography, drawing "a clear line of partition" between "the two great groups" of mankind (the saved, and the rest) (262). This moral *cordon sanitaire* governs his condemnation of Ruth: if good depends on its separation from evil for its continued existence, then the innocent must be kept apart from the tainted. A "fallen and depraved" woman is not fit to associate with his "pure children" (284). His logic leads ineluctably to condemnation of her child, that "heir of shame" whose association with his "innocent" children could have "contaminated" them (275). He repeats the charge to Benson: "the usefulness [of employing Ruth in Bradshaw's home] was to consist in contaminating my innocent girls" (283).

In 1853, Bradshaw's rhetoric would have been perceived to depend on shaky foundations. Lazarettos and quarantine policies were the subject of political and medical controversy in the late 1840s. Criticism of quarantine was not confined to those with economic interests in its relaxation: popular opinion held that Britain's quarantine laws were inhumane and ineffective, particularly in the aftermath of the 1845 *Eclair* controversy, as Mark Harrison has shown. The *Eclair*, a steam-sloop deployed by the British navy against the West African slave trade, had a disastrous return voyage from Sierra Leone, losing most of her crew to what was probably yellow fever.[5] When the ship returned to Britain on 28 September 1845 with less than a third of its original crew, she was placed in quarantine at Stangate, where five more men became sick and died (Health, 1852, 93). These deaths in British quarantine were regarded as a national disgrace, the unnecessary consequences of an archaic practice, and were criticized in strong terms in the press and by the Navy (Harrison 80–101). The *Eclair* is cited in the General Board of Health's first *Report on Quarantine* (1848), which argued that local atmospheric and sanitary conditions, not contagion, were the most important factors influencing the spread of disease, and therefore proposed "the entire discontinuance of the existing quarantine regulations in this country and the substitution of sanitary regulations" (Health 127).[6] Although *Ruth* represents typhus as a contagious disease, like most of her contemporaries, at this time when anticontagionism was at its height, Gaskell's idea of epidemic disease was influenced by anticontagionist thought. Her husband William Gaskell worked with a sanitary committee to plan for potential cholera epidemics, and in a letter of 1854 on the Soho cholera epidemic (the same that was mapped by John Snow), she deferred to Florence Nightingale as the last of several authorities who held cholera to be "*not* infectious" (Uglow 300; *Letters* 211). Quarantine, in 1853, was an unpopular practice, seen as archaic, unnecessary, and inhumane. It has no part to play in *Ruth*, neither as a medical protocol, nor as a model for the moral management of fallen women. It is the treatment of the sick *within* the community that stems the typhus epidemic, and it is the acceptance of the fallen woman *within* the community, not Bradshaw's programme of exclusion, that allows Ruth to escape the usual fates of fictional fallen women.

---

[5]   An epidemic fever devastated Boa Vista, one of the Portuguese Cape Verde Islands, shortly after the *Eclair* was permitted to dock there. Local voices identified the *Eclair* as the origin of the disease, but to have admitted the identity of the fevers of the *Eclair* and Boa Vista would have been problematic for the Portuguese authorities. See Harrison on the official Portuguese investigation, the various reports commissioned by the Admiralty, and their reinterpretation by the anticontagionist General Board of Health (80–101).

[6]   The *Eclair* controversy is also discussed at great length in the General Board of Health's Second *Report on Quarantine* (89–118).

Ruth's Map: Imagining Distance

Jonathan Grossman recently has shown how Dickens's novels create ways of understanding the rise of a networked community structured by integrated, extensive public transport systems. Most pertinent to the present discussion is Grossman's fine reading of interconnectedness and perspective in *Little Dorrit* (1855–1857), in which two intertwined plots reveal an extended, international community formed of overlapping social, temporal and physical connections, few of which are visible or comprehensible to the novel's characters. In *Dorrit*, he explains, the "density and extensivity of people's interconnections exceeds their capacity to grasp them" (195). A similar challenge faces the reader of *Ruth*: a dense and extensive network of connections must be inferred if we are to make sense of Eccleston's typhus epidemic, but that network's existence is only dimly and fitfully grasped by the characters. Like *Little Dorrit*'s cast of international travelers, *Ruth*'s characters are repeatedly surprised by apparent coincidences and truncated chains of separation. The distinction I draw between *Dorrit* and *Ruth* is the visibility of the network within the diegesis. Dickens's characters, Grossman observes, "project an omniscient-like view" of the system within which they know themselves to be circulating; their difficulty is that they know their understanding of their network can only ever be partial (195). In contrast, *Ruth*'s characters consistently fail to imagine the network's existence, their understanding lagging behind its rapid development. The novel depicts a society in transition, one that has not yet grasped the impact on "remote" communities of the extension of the canal, road and railway networks, innovations in road surfacing, expansion of commercial shipping, increased international trade, and military action overseas. Such political and commercial "imperial networks" both "increased the speed and frequency of communications between hitherto disparate territories" and "presented new opportunities for the passage of disease" (Harrison 81). *Ruth* draws attention to the disparity between the perceived remoteness of any given community and its actual connectedness within imperial networks. Regular, predictable, systematized connections link the novel's loci (Fordham, Llan-dhu, Eccleston, Abermouth) to the capital and to each other; but the novel's characters, particularly Ruth, perceive them to be more remote than they are proved to be by the typhus epidemic.

On two occasions, Ruth's difficulty in thinking about distance leads to crisis. Her mistaken belief that her childhood home is inaccessible from Fordham enables Bellingham to gain her confidence: Ruth's nostalgic lament for "the dear old Grange, that I shall never see again" is punctured by his practical correction that "it is only six miles off; you may see it any day. It is not an hour's ride"; if they walk, they could manage the journey in two and a half hours "without hurrying" (36). In Llan-dhu, Ruth continues to struggle to understand distance. The village, easily accessible by mail coach and packed with tourists, is not actually remote, yet she is baffled by Benson, an Englishman who "knew the country and the paths so perfectly he must be a resident" (56). Bellingham and Benson are both repeat visitors, familiar enough with the village to know its terrain, to be on friendly terms with its residents, and in Benson's case, to have learned its language. This familiarity with the landscape and people of the national periphery is made possible by the stagecoach's contraction of travelling time. Abandoned by Bellingham, watching his coach climb the mountain pass to Pen trê Voelas, Ruth does not understand that what appears to be "a snail's pace" is actually much faster than her best speed on foot, and so ensues the tragic spectacle of Ruth attempting to overtake a coach: "Every time it was visible it was in fact more distant, but Ruth would not believe it" (76–7). Ruth's imagination remains that of the pedestrian. As she descends into despair, William Wynn, the village post boy, traverses the "barrier horizon" multiple times, travelling by coach between Llan-dhu and Pen trê Voelas with letters about Ruth.

The relative ease and speed of the journey from Llan-dhu to Eccleston by mail coach ought to have warned Ruth and the Bensons that Ruth's false identity would one day be discovered. They are not journeying to a remote sanctuary; they are speeding through an efficient, well-traveled network. That efficiency, and the technological innovation that made it possible, is signaled by the Bensons' method of travel. The Bensons travel outside the coach for economy, a mode of transport enabled, as Grossman notes, "by the smoothing power of engineered roads and effective spring-suspension systems" (34). They are accompanied on their journey by a jolly woman who tells of her three sons, all soldiers and sailors, living "here, there, and everywhere," in America, China, and Gibraltar (107). This cameo from a fellow traveler is a rare articulation of the "meanwhile" plot structure: the jolly mother "can laugh and eat and enjoy" while her son is "in China, making tea" precisely because she can imagine her son's simultaneous existence, though they are separated by distance (107). Ruth never attempts this imaginative leap, never speculating as to what Bellingham might be doing while she is suffering. He has left: he is lost to her. Ruth's sense of a bounded world prevents her from imagining the mundane continuation of existence beyond her immediate environment. Her idea of community depends on place rather than time, hence her unformed plan to expunge memory of her disgrace by going "away," a stratagem that depends upon a wholly spatial, atemporal model of community. Simultaneity and the idea of "meanwhile," form no part of Ruth's imagined community.[7] *Ruth*, however, gradually discloses an idea of community dependent less on space than on connections extending through time.

Two coincidences, necessary for the advancement of the plot, are made plausible by the novel's attention to geographical and social connectedness. The political maneuvers of Bradshaw will eventually bring Bellingham to Abermouth, where he will confront Ruth, and the mercantile ambitions of Mrs. Pearson, a relative of her former employer, will bring knowledge of Ruth's past to Eccleston. Traveling is thought to be difficult; it proves to be easy and efficient: Abermouth, which

---

[7]   Ruth's idiosyncratic, problematic experience of time intersects with Mullen's revision of Anderson's model. Unable to experience the common understanding of time exemplified by her commercially minded fellow traveler, Ruth is, at this point of the novel, not a constituent of any community.

Leonard believes is "far more distant and inaccessible than the beautiful blue sky," can be reached by rail in time for dinner (210).[8] The mechanism of Ruth's public disgrace reveals her social network. The catastrophe of Ruth's life—the revelation of Leonard's illegitimacy to Eccleston—is brought about by the movement of information through a network of acquaintances, and through a branch of which she has no knowledge. Disaster is precipitated by a chance conversation between Jemima Bradshaw and Mrs. Pearson, who passes information about Ruth to the gossips of Eccleston. Ruth does not know of, and never meets, Mrs. Pearson. Even before typhus makes visible the density and extension of Ruth's community, the existence of a network is evident in the movement of information. The Bensons brought Ruth to Eccleston in the belief she could "go into quite a fresh place, and be passed off as a widow," but their idea of a fresh place is a relic of an earlier time, when the nation was less densely interconnected (99). As Faith Benson attempts to teach Ruth about Eccleston, her new home, Ruth is likened to "a child who gets a few pieces of a dissected map, and is confused until a glimpse of the whole unity is shown him" (116). The map represents Ruth's community, its dimensions and hierarchies patiently delineated by Faith Benson; but as the novel's perspective expands to register Parliament in London and the slow progress of typhus, the dissected map becomes emblematic not only of Ruth's (in)comprehension, but of the general condition of knowledge. A community is always greater than any constituent's concept of it.

The pieces of the dissected map come together in the novel's closing chapters, revealing the community's extent and dimensions through the communication of typhus. It comes "creeping, creeping, in hidden slimy courses" in a wet and cold "early autumn," in the immediate aftermath of a "national triumph of arms" that opens "a new market for the staple manufacture" of Eccleston, bringing to an end a "year or two" of depressed trade (342). Typhus is introduced through a "meanwhile" plot structure: Gaskell quickly sketches three plots (the revival of trade, a projected election, and balls for the "shopocracy") that develop concurrently with typhus' progress through the community (342). "*While* the town was full of these subjects by turns," typhus is detected "in the low Irish lodging-houses" by Catholic priests (342, emphasis added). Attacking first the impoverished and disenfranchised, it spreads in advance of the capacity of individual medical practitioners to determine its epidemic status:

> Before the medical men of Eccleston had had time to meet together and consult, and compare the knowledge of the fever which they had severally gained, it had, like the blaze of a fire which had long smouldered, burst forth in many places at once—not merely among the loose-living and vicious, but among the decently poor—nay, even among the well-to-do and respectable. (342)

Typhus' virulence reveals the real nature and composition of the community of Eccleston—the co-existence of the respectable, the decently poor, and the

---

[8]   Rob Burroughs's essay in this collection identifies Abermouth as a critical site where past and present can be brought together.

previously unmentioned Irish. Moreover, Gaskell's careful delineation of the situation in which typhus becomes epidemic—the decline and revival of trade, the national triumph of arms, the existence of an impoverished migrant community—represents Eccleston in a new aspect. Ruth's remote sanctuary is incorporated within national political networks and international trade networks, it has a large migrant community, and it is dependent on international military action for its economic prosperity. *Ruth* charts the integration of remote communities within the informal imperial network using that most visible of biomarkers: communicable disease. Ruth lives in a time of increasingly rapid circulation of people, goods, rumors and disease; had she lived in a less mobile age, she might have been able to escape her past.

Isolating Typhus

Gaskell makes the movement of typhus an index of the true scale and connectedness of the community, but typhus is not a neutral biomarker. A generic fever would have served the purpose of dispatching the heroine, and in earlier episodes in the novel, Gaskell is content to leave the nature of disease unspecified. The late introduction of a specific disease, and one that was generally accepted to be contagious (except by the most extreme proponents of anticontagionism), is significant. Typhus was a migrant who had settled in Britain's slums. In the Victorian popular imagination, typhus was the virulent "gaol fever," "ship fever," "Irish fever," and "camp fever" that destroyed armies. It was associated with overcrowded prisons and ships, with famine and diaspora, with urban degradation, and with international conflict. Typhus had been the constant attendant of war in Europe since the sixteenth century, and in living memory, it "held the epidemiological sway" in the Revolutionary and Napoleonic Wars (Smallman-Raynor and Cliff 102). It was the predominant cause of mortality in the retreat from Corunna, and it was typhus that ended Napoleon's Russian campaign (Smallman-Raynor and Cliff 104–8; Talty). It wrought devastation on the malnourished, vulnerable population of Ireland during the Famine, and on the Irish diaspora who lived in overcrowded accommodation in British urban centers. Primarily a louse-born disease, typhus increases in prevalence in overcrowded environments and where personal hygiene is neglected. Of the communicable diseases, only typhus and tuberculosis have such a "broad environmental ecology," the key determining factors in typhus prevalence being "domestic and working conditions, … cleanliness, ventilation, and personal hygiene, and the economic rhythms of society" (Hardy 191–2). Hardy notes that typhus "appears wherever poverty, crowding, and insanitary conditions prevail, in times of social dislocation, and principally in the winter months" (Hardy 191–2). Gaskell's attention to temperature, economic depression, and overcrowding is astute. Prison reform, improved conditions in military hospitals and on board naval ships, and the sanitation movement achieved a dramatic decline in incidence over the course of the century, but at the time of *Ruth*'s genesis, typhus' impact on the urban poor and those who attended them was severe (Spink 10–11, 323;

Zinsser 279, 288–93). Typhus had been epidemic in England in every year since 1837, reaching peak mortality in 1847 (Loether 113–14, 284–5). It was increasing in incidence and in visibility, appearing more frequently in mortality statistics, recorded hospital admissions, and as the subject of published lectures, treatises, and case histories.

Gaskell's depiction of the management of typhus in the Eccleston Infirmary correlates with its management in mid-century Manchester. The Eccleston Infirmary shares key practices with the Manchester Royal Infirmary and the Manchester House of Recovery, a specialist fever hospital. The House of Recovery was established in 1796 "to meliorate the condition of the poor, to prevent the generation of disease, to obviate the propagation of them by contagion and to mitigate those which exist by providing comforts and accommodation of the sick" (Sutherland 23). Patients were carried to the House in a sedan chair reserved for their use, and upon admission their linen and bedclothes were removed, washed, and aired on the House's own drying green (25). No visitors were admitted without authorization from a doctor, and although the attending physicians held positions at other institutions, the House had its own Resident Clerk, Matron, fever nurses, and servants (25). The 1847–1848 typhus epidemic overwhelmed the House: in 1847, every bed was full and a temporary hospital was established to accommodate the overflow (36). By 1850, the funds of the House were depleted by the expense of treating epidemic fever and the withdrawal of financial support from the civil authorities, and the House was incorporated into the Infirmary in 1852 (Sutherland 36–8; Pickstone 102–6). The civil authorities seem to have been persuaded by the General Board of Health's argument that it was the *concentration* of cases in confined spaces, not contagion, that increased typhus' virulence and caused epidemics, and advised the Infirmary to house fever patients on the general wards (Health 45–6). The Manchester trustees were unconvinced and separated the Infirmary's new fever wards from the general wards with partitions and a dedicated access staircase (Renaud 132; Sutherland 38). Although incorporated within the financial and physical structure of the Infirmary, the House's architecture of isolation continued to govern the treatment of fever patients and the organization of staff. Gaskell recreates these conditions in the Eccleston Infirmary. Gaskell stresses the isolation of cases within dedicated fever wards staffed by specialists—the "customary staff of matrons and nurses"—and swift isolation and transport of patients: "[a] portion of the Infirmary of the town was added to that already set apart for a fever-ward; the smitten were carried thither at once, whenever it was possible, in order to prevent the spread of infection; and on that lazar-house was concentrated all the medical skill and force of the place" (343). Access is restricted, and Ruth lives within the Infirmary during her tenure.

The years of typhus' peak incidence and the closure of the House coincided with Gaskell's acquaintance with Charles William Bell, a Manchester physician with a special interest in fever who worked at the House and Infirmary. The Gaskells and the Bells socialized together and assisted each other: in 1850, Gaskell informed Eliza Fox that she had involved Bell in a plan to honor the philanthropy of Thomas Wright, and was also reading his daughter's manuscript novel (*Letters* 63). Bell, nephew of the surgeon and anatomist Sir Charles Bell, had become interested in fever during his early career in Persia. He was appointed at the Manchester Royal Infirmary in 1847, and was attending physician at the House from 1848–1852, the period of typhus' greatest prevalence and mortality (Brockbank 25–7). Bell seems a plausible source for *Ruth*'s representation of typhus and its treatment.

In the immediate aftermath of the Manchester typhus epidemic, Bell developed a theory of fever causation. The prompt for this appears to have been a lecture on typhus delivered at the 1848 meeting of the Provincial Medical Association by William Davies of Bath, which Bell praised for its distinguishing of communicable and non-communicable fevers (Bell, "Lecture" 647). In the following year, Bell delivered the address in medicine to the Association, and he complicated Davies's theory. Like many of his contemporaries, Bell responded to anticontagionism by developing a multifactorial idea of disease causation informed by Justus von Liebig's organic chemistry (Pelling 324). There were, Bell argued, three causes of epidemics: specific poison, which always produced contagious disease; putrefaction of organic matter, which could be communicated but did not necessarily produce contagious disease; and epidemic influence, which was never contagious. Bell's classification of typhus overlaps with the characterization of typhus in *Ruth*. Bell classed "Irish typhus" as a combination of the first and second classes: it had been brought to Britain by Irish refugees from famine, and had combined with endemic "putrid fever" (Bell, "Address" 20). So too in *Ruth*, typhus is an endemic "fever which is never utterly banished from the sad haunts of vice and misery," but becomes epidemic within the Irish population (342). It is also, clearly, a contagious disease, as Bell insisted in his writings on typhus. When asserting the contagiousness of typhus, Bell referred back to Davies's lecture, specifically to his account of his first encounter with typhus, in which he was able to conduct a miniature epidemiological study and trace the outbreak "distinctly to an individual" (Bell, "Address" 22). The name of that individual and the progress of typhus charted by Davies will be familiar to readers of *Ruth*. On 4 March 1848 a man "named John Dunn" was admitted to the Bath United Hospital with typhus, which his neighbor in the ward then contracted (Davies 10). Bellingham, at the time he lies delirious with typhus in *Ruth*, is known as Donne. Davies described a second history of infection from the same epidemic, in which a ward nurse contracted typhus from a female patient whose "delirium [was] of a more active character than usual," which therefore brought the nurse into "more frequent and immediate contact with her than is commonly necessary" (10). Bellingham shares this atypical mania: in his typhus delirium he becomes a "wild, raging figure" (357). A third case was traced to an "Irish woman" (Davies 9). The parallels between Davies's published lecture and *Ruth* are intriguing: Dr. Davies of Bath becomes Mr. Davis, surgeon; the Irish woman becomes the Irish population; Dunn becomes Donne; and Donne/Bellingham acquires the unusually active delirium of the patient who exhausted the nurse. It is by no means certain, or even probable, that Gaskell read Davies's published lecture; but her familiarity with Bell at the time of Manchester's typhus crisis makes it plausible that she heard a version of Bell's favorable account of Davies's small but compelling demonstration of typhus' contagiousness.

Bell wrote forcefully on the malign consequences of denying the contagiousness of typhus. Contrary to the stated opinion of the General Board of Health, he wrote, "contagion is the one and only means by which this disease is propagated ... though its diffusion may be favored by atmospheric and other causes" (Bell, "Address" 21). It did not necessarily follow, however, that typhus should be made a quarantinable disease. Although Bell believed that "an efficient system of quarantine against the introduction of specific typhus from Ireland" could have saved thousands of lives, he concluded that, with the disease already in circulation in Britain, "it would be absurd to maintain quarantine for this purpose" (Bell, "Address" 34–5). As with *Ruth*'s dreams of a moral *cordon sanitaire*, quarantine is dismissed as an idealist's fantasy. This should not, though, dissuade medical practitioners from isolating the sick in fever hospitals: this practice, he insisted, was "the only means by which the poor have it in their power to preserve their families and neighborhood from infection" (Bell, "Address" 39).

Purification

Bell acknowledged that quarantine could have prevented typhus from becoming epidemic, but he insisted that to attempt it in the present age was futile. The barrier between England and the domain of typhus had already been breached, and the disease had become endemic. *Ruth* makes a similar criticism of moral *cordon sanitaires*. In a densely interconnected and extended community, the isolation of the impure from the pure, even if we admit the categories, is impossible. Gaskell develops an alternative way of imagining moral impurity, one more in sympathy with her Unitarian faith, which reconfigures purity as a gradual, effortful process of purification. Ruth's purification takes the form of reconciliation with her community and, ultimately, improves that community's knowledge of itself. As such, her purification overlaps with the Unitarian idea of atonement as a state of being at one with fellow humanity (literally "at-one-ment") (Webb 166). She who in Bradshaw's moral schema would be separated from the community for fear of staining the pure, is instead expected to work out her redemption within the community. Real at-one-ment must be instantiated in a social setting, and cannot take the form of lonely penance. In Ruth's work as a nurse, a healer, and a moral exemplar, we can see Gaskell imagining a form of domestic mission. Unitarian domestic missions established to relieve poverty, Webb observes, emphasized individual moral examples, one-on-one relationships, and common humanity (147). Ruth's career fulfills the demands of atonement and the domestic mission. In the fellowship she establishes with and between sufferers, she achieves atonement not through her death, but through her reconfiguration of her community.

Before Ruth returns home from the Infirmary, she submits to a procedure of "purification" recommended by Davis, the Infirmary's surgeon (347). The term "purification" is, by this late point in the novel, strongly associated with moral and spiritual improvement. Gaskell's application of "pure" and "impure" differs from conservative Victorian usage: "pure" is repeatedly applied to Leonard, the illegitimate child (132, 134); to the "Christian standard—that divine test of the true and pure" that Bradshaw fails to meet in his electioneering (212); and to Ruth's love for the father of her child (156). In place of the absolute dichotomy of purity and impurity, Gaskell substitutes a process of purification. This process was foreseen by Benson for Ruth from the moment they learn of her pregnancy: her reverence for her child, he asserted, "will be purification" (97). And, just as Benson predicted, at moments of crisis—when Leonard is born, when she meets Donne/Bellingham—Ruth prays for purification. This desire is natural to motherhood, Gaskell stresses: mothers "pray to God to purify and cleanse their souls," for their children's sake (133), and it is in the immediate aftermath of Leonard's birth that Ruth begins the "hours of spiritual purification" that bring painful consciousness of Bellingham's selfishness (134). Purification is equated with a mother's (not a maiden's) love, selflessness, and hard-won knowledge. Purity here, notably, is *not* innocence: it is an aspiration engendered by knowledge of one's own imperfection.

Initially, the concept proves difficult to grasp: Faith Benson holds the doctrine to be "questionable morality," and Jemima Bradshaw is reluctant to accept that Ruth might have "worked her way through the deep purgatory of repentance up to something like purity again" (97, 265). It is recognition of her own imperfection that enables Jemima herself to be "purified from pride" (299), and to accept that there is not "the faintest speck of impurity" in Ruth (211). *Ruth* is not a story of fall and delayed punishment; it is a story of coercion, stigmatization, and communal reconciliation. It describes the reconfiguration of the meaning of impurity and recognition of common imperfection. Purity, an ideal, absolute state, becomes a process of *purification*, in which that which is contaminated may be healed.

Hostile reviews of *Ruth* challenged its critique of the rhetoric of moral quarantine. Purification reverted to purity in *Sharpe's London Magazine*'s protest against the "communion" of the maiden and the "spotted woman" (Easson 209). The *Christian Observer*'s critique was an explicit defense of the moral *cordon sanitaire*:

> "Ruth," the heroine of the volumes, has offended against those laws of God and man which bind a woman to purity of life and conversation … [W]e ourselves, poor offending creatures, ought to forgive her. But we believe that society would sustain the deepest injury if, in virtue of this act of forgiveness, we were to rebuild the bridge of general intercourse between the guilty and the pure … Virtue needs all the guardians she can have in this "naughty world," and one of them is, those fences which society has erected to exclude from the common haunts of society the notoriously guilty, though they may also be the sincerely contrite. (Easson 314–15)

Conversely, favorable reviews embraced the novel's reconfiguration of the language of disease and purification. George Henry Lewes set Bradshaw's favorite slur in scare quotes: "If she be *called* a widow, no one will be 'contaminated' by her" (Easson 216). John Forster enthusiastically adopted Gaskell's language and idea of purification:

> Ruth grows in purity and goodness; whatever had been weak in her character becomes strong for her child's sake ... the very mark of her shame (a thought worked out to the last of this book with wonderful spirit and unflinching truth and courage) become the motive and the means of her purification. (Easson 221)

Similarly, *Bentley's Miscellany* recognized *Ruth* as "the history of one strengthened and purified by a fiery trial ... a leper whose leprosy is cleansed" (Easson 240).

I would take this assessment further, and reiterate that which Nightingale stressed: *Ruth* celebrates the possibility of healing and the achievements of medical professionals. *Ruth* predates the secular beatification of Nightingale, but its recognition of nursing as a profession, particularly the special professional and *moral* identity of the fever nurse, is in line with contemporary medical opinion. For example, the physician Robert Graves stressed the special skillfulness of the fever nurse, particularly in managing patients "who are ... in a state analogous to insanity ... during a course of typhus fever. There is a necessity for moral management in fever as well as in insanity, and this is understood only by an experienced nurse" (115). Ruth's career, and her purification, should be understood in this context.

The scene beneath the Infirmary's window, in which Leonard hears the families of those Ruth has served praise her skill, contains a passionate rejection of the reading of Ruth's service as degradation. Such service strengthens and purifies. To the accusation that "she has been a great sinner, and this is her penance," an old man whose daughter died in Ruth's arms responds angrily that Ruth "has never been a great sinner; nor does she do her work as a penance, but for the love of God" (346). His clarion call is answered by "a clamour of tongues, each with some tale" of Ruth's work (347). Here Gaskell reveals the invisible network Ruth has circulated within, the scale and extent of her movements unknown until this moment, when typhus draws the community together. "Few were aware how much Ruth had done," for she does not speak of her activity: like the silent and invisible movement of typhus among the Irish poor, Ruth's silent and invisible work has gone unwitnessed until it suddenly breaks out into the open, made known at last through the overwhelming clamor of the crowd (347). The force of this moment compels Leonard to make contact with the community for the first time since he learned of his disgrace, drawing him into the crowd and prompting his proud declaration of affinity with Ruth.

Ruth closes with markers of the community's esteem for its savior: the praise of the massed poor, the formal thanks voted by the Board (presumably the local Board of Health), and the crowd at Ruth's funeral sermon. It is meaningful that this gathering is composed both of Ruth's intimate associates and a mass of unknown figures. As typhus revealed the extent of the community, bringing it into view at the Infirmary, so the sermon reveals Eccleston's unknown, unrecognized aspect. The community is no longer unimagined, but nor does it need to be imagined, for in the closing pages of the novel the community is *represented* in its entirety, in one place, at one time, brought together by their common loss. The whole community can be perceived from a single point of view—that occupied by Mr. Benson in the pulpit:

> From the pulpit, Mr. Benson saw one and all—the well-filled Bradshaw pew—all in deep mourning, Mr. Bradshaw conspicuously so … —the Farquhars—the many strangers—the still more numerous poor—one or two wild-looking outcasts, who stood afar off, but wept silently and continually. (368)

The ranks of those whom Ruth has served and saved, that vast network encompassed by "one and all," greatly exceed the small community described by Faith Benson when Ruth first came to Eccleston. Beneath the windows of the Infirmary and from Benson's pulpit, the reader of *Ruth* finally glimpses that vision of "the whole unity" that Ruth could *not* see in her dissected map (116). The respect paid to the purified woman by those she has healed and the revelation of the community's true size and extent is a powerful rejoinder to the rhetoric of moral contamination.

Works Cited

Anderson, Amanda. *Tainted Souls and Painted Faces: The Rhetoric of Fallenness in Victorian Culture*. Ithaca: Cornell UP, 1993. Print.

Anderson, Benedict. *Imagined Communities: Reflections on the Origin and Spread of Nationalism*. 2nd ed. London: Verso, 2006. Print.

Bell, Charles William. "Lecture on the Nature & Treatment of Cholera, Considered with Reference to its Analogy with Congestive Agues of Quotidian Type." *Provincial Medical & Surgical Journal* 24–26 (1848): 645–54, 673–81, 701–7. Print.

———. "The Address in Medicine, Being an Essay on the Principal Causes which Unite in Producing and Diffusing Disease; Read before the 17th Annual General Meeting of the Provincial Medical and Surgical Association, held at Worcester, August 1st and 2nd, 1849." *The Transactions of the Provincial Medical and Surgical Association* ns 5 (1850), 1–47. Print.

Brockbank, William. *The Honorary Medical Staff of the Manchester Royal Infirmary 1830–1948*. Manchester: Manchester UP, 1965. Print.

Christensen, Allan Conrad. *Nineteenth-Century Narratives of Contagion: Our Feverish Contact*. London: Routledge, 2005. Print.

Davies, W[illiam]. *Fever, in Its Relations to Sanitary Reform, Being the Address in Medicine, Delivered at the Sixteenth Anniversary Meeting of the Provincial Medical and Surgical Association, Held at Bath, August 16th & 17th, 1848*. Worcester: Deighton, 1848. Print.

Easson, Angus, ed. *Elizabeth Gaskell: The Critical Heritage*. London and New York: Routledge, 1991. Print.

Flint, Kate. *Elizabeth Gaskell*. Plymouth: Northcote House, 1995. Print.

Gaskell, Elizabeth. *The Letters of Mrs Gaskell*. Ed. J.A.V. Chapple and Arthur Pollard. Manchester: Manchester UP, 1966. Print.

Graves, Robert J. *Clinical Lectures on the Practice of Medicine*. Ed. J. Moore Neligan. 2nd ed. Vol. 1. Dublin: Fannin; London: Longman; Edinburgh: Machlachlan, Stewart, 1848. Print.

Grossman, Jonathan H. *Charles Dickens's Networks: Public Transport and the Novel*. Oxford: Oxford UP, 2012. Print.

Hardy, Anne. *The Epidemic Streets: Infectious Disease and the Rise of Preventive Medicine, 1856–1900*. Oxford: Clarendon, 1993. Print.

Harrison, Mark. *Contagion: How Commerce Has Spread Disease*. New Haven and London: Yale UP, 2012. Print.

Health, General Board of. "Report on Quarantine." London: Clowes & Sons for HM Stationery Office, 1849. Print.

Health, General Board of. "Second Report on Quarantine. Yellow Fever." London: Clowes & Sons for HM Stationery Office, 1852. Print.

Jenner, William. *Typhus Fever, typhod [sic] fever, relapsing fever, and febricula, the diseases commonly confounded under the term continued fever. Illustrated by cases collected at the bed-side*. London: W. Tyler, 1849–1851. Print.

———. *The Identity or Non-Identity of Typhoid and Typhus Fevers*. London: John Churchill, 1850. Print.

Levy, Heather. "'With Arms Entwined': Deadly Deceit and Romantic Friendship in Ruth and Lois the Witch." *Elizabeth Gaskell, Victorian Culture, and the Art of Fiction – Original Essays for the Bicentenary*. Ed. Jung, Sandro. Gent: Academia, 2010. 83–98. Print.

Loether, Herman J. *The Social Impacts of Infectious Disease in England, 1600 to 1900*. Lewiston, NY: Edwin Mellen, 2000. Print.

McDonald, Lynn, ed. *Florence Nightingale on Society and Politics, Philosophy, Science, Education and Literature*, vol. 5. 16 vols. Waterloo, ON: Wilfrid Laurier UP, 2003. Print.

Pelling, Margaret. "Contagion/Germ Theory/Specificity." *Companion Encyclopaedia of the History of Medicine*. London: Routledge, 1993. 309–34. Print.

Pickstone, John V. *Medicine and Industrial Society: A History of Hospital Development in Manchester and Its Region, 1752–1946*. Manchester: Manchester UP, 1985. Print.

Renaud, Frank. *A Short History of the Rise and Progress of the Manchester Royal Infirmary*. Manchester: J.E. Cornish, 1898. Print.

Smallman-Raynor, M.R., and A.D. Cliff. *War Epidemics: An Historical Geography of Infectious Diseases in Military Conflict and Civil Strife*. Oxford: Oxford UP, 2004. Print.

Spink, Wesley W. *Infectious Diseases: Prevention and Treatment in the Nineteenth and Twentieth Centuries*. Minneapolis, MN: U of Minnesota P, 1978. Print.

Sutherland, D. Sage. *The Manchester 'House of Recovery' and 'Board of Health' 1796 to 1852: The History of the Manchester Fever Hospital*. Manchester: Richard Bates, 1929. Print.

Talty, Stephan. *The Illustrious Dead: The Terrifying Story of How Typhus Killed Napoleon's Greatest Army*. New York: Crown, 2009. Print.

Thornton, Robert J. *Unimagined Community : Sex, Networks, and Aids in Uganda and South Africa*. California Series in Public Anthropology. Ed. Robert Borofsky. Berkeley, CA: U of California P, 2008. Print.

Uglow, Jenny. *Elizabeth Gaskell: A Habit of Stories*. London: Faber and Faber, 1993. Print.

Webb, R.K. "The Gaskells as Unitarians." *Dickens and Other Victorians: Essays in Honour of Philip Collins*. Ed. Joanne Shattock. Houndmills: Macmillan, 1988. 144–71. Print.

Zinsser, Hans. *Rats, Lice and History: A Chronicle of Pestilence and Plague*. Boston, 1935. New York: Black Dog & Leventhal, 1976. Print.

Chapter 6
Temporally out of Sync: Migration as Fiction and Philanthropy in Gaskell's Life and Work

Fariha Shaikh

Migration is a crucial, yet often overlooked, theme in Elizabeth Gaskell's fiction. Her most famous—and most contentious—use of the motif is at the end of *Mary Barton* (1848), where Jem and Mary move away from Manchester to settle in Canada. Given that the novel grapples with the condition-of-England question, its resolution has been seen as a failure on Gaskell's part to provide an effective solution to the problems of industrialization that she raises. Despite her subsequent, recurrent use of emigration in her literary work, contemporary critical scholarship has remained fixated on the ending of *Mary Barton*. This refusal to situate the novel within the broader context of her work and life has prevented the development of a subtler, more nuanced understanding of Gaskell's stance on emigration. To this end, in this chapter I bring the ending of *Mary Barton* into conversation with "My French Master" (1853) and *Lois the Witch* (1859). The 1850s was one of the peak periods of emigration in the nineteenth century. Eric Richards calculates that in 1852 alone, over 365,000 people left to settle elsewhere (11). Although we do not have an exact figure for the decade, the increasing popularity of emigration is attested to by the numerous schemes that sprang up around this period. While the majority of emigrants were self-financed (11), a large number also emigrated on government-supported schemes, while still others emigrated through philanthropic endeavors that were run by keen supporters of emigration. Caroline Chisholm, for example, founded the Family Colonization Loan Society in 1849, which lent money to families emigrating to Australia on an interest-free basis for two years or longer. In the same year, Sidney Herbert founded the scheme "Emigration of Distressed Needlewomen" and advertised it in *Sharpe's London Magazine*, noting "[h]ow easy it would be for two or three ladies to subscribe the necessary sum for sending out one emigrant" (103).[1]

---

[1] Throughout the course of the century, settler colonies such as Canada, Australia, and New Zealand were popular destinations—South Africa less so. Notwithstanding her political differences with Britain, North America remained the most popular destination with emigrants throughout the course of the century. Other colonies, such as India, were felt to be possessions, rather than a part, of England. See Margot Finn, "Victorianism at the Frontier: The White Settler Colonies."

In spite of this increased interest, Gaskell narrates emigration through a temporal shift in each of the stories under consideration here: Canada is imagined as a pre-industrialized, pastoral place at the end of *Mary Barton*; "My French Master" is set during the French Revolution; *Lois the Witch* is a historical retelling of the Salem Witch Trials of 1692. In this chapter, I argue that Gaskell's use of this temporal shift changes as she develops as a writer. In *Mary Barton*, the pastoral colony speaks of new beginnings. Gaskell's decision to have her small Manchester community emigrate is not an escapist fantasy: it stems from her wholehearted support of emigration as a solution to the problems of industrialization. By the end of the decade, Gaskell's emphasis has changed. Both *Lois the Witch* and "My French Master" are works of historical fiction: this temporal distancing allows her to remove herself from the emigration debates surrounding her at the time and explore a different rhetoric surrounding migration and global mobility. Both short stories deal with the complex difficulties of making a new home abroad. Through Lois and Monsieur de Chalabre, the "French Master," Gaskell explores themes of loss, remembrance and community—themes that are as relevant to the phenomenon of nineteenth-century emigration that she was witness to as they were at the historical time in which the stories are set.

Discovering Pasley

In January 1850, Gaskell helped a 16-year-old girl by the name of Pasley emigrate to South Africa. Gaskell had come across Pasley on one of her many visits to the New Bailey Prison in Manchester: Pasley was a vagrant, an alcoholic, and a prostitute. When the two women met, Pasley had only a few more days left to serve, but Gaskell feared that her life would continue on the same downward trajectory once she was released: waiting for her when she came out were "two of the worst women in the town who have been in prison with her, intending to way-lay her" (*Letters* 61). Desiring "to keep her out of all temptation" and "even chance of recognition," Gaskell decided that the best course of action would be for Pasley to emigrate. She wrote hastily to Charles Dickens asking if there is any possibility for the young girl to be admitted in Urania Cottage, the house for fallen women that he had set up a few years earlier with the help of Angela Burdett-Coutts (Hartley 49–50). In her letter, Gaskell paints Pasley's life as a bleak series of disasters—her father had died when she was two; her mother had remarried and "had shown most complete indifference" to her situation; the dressmaker she had been apprenticed to had "failed, and had to dismiss all her apprentices"; the seamstress under whose care she was then placed "connived at the girl's seduction by a surgeon in the neighbourhood who was called in when the poor creature was ill"; she entered a penitentiary in the hope of gaining salvation, where she met a woman who led her into prostitution. In the short four months between leaving the penitentiary and landing in prison, Pasley found herself leading a "most miserable life" (*Letters* 61).

Despite Gaskell's advocacy, Dickens felt he and Burdett-Coutts could not take Pasley into Urania Cottage without "personal knowledge of her from our own observation." Furthermore, "as she is not altogether a helpless outcast, but may get abroad without her [Burdett-Coutts's] help," because of a small inheritance from her father's family, Dickens wrote to Gaskell that he "doubt[ed] Miss Coutt's [sic] inclination to admit her" (*Letters* Vol. 7, 7). Burdett-Coutts never corresponded directly with Gaskell on the matter, but she sent many suggestions for her through Dickens. Gaskell acted upon her advice, and within a few weeks, found a family immigrating to South Africa who were willing to take Pasley with them.

We know nothing more of Pasley apart from what is left behind in Gaskell's letters. The record relating to her at the New Bailey Prison has been lost, and she never kept in touch with Gaskell after she emigrated (assuming that she could write at all). Nonetheless, her life resonated powerfully with Gaskell over the coming years. Gaskell had already shown an interest in the fallen woman as a legitimate character for fiction: "To whom shall the outcast prostitute tell her tale," she asks rhetorically in *Mary Barton* (158). She herself takes up this cause in the novel through the figure of Esther, Mary's aunt. It is therefore unsurprising that the next piece she wrote after having met Pasley, the short story "Lizzie Leigh" (1850), is based on a young girl who has a child out of wedlock. Three years later, in *Ruth* (1853), Gaskell would finally gain the courage to turn the fallen woman into the protagonist of a novel. Gaskell's preoccupation with the fallen woman falls into a larger interest at the time in the fallen woman[2] but Pasley's story is only partially a story of Victorian social mores, their sexual politics, and the fallen woman. It is also a story of nineteenth-century settler emigration and the promise of new beginnings that it was supposed to bring. Just as settler colonies in mid-nineteenth-century novels are a partial presence, a place from which people and wealth magically appear and disappear (Said 102–7), so too, in the story of Pasley, the narrative fades out when it reaches South Africa.

Mary Barton: Escaping by Emigrating?

Gaskell saw emigration as the only hope left for Pasley. There was no possibility, in her eyes, of improving Pasley's life in the dirty, crowded streets of industrial Manchester where vice and temptation were always around the corner. In *Mary Barton*, Gaskell resorts to a similar narrative resolution. Though the fallen Esther dies, Mary, Jem, and his mother move away from Manchester to settle in Canada. At the end of the novel, the reader is given a scene from Mary and Jem's new life:

> I [the narrator] see a long, low wooden house, with room enough and to spare. The old primeval trees are felled and gone for many a mile around; one alone remains to overshadow the gable-end of the cottage. There is a garden around the dwelling, and far beyond that stretches an orchard … At the door of the house, looking towards the town, stands Mary, watching the return of her husband from his daily work. (392–3)

---

[2]   See, for example, Sally Mitchell, Judith Walkowitz, and Amanda Anderson.

This is an image of a perfect Eden: the small clearing is a testament to Jem's hard work at making a home for his small family and mother. The fact that their house has "room enough and to spare" is surely a comment on the scenes of working-class living conditions that Gaskell outlined earlier: the "unpaved" streets where pools of "household slops of every description … ran into the next pool, which overflowed and stagnated," and the Davenport's home where John Barton and George Wilson see through "the thick darkness … three or four little children rolling on the damp, nay wet brick floor, through which the stagnant, filthy moisture of the street oozed up" (60). In Canada, caring for one's children is not a daily struggle: Mary and Jem's child, Johnnie, sings gaily of his "daddy" who returns from work "With his pocket full of plums, / And cake for Johnnie" (393).

Perera Suvendrini argues that "the migrations and overseas voyages in novels such as *Mary Barton*, *Alton Locke*, *David Copperfield*, and *Great Expectations* are often read within a different frame of reference—one of 'magic' or 'escape'—rather than as part of the novel's processing and configuration of the specific social situation seen as its main concern: they are not 'read within the same interpretive framework as the rest of the narrative'" (52). However, it is precisely *because* the emigration scene is displaced from the realist field of narration that it offers such a powerful image of escape on both social and political fronts, an escape that is found with equal vigor in emigration literature. As if to stress that Canada is enough of a geographical elsewhere to provide Mary and Jem with complete reprieve from any social stain whatsoever, Gaskell refuses to narrate the colony through the realist mode in which the rest of the narrative is written: the narrative voice at the end takes on a peculiar dream-like quality as it relates from England what it can "see" of Jem and Mary's life. By imagining the colony through the pastoral mode, Gaskell suggests that it is a temporal elsewhere: as Coral Lansbury argues, the "evocation of a pastoral age was accompanied by the belief that it was … the source of virtue and happiness" (33), a utopian way of living in a pre-industrial age. In *The Country and the City*, Raymond Williams argues that this "backward reference" (35) inherent in pastoral literature is based "on a deep desire for stability": in actual fact, it "served to cover and evade the actual and bitter contradictions of the time" by offering readers a vision of an ideal past (45). For him, the ending of *Mary Barton* is similarly evasive: rather than offering a "solution to the poverty and overcrowding of the cities," the novel "ends in Canada, in a mood of rural idyll and escape" (281). Lynette Felber takes a similar line of argument: "the scene is underdeveloped," she argues "and lacks continuity with the primary narrative; as a solution to the industrial problem" (60). Crucially, however, Gaskell's use of the pastoral looks forward to a better future even as it refers to an idealized pre-industrialized past. Jem's job as "instrument-maker to the Agricultural College they are establishing at Toronto" (375) suggests that Canada has the potential to move forward into an industrial age that will not mimic Manchester. The fact that Margaret and Will follow Mary and Jem to settle in Canada intensifies the disjuncture between England's industrial centers and her colonies. In another chapter in this book, Emily Cody identifies Gaskell's use of "confined spaces" to explore the entrapment of the working classes, and the "ever-escalating pressures" that they face as a result of unemployment and industrialization. Canada is a spacious reprieve with potential for a more humane development and growth (Cody 94). In short, the colony offers better opportunities than Manchester for making a life and a home: it is a better reflection of England. This asymmetrical mirroring of both home and colony maintains the colonial ideology of the colony as home, as well as upholding one of the central rhetorical points of emigration propaganda that the colonies are a better place for starting again.

To its supporters, emigration seemed to offer the perfect solution to a seemingly over-populated and under-resourced England. "[I]t is melancholy to reflect," wrote Caroline Chisholm in *Household Words*, "that thousands of British subjects should wander about, more like spectres than beings of flesh and blood; and that hundreds should die from starvation, while our vast colonies could provide abundantly for them" ("Bundle" 19). *Wiley and Putnam's Emigrant's Guide* (1845) draws a similar comparison: whereas "Great Britain teems with a vast surplus population and tens of thousands are crowded out from the means of gaining a scanty subsistence," "America offers a boundless field for industry" (iii). Tales of individual, personal success also circulated in print. One emigrant, for example, wrote home requesting that his letter be shown to his friend in order that he may be convinced that "we have plenty of game here, and deer plenty" (*Letters from Settlers* 7); another strives to assure his readers that "we have not hopped out of a frying pan into a fire, but out of a fire into a frying pan" (*Copies and Extracts* 6); another, less rhetorical figure claims that he and his family "have plenty of potatoes, fruit, vegetables, corn, everything; pumpkins, melons; [and a] well furnished house" (Chisholm, *Comfort* 9).

Thus, the shift at the end of *Mary Barton*, from a realist mode of narration to pastoral, allows Gaskell to draw on the narratives of success that were circulating in emigrant propaganda. The temporal shift inherent in this shift in narrative style is not, however, the static backward gaze of nostalgia. Rather, it is an enabling backward glance that simultaneously gestures to the possibilities of moving into an industrialized age in a more humane fashion. Emigration was an important feature of Gaskell's philanthropic work at this time: Pasley is the most prominent example of what seems to be a broader interest in emigration: in her letters, she writes of having "already received the kind offices from Mrs. Chisholm in helping out a family of emigrants" (*Letters* 62) and of wanting to know more of the "Plymouth Ladies" (*Letters* 62), presumably a group of female philanthropists running an emigration scheme. For her, emigration is not an escapist fantasy but a cogent and coherent solution to the problems of industrialization. In a few years' time, this unambiguous, wholehearted support for emigration would be replaced with a more nuanced outlook, as she sought to problematize the fact of global mobility.

New Communities: *Lois the Witch* and "My French Master"

Unlike *Mary Barton*, which depicts nineteenth-century settler emigration, "My French Master" and *Lois the Witch* both look back to historical instances of migration. Monsieur de Chalabre, the protagonist of "My French Master," is a member of the French aristocracy who has been forced to flee France and settle in England in the aftermath of the French Revolution. The short story is told through the eyes of an elderly woman whom de Chalabre had taught when she was a young girl. Although Chalabre is well-loved and respected by the English villagers, he tries to return to France, but fails. He has been forgotten by all those who knew him: his wealth and status mean nothing to those now in power. Distraught, he returns to England and settles down by marrying an English girl, Susan Dobson. *Lois the Witch* looks back to an even earlier moment: the Salem Witch Trials of 1692. Drawing on what she had read of the trials in Charles Upham's *Lectures on Witchcraft, Comprising a History of the Delusions in Salem* (1831),[3] Gaskell imaginatively recreates the life of one particular "witch," Lois Barclay. Left an orphan by her dying mother, Lois emigrates to America to reunite with her maternal uncle and his family, but she finds a cold community too steeped in their own superstitions to welcome outsiders. Eventually, she becomes the unwitting victim of the jealousy of her two cousins, Faith and Prudence, who spread rumors that she is a witch. To punish her for her sins, the Salem community eventually hangs her. In tone, the two stories could not be more different: "My French Master" is lighter; the first person narrator looks back on her simple, rural childhood in the New Forest with gentle humor. *Lois the Witch*, on the other hand, attempts "to create the atmosphere of mental tyranny" and portray "the psychology of a people driven by the pitiless logic of their own premises to a conclusion from which they firmly believed there could be no shrinking" (Hopkins 257). Despite the differences in tone and plot, both stories interrogate the ways in which resettlement puts pressure on the emigrant's position in their new community and their attachments to their homeland. This problematized approach to migration is a marked departure from the pro-emigration stance of *Mary Barton*, where emigration is a straightforward formula for success.

   In contrast to the vast majority of mid-Victorian fiction, where the places to which the emigrants travel are at best a partial presence, Gaskell follows Lois and de Chalabre to their lands of exile in order to explore their sense of loss. When de Chalabre flees to England, he forfeits his "considerable estates in Normandy" and his "old Château Chalabre" (77). More importantly, however, he unwittingly forfeits his fame. When he goes to meet Louis XVIII in London, he finds that his name, which was once "a name of note in Normandy," has faded in the memories of the French aristocrats as a result of his "long years of exile" (78). For de Chalabre, emigration entails not only a loss of wealth and power, but also the friendship circles and networks of influence that he once knew. In England, he gains a new community's affections: he is "a favourite in all the forest circle," a "great acquisition to the sociable dinner parties" (75). As the years pass by, the community's love for and trust of him does not waver: as the narrator grows with her sister "from children to girls—from girls into women … still M. de Chalabre

---

[3]   Charles Upham was a US Representative in Massachusetts. He lived in Salem, Massachusetts for most of his life and was there at the time of the trials.

taught on in the forest; still he was beloved and honoured; still no dinner-party within five miles was thought complete without him" (75–6).

Lois is as hated by the Puritans of Salem as de Chalabre is loved by the villagers in the forest. Upham's lectures feature no emigrants: the fact that Lois is English makes her sense of otherness much more pronounced. Throughout the novella, she is always referred to as the "English girl" (22), who looks around her "with an English eye" (15). Her uncle is on his deathbed when she arrives. After his death, she has no blood relations to look after her. The "ungracious reception" (17) her aunt and cousins, Manasseh, Faith, and Prudence, give her is an indication of their behavior in the days to come: her aunt "look[s] askance at her for many reasons" (22), and Lois senses that she "irritate[s] Manasseh past endurance" (23) with her stories of Barford. It is Faith and Prudence, however, who secure her notoriety as a witch. When Faith finds out that the man she loves, Pastor Nolan, has affections for Lois and not herself, she is driven on by "enmity with all the world in her bitter jealousy of heart." "Take care," she hisses, "how you meddle with a witch's things" (65). Prudence takes up the taunt: "'Witch Lois! Witch Lois!' said she at last, softly, pulling a childish face of spite at her" (65). A short while later, when all three are at the hanging of the Indian "witch" Hota, Prudence pretends to have (or has) an epileptic fit and blames Lois for it. Lois feels "every eye" of the crowd "fixed upon her in hatred and dread" (69): with no further questioning, she is taken by the crowd, thrown into prison, and hanged in the following days.

Ironically, however, Lois emigrates in order to strengthen her ties with her extended family. In her small village of Barford, the only person who has the means to offer Lois a home after her mother's death is the rich Miller Lucy. However, as Lois is in love with the miller's son, Hugh Lucy, the miller "think[s] it more prudent not to offer the orphan a home" (4). She experiences such "outrageous threats and expressions of uncontrolled vehemence" from him that she decides to leave for America as "her absence might soften down matters" (5). Clearly, the possibility of marriage and starting her own family is not open to her. She is further led on by her mother's conviction that her uncle, Ralph Hickson, will "take thee in, and love thee as a child, and place thee among his children," and that she will be treated "as if thou wert his own flesh and blood, as indeed thou art" (5). The family was an important conceptual unit of nineteenth-century emigration. Young couples were the most likely to be successful colonists, as they had the ability to withstand and adapt to life in the bush, and they would soon populate the colonies. Caroline Chisholm's Family Colonization Loan Society aimed to reunite families who had been split by emigration by prioritizing those who had already had family members in Australia. Furthermore, the emigration of families was considered morally safer than that of the emigration of single young men or women. Tellingly, Gaskell feels that only by sending Pasley out with a family is her mobility made safe, and the ending of *Mary Barton* is filled with the happy migration of families. Clearly, in *Lois the Witch* and "My French Master," Gaskell problematizes the familiar coupling of migration and the family she used so readily in her earlier work. Instead, she explores the conflicted and contested nature of trying to make a home in a foreign land, while not forgetting the one left behind.

To remind themselves of the lives and communities they had left behind, nineteenth-century emigrants frequently traveled with tokens of remembrance. Often these could be material artifacts, such as coins, or other objects with affectionate messages engraved on them (otherwise known as "love tokens"; Field 1–4), but sometimes they could be more abstract. One emigrant, for example, gave Chisholm the memory of "my wife, her sister, and husband came to see me when I received sentence of death, for taking fire-arms from a constable in a tithe row" (Chisholm, *Emigration* 29).

In their respective ways, Lois and de Chalabre also have their own "emigrant's tokens." For Lois, they are particular vignettes associated with England. Sitting on the casks of the ship, waiting for Captain Holdernesse, her mind drifts back to what she has left behind: in front of her "aching eyes," "there rose the little village church of Barford ... the old parsonage too, the cottage, covered with Austrian roses and yellow jasmine, where she had been born ... the path, not a hundred yards long, from the parsonage to the vestry door" (3–4). She entertains Faith by telling her "her old stories of English ways and life" (25), and the "dear old ways at home" (28). In a place where the mere "rumour" of witchcraft is "like the echo of thunder among the hills" (52), where Lois "shiver[s] and tremble[s] with affright at [a particular] narration" (56), where "weird stories" told by a "lurid light" blend into reality (24), Lois's own stories of life in England provide a reassuring sense of the normality that she once knew.

De Chalabre chooses to remember his affiliation to France through flowers. In the simple, country way of living, it seems apt that flowers become a complex site through which de Chalabre negotiates his identity and sense of allegiance to France. He "long[s] in secret" for his "rose garden" and "orangerie" at Chalabre (77), but must content himself with the English "carnations and roses" (71) that the narrator's mother picks out for him. The code names that the narrator's parents use to refer to the executions of Louis XVI and Marie Antoinette—the "Iris" and "White Lily" (73) respectively—are, tellingly, the names of English flowers. When de Chalabre returns from France, he places "immortelles" (80) on the grave of the narrator's mother—in one simple gesture, tying together his undying fondness for her and his love for France. Whereas Lois looks on at the American landscape with foreign eyes, de Chalabre uses the English flora to articulate his sense of loss. The culmination is when he marries the "buxom, red-armed, apple-cheeked" Susan Dobson—the epitome of an English country girl—"[n]o word, nor allusion, nor expressive silence, nor regretful sympathetic sighs [from her], could remind M. de Chalabre of the bitter past, which he was evidently striving to forget" (82). If the "tale's central story is of fidelity to the past" (Glen xxvi), then so too, is this the migrant's concern. Moving away from all that they had known and that was familiar, Lois and de Chalabre both strive to retain a relationship with their past through the retelling of stories and the gifting of flowers respectively. Although Gaskell draws on the popular symbolic meanings of flowers elsewhere in her work (Eve 1–15), here, Lois and M. de Chalabre use flowers to remember their homelands in private and individual ways.

Both "My French Master" and *Lois the Witch* were written during "a period rich in fiction": as Jenny Uglow argues, Gaskell wrote much of her short fiction during the mid-1850s, "in which she battled with disturbing questions of gender, faith, authority, power and pain" (459). Shelston argues that in her short stories, Gaskell crosses social, cultural, and geographical boundaries to "move into new ground and operate ... experimentally" (Shelston 16–17). It is in the historical turn of both "My French Master" and *Lois the Witch* that Gaskell is at her most experimental. "My French Master" and *Lois the Witch* are both intimately concerned with loss and remembrance, two defining features of the emigrant's experience that are entailed by the emigrant's geographical distance from their homeland. This extends beyond the ways in which Lois and de Chalabre try to remember their homelands to the narrative form itself: historical fiction itself is an act of cultural remembering, as the novelist recalls and reshapes the past and brings it to bear upon the present moment.

Migration Troubled

It is perhaps unsurprising that Gaskell chose to explore the migrant sensibility in her work at a time when events in her personal life were bringing home to her the possibilities, potentials, and pitfalls of relocating. All around her people were moving, or were given the opportunity to move. In 1857, her daughter Meta became engaged to Captain Charles Hill, whom she had met in Rome. Meta eventually broke off the engagement, but prior to this, Gaskell herself had contemplated that she might go out to India when "the day draws nearer for my daughter to join him" (*Letters* 367), and was excited at the prospect of doing so. Two years later, her husband William had been "urged and reurged" to consider a job in London. He declined, and in Gaskell's opinion, "wisely and rightly": "He could never get in London the influence and good he has here; and he is too old to be taken up by the roots and transplanted merely for an extra hundred or so a year" (*Letters* 421). This unease with the condition of being mobile extends to emigration and is reflected in her letters. In 1857, she wrote to Charles Eliot Norton, her North American friend, asking what the possibilities of a young boy succeeding in North America would be, if she were to send him over:

> IF I send a boy over to you three years hence or so, can he earn his liveliehood [*sic*]? That is a comprehensive question, but I mean here is a stout strong good intelligent friendless boy, knowing (from the circumstances of his parentage) both French & English, & learning a good solid homely quantity of arithmetic &c, – and could he at 14 do in America?—earn enough to keep him,—and get on, if he deserved it? If he came, I know you would have an eye upon him, so I don't ask that—but could one get on in the world? (*Letters* 374)

Question after question after question: we have here the same urgent enquiring in the letter that Gaskell wrote to Dickens about Pasley. But whereas Gaskell's questions then enthusiastically explored the different ways in which Pasley could emigrate, here, her questions stem from doubt: sending the young 14-year-old to America might not be the best way out of his situation. Gaskell's anxieties cluster around the young boy's ability to better his material conditions—whether or not he could "earn enough to keep him" and "get on in the world" to make something of himself. Her faith in migration as a force for social good, or as a means of social reform, seems to have been shaken. In "My French Master" and *Lois the Witch*, Gaskell does not reproduce the familiar emigration-as-solution narrative that she used so readily in the earlier *Mary Barton*. Instead, she probes the idea of migration more broadly by looking to earlier instances of migration and questions what mobility and resettlement might mean for those on whom it has been forced, and for those who are not accepted by the host community. This emphasis on the fractures and frissons within the migrant experience is sustained throughout her fiction in this period. In *Cranford* (1853), Peter Jenkyns settles in India for the better part of his life after having been forced away by his father; in *North and South* (1855), Margaret's brother, Frederick, is forced to migrate to Spain after becoming involved in a mutiny while serving in the British navy; in *Cousin Phillis* (1864), Edward Holdsworth emigrates to Canada, leaving behind a lovesick Phillis. Critics give an undue prominence to *Mary Barton* in their discussions of Gaskell and emigration: what they miss is that the upbeat, pro-emigration stance at the end of the novel is only the beginning of rich, nuanced literary and philanthropic engagements with emigration: emigration is, more often than not in Gaskell's work, a troubled site of loss, anxiety, and pain, through which she interrogates the shifting boundaries of "home" in a world of rapid change and mobility.

Works Cited

Anderson, Amanda. *Tainted Souls and Painted Faces: The Rhetoric of Fallenness in Victorian Culture*. London: Cornell UP, 1993. Print.

Chisholm, Caroline. "A Bundle of Emigrant Letters." *Household Words*, 30 March 1850. Print.

———. Comfort for the Poor! Meat Three Times a Day!! Voluntary Information from the People of New South Wales, Collected in that Colony by Mrs. Chisholm in 1845–46. London: John Ollivier, 1847. Print.

———. Emigration and Transportation Relatively Considered in a Letter, Dedicated, By permission, to Earl Grey. London: John Ollivier, 1847. Print.

Copies and Extracts of Letters from Settlers in Upper Canada. London: Marchant, 1833. Print.

Dickens, Charles. *The Letters of Charles Dickens*. 12 vols. Ed. Madeline House and Graham Storey. Oxford: Clarendon, 1965–2002. Print.

Eve, Jeanette. "The Floral and the Horticultural in Elizabeth Gaskell's Novels." *Gaskell Society Journal* 7 (1993): 1–15. Print.

Felber, Lynette. "Gaskell's Industrial Idylls: Ideology and Formal Incongruence in *Mary Barton* and *North and South*." *Clio* 18.1 (1988): 55–72. Print.

Field, Michele. "Introduction." Michele Field and Timothy Millett. *Convict Love Tokens: The Leaden Hearts the Convicts Left Behind*. Kent Town: Wakefield, 1998, 1–4. Print.

Finn, Margot. "Victorianism at the Frontier: The White Settler Colonies." *The Victorian World*. Ed. Martin Hewitt. London: Routledge, 2012. 656–70. Print.

Gaskell, Elizabeth. *The Letters of Mrs Gaskell*. Ed. J.A.V. Chapple and Arthur Pollard. Manchester: Mandolin, 1997. Print.

———. *Lois the Witch*. 1859. London: Hesperus, 2003. Print.

———. *Mary Barton: A Tale of Manchester Life*. 1848. Penguin: London, 1996. Print.

———. "My French Master." 1853. *Cousin Phillis and Other Stories*. Oxford: Oxford UP, 2010. Print.

Glen, Heather. "Introduction." *Cousin Phillis and Other Stories*. Oxford: Oxford UP, 2010. Print.

Hartley, Jenny. *Charles Dickens and the House of Fallen Women*. London: Methuen, 2008. Print.

Hopkins, Annette B. *Elizabeth Gaskell: Her Life and Work*. London: John Lehmann, 1952. Print.

Lansbury, Coral. *Arcady in Australia: The Evocation of Australia in Nineteenth-Century English Literature*. Melbourne: Melbourne UP, 1970. Print.

Letters from Settlers in Upper Canada. London: Marchant, Printer, 1834. Print.

Mitchell, Sally. *The Fallen Angel: Chastity, Class and Women's Reading 1835–1880*. Bowling Green, OH: Bowling Green State UP, 1981. Print.

Perera, Suvendrini. *Reaches of Empire: The English Novel from Edgeworth to Dickens*. New York: Columbia UP, 1991. Print.

Richards, Eric. *Britannia's Children: Emigration from England, Scotland, Wales and Ireland since 1600*. London: Hambledon and London, 2004. Print.

Said, Edward. *Culture and Imperialism*. London: Chatto & Windus, 1993. Print.

W., J.M. "A Few Words about Mr. Sidney Herbert's Emigration Scheme," *Sharpe's London Journal*, 12 July 1850, 99–103. Print.

Shelston, Alan. "Exploring the Boundaries in Elizabeth Gaskell's Shorter Fiction." *Elizabeth Gaskell and the Art of the Short Story*. Ed. Francesco Marroni, Renzo D'Agnillo and Massimo Verzella. New York: Peter Lang, 2011. Print.

Uglow, Jenny. *Elizabeth Gaskell: A Habit of Stories*. London: Faber and Faber, 1993. Print.

Upham, Charles W. *Lectures on Witchcraft, Comprising a History of the Delusion in Salem, in 1692*. Boston, MA: Carter, Hendee and Babcock, 1831. Print.

Wiley and Putnam's Emigrant's Guide, Comprising Advice and Instruction in Every Stage of the Voyage to America. London: Wiley and Putnam, 1845. Print.

Walkowitz, Judith. *Prostitution and Victorian Society: Women, Class and the State*. Cambridge: Cambridge UP, 1980. Print.

Williams, Raymond. *The Country and the City*. London: Chatto and Windus, 1973. Print.

Chapter 7
Moving Between *North and South*: Cultural Signs and the Progress of Modernity in Elizabeth Gaskell's Novel

Lesa Scholl

The 2004 BBC adaptation of *North and South* creates a sense of historical immediacy by adding a scene where several of the central characters travel by the newly popular railway, converging at the Crystal Palace for the Great Exhibition of 1851. While this historical event is not included in Gaskell's original text, it is a valid addition: The Great Exhibition of the Works of Industry of All Nations focalizes the impetus of progress in Gaskell's text, as well as the crises of modernity, both spatially and culturally, within mid-nineteenth-century Britain. London's centrality to the Empire is critiqued most often through Mr. Thornton's arguments against centralized government, but even more crucially, we vividly encounter the unrelenting speed of change and progress. In a manner that resonates with cultural anxieties of the early twenty-first century, nineteenth-century culture and society were running to catch up with the ethical and philosophical implications of rapid scientific and technological advancement. In terms of transportation, the advancement of the railway meant not only more extensive travel, but also faster travel—which both literally and metaphorically represented the increased physical access to other cultural spaces. This meant an increased possibility of cultural conflict, not just in terms of colonial encounters or traveling to the exotic Orient or the East, but even within the borders of Great Britain. In Gaskell's *North and South* (1854–1855), the conflict is even more localized, specifically within England. The term "foreigner" is used repeatedly, not just for the imported Irish "knobsticks" (233), but also for those who move from the South of England to the North. Although the South is part of the same nation, it is being written in terms of a different country, with different cultural values, social and political systems, and language.

The advent of the railway led to a rapid transformation of the English landscape, which broke down class boundaries as well as geographical ones. This technological advancement worked alongside the industrialization of Britain, which, as Jill Matus observes, "precipitated rapid shifts of population into the cities to seek work in the factories" ("*Mary Barton* and *North and South*" 27). Transportation to and within Britain became much more accessible and cheaper, making migration more possible. The presence of the Irish in *North and South* amplifies not just the sense of national crisis in terms of the pressures on Britain's social and economic infrastructure, but also the challenge of foreignness in a nation trying to maintain a sense of cultural unity. As Mary Mullen argues, "[t]he Irish hands and Irish characters … of the novel reveal the limits of the nation's capacity to incorporate difference" (113). Resistance to change leads to extinction in Gaskell's vision, yet questions remain as to how adaptation and change should manifest. The increased demographic mobility had a resounding effect on the make-up and expectations of English society, requiring a rethinking of national identity as the need to adapt quickly to the changes grew more and more apparent. Gaskell's narrative thus both celebrates and critiques the possibilities of progress and social evolution.

Gaskell shows the "turbulence, upheaval, and disruption in changing social conditions" (Matus, "*Mary Barton* and *North and South*" 35), but in the midst of this conflict, the fluidity of transportation also allows for the possibility of mediation between cultural spaces, for cross-cultural understanding, and what Stuart Hall refers to as taking on a "second cultural repertoire" (206). Margaret Hale's experiences in moving from the South to the North, as well as back and forth to London, can be understood in terms of cultural translation, as well as social evolution. While Matus perceives that Gaskell absorbs the "language of shock and horror" into the "realist texture of the novel's narrative" in order to normalize the trauma of change—to construct it as a part of the "ordinary workaday world" ("*Mary Barton* and *North and South*" 39)—my reading takes this idea further to suggest that Margaret's ability to absorb the shock and horror is what gives her the strength to adapt, and therefore survive. As Wendy Parkins astutely observes, "Margaret is not merely the mediating point of social disruptions and dislocations, she *lives* these disruptions, represented first and foremost through her mobility: her shifting perspective from which the problems of modernity and modern social relations can be resolved" (507).

The connection between language, narrative, mobility, and adaptation has been brought into focus by Matus:

> North and South may be opposed in various ways, but it is significant to note that in this newly industrialized world they are readily accessible to each other. Railway transport connects all parts of the country. There is certainly a contrast between the railway stations of the North and those in the South, but the point is *that the country is traversed with lines of communication*. (*Shock* 66, emphasis added)

Throughout Gaskell's novel, it is not just Margaret's physical mobility, but her willingness to be mobile in her use of language that enables her to communicate effectively across cultures, as well as to mediate between them. It is through both physical and linguistic transportation that cultural adaptation is made possible. In this chapter, I combine theories of cultural translation with ideas of evolution to explore Gaskell's use of cultural signs and symbols of progress to shape a vision of positivist modernity. It is a vision that incorporates the meritocracy and interdependence of Political Economy with Darwinian ideas of adaptation and extinction. These ideas, often seen as mutually exclusive, speak to each other throughout Gaskell's work.[1] While Adam Smith saw the limits of self-interest and the problems of monopolies, the ideal of Political Economy was that if human beings pursued their "rational self-interest" (with the critical emphasis on "rational"), it would lead to "economic optimality and market equilibrium for society in general" (Gagnier 25). Gordon Bigelow has shown the way in which *North and South* expresses the development of this kind of equilibrium in the midst of industrialized selfishness (174), but at the same time the poverty and scarcity of Gaskell's Milton refuses to ignore the competitive, often destructive, angst necessitated by the "survival of the fittest" construct. Within these often conflicting agendas, Gaskell brings to the fore the most powerful tension within Social Progress: utilitarianism and the future growth of the community, city, and nation, versus the value of the immediate individual.

North and South opens with ideas of traveling across national boundaries, with mention of Edith's wedding tour to Scotland as well as her husband's posting in Corfu. This mobility speaks to progress in that these places become a normalized part of the English experience, yet it is also destabilizing and chaotic because it is linked to war. The Crimean War, which was occurring when Gaskell wrote *North and South*, had astonishing effects in terms of breaking down longstanding lines of national division, for example through England's alliance with France against Russia. Stefanie Markovits argues that while it does not talk directly about the war, Gaskell's text is highly influenced by it. The civil unrest that is represented reflects, and is perhaps exacerbated by, the greater international crisis England was facing. There was a growing discourse in which the external war and the threats of civil unrest spoke to each other, worsened by the breakdown of community due, to a large extent, to poverty and mobility. Within the need to hold fiercely to a sense of parochial identity, the internal unrest was written in terms of war. In 1864, Matthew Arnold would write:

> the provincial spirit … does not persuade, it makes war; it has not urbanity, the tone of the city, of the centre, the tone which always aims at a spiritual and intellectual effect, and not excluding the use of banter, never disjoins banter itself from politeness, from felicity. But the provincial tone is more violent … it loves hard-hitting rather than persuading. (249)

In Gaskell's text, the provincial warfare dominates the entire geography of the nation, until it is mediated by Margaret's body and language. Apart from her physical travel, Margaret is positioned metaphorically as mediator through her fluid use of regional dialects, and then literally as she stands between Thornton and the strikers. It stands to reason, then, that she is the character who is invigorated by

---

[1]   The influence of both Smith and Darwin is evidenced throughout Gaskell's *Letters*. Darwin was Gaskell's cousin (*Letters* 99) who often visited the Gaskells at Plymouth Grove, while Gaskell famously implored her eldest daughter, Marianne, not to "make up [her] mind … on the subject of Free Trade" until after they had read together Smith's *Wealth of Nations* (93).

thoughts of travel, as well as the most able to adapt to different cultural contexts. The text takes up, according to Markovits, the growing emphasis on "human interest" stories coming out of the war (469). In a similar manner, Margaret, as mediator and a figure of cultural adaptation, begins to feel a connection to Milton and the city's concerns once she comes to know individual inhabitants of the place. Markovits argues that the ending of the book "signif[ies] a larger bond than just between one man and one woman" (490), just as the stories of individual soldiers that were coming out of the war built empathy and concern for the cause as a whole.

Margaret's relationship to place and people situates her as a signifier of progress and social evolution. She resolutely refuses to draw back, mediating and enabling social change, thus providing an example of cultural adaptation. Margaret initially idealizes Helstone, describing it to Henry Lennox as being "like a village in a poem—in one of Tennyson's poems" (*NS* 14). Her first response to her father's announcement that they are leaving Helstone for Milton, however, is one of resolve: "Was it to be so sudden then? thought Margaret; and yet perhaps it was as well" (38). She therefore shows her "adaptability to the changes of modernity ... and her recognition of a certain instability in her own subjectivity which matches the upheaval around her" (Parkins 510). Yet what Margaret does withdraw from is the expectation that she break the news to her mother, whose response provides a drastic contrast to Margaret's. Matus suggests that Mrs. Hale is "rendered frail and sickly by the move to Milton" ("*Mary Barton* and *North and South*" 36), which implies that unlike Margaret, her mother is not capable of adaptation—and therefore she cannot survive. Even before the move, though, Mrs. Hale is considered weak in health. Margaret tells her that she thought she would be "glad to leave Helstone ... You have never been well in this air, you know" (*NS* 46), and it is also clear that Mrs. Hale had never adapted to her married life. Her frailty is evidence of her inability to move with change, and as a result she becomes a burden. It is Margaret who must take charge and give the family hope of survival through her ultimate willingness to move: "Mrs. Hale, overpowered by all the troubles and necessities for immediate household decisions that seemed to come upon her at once, became really ill, and Margaret almost felt it as a relief when her mother fairly took to her bed, and left the management of affairs to her" (50). Mrs. Hale's demise, then, is inevitable in the trajectory of the novel. As Parkins points out, in *North and South* "immobility is not an option; like the most strident celebration of modernity, *North and South* makes clear that stasis equates with death and that a certain degree of mobility and change is inevitable in modern life" (513).

Margaret is positioned from the onset as an intrepid traveller; where Edith pretends "to shiver and shudder" (*NS* 9) at Captain Lennox's accounts of his adventures abroad, Margaret "glow[s] as she listen[s]" (9). Within these two female bodies, Edith's physical response represents resistance to change, while Margaret is physically energized by it. It is Margaret's fluidity, her ability to travel and adapt, that enables her to survive the changing landscape of England. Yet that is not to say the transition is easy for her. Her departure from Helstone suggests the lack of power Margaret has over change. Just as "[r]ailroad time inexorably wrenched [the Hales] away from lovely, beloved Helstone" (57), England was being wrenched into the industrial age. Yet while Margaret cannot resist the changing landscape that they travel through, she finds agency in choosing to adapt to the new cultural spaces she enters.

As with many cross-cultural encounters, Margaret's experience is often ambivalent, if not acrimonious. However, the fact that she has been displaced from childhood, from the moment she was sent to London to live with her aunt and cousin, means that she is an ideal figure to implement and represent social progress. In a sense, Margaret does not wholly belong anywhere. Because her identity cannot be located in a sense of home, she does not have the strong ties to location that Edith does. While Edith finds "anything of a gipsy or make-shift life ... distasteful" (9), Margaret's life has been one of shifting. The two young women, therefore, set up the oppositions between stability and dislocation, and conservatism and progress. Margaret does gain this attachment for a short time, when she first returns to Helstone, which she refers to as home. She believes she will be content within the quiet country life, even though this, too, requires her to readapt after living in London for most of her formative years. Yet as a figure of adaptation, she cannot remain long within the fairytale-like, pastoral village, which has a sense of existing outside of time and therefore outside the unrelenting progress that is taking place everywhere else. Having lived in London for so long, her experiences in the city cannot be wholly removed from her renewed life in Helstone. She is not only older and more mature, her memories propel her forward. Although she speaks of having tired of riding in Aunt Shaw's carriage as a reason for why she enjoys walking so much in Helstone (20), her walking suggests a level of restlessness and compulsion for movement: "with the soft violence of the west wind behind her ... she seemed to be borne onwards, as lightly and easily as the fallen leaf that was wafted along by the autumnal breeze" (20–21). While this image is predominantly pastoral, the violence of the wind reflects the changing world, and in line with this resonance, the comparison of Margaret to an easily moved leaf acts as a reminder that she is designed for mobility, even though she seeks to ignore that impulse.

In Milton, though, the changing world cannot be ignored. Margaret's foreignness and isolation are constantly reinforced through her lack of understanding of language and cultural forms, as well as her displacement within the Milton social hierarchy. Her culture shock is expressed through her violent experience of being out of step and out of time with Milton's native inhabitants:

> Until Margaret had learnt the times of their ingress and egress, she was very unfortunate in constantly falling in with them. They came rushing along, with bold, fearless faces, and loud laughs and jests, particularly aimed at all who appeared to be above them in rank or station. The tones of their unrestrained voices, and their carelessness of all common rules of street politeness, frightened Margaret a little at first. (72)

As a migrant, she exists between cultures: she does not belong to the North, but at the same time she is increasingly disconnected from the South. However, the fact that she was frightened "at first" reveals that she grows accustomed to the northern cultural forms. While she feels disconnected from the moment her father decides to move his family due to his religious dissent, Margaret's sense of displacement and fear lessens as she adapts to her new environment. From this position, Margaret is able to act as a mediatory force between the two cultures. It is first necessary, though, for her not only to learn the language and cultural forms of the North, but to incorporate them to some degree in her cultural repertoire.

The connection between cultural adaptation, language, and progress is focalized in Margaret's body. Physically, Margaret does not fit the mould of regular beauty: "Sometimes people wondered that parents so handsome should have a daughter who was so far from regularly beautiful; not beautiful at all, was occasionally said. Her mouth was wide; no rosebud that could only open just enough to let out a 'yes' and 'no,' and 'an't please you, sir'" (18). On one level, this description shows how Margaret is not like other women: it focuses on her mouth, and her lack of regular beauty is tied up in her ability to say more than yes or no. Her capacity to speak puts her outside the norm, and outside the convention of female beauty. But taking this idea further, it is Margaret's ability to speak that enables her ability to move and adapt within different cultural contexts. Her lack of conventional beauty speaks to Darwin's discussion of monstrosity and variety in evolution:

> We have also what are called monstrosities; but they graduate into varieties. By a monstrosity I presume is meant some considerable deviation of structure in one part, either injurious to or not useful to the species, and not generally propagated. Some authors use the term "variation" in a technical sense, as implying a modification directly due to the physical conditions of life. (29)

Furthermore, the fact that Margaret is so different from her parents is also significant:

> Whatever the cause may be of each slight difference in the offspring from their parents—and a cause for each must exist—it is the steady accumulation, through natural selection, of such difference, when beneficial to the individual, that gives rise to all the more important modifications of structure, by which the innumerable beings on the face of this earth are enabled to struggle with each other, and the best adapted to survive. (107)

Margaret's parents may be considered beautiful, but in terms of cultural adaptation they are both ultimately weak and cannot survive. Margaret's adaptive variations, then, can be seen as necessary to progress and the development of the species. Her lack of beauty can be seen as a monstrosity, with a deviation of structure in one significant part—her mouth—yet she is the variation necessary to progress.

The idea of Margaret as a monstrosity is reinforced in that she is physically displaced in her aunt's home, and no longer of use there once her cousin is married. She experiences a similar sense of uselessness and idleness when she returns to London after her parents' deaths. Yet her positioning changes to one of variety when she moves to the North. In the North she is found to be highly beautiful and attractive; in this sense her relocation positions her where her traits are desirable for adaptation and progress through cross-fertilization. Similarly, Thornton and Nicholas are both described in terms attributable to monstrosity or hybridity. Nicholas describes Thornton as "two chaps ... bound up in one body" (*NS* 331), while Nicholas speaks of Thornton staring at him "as if [he] were some strange beast newly caught in some of the zones" (331). They therefore resonate with Darwin's ideas of natural selection and variety:

> As many more individuals of each species are born than can possibly survive; and as, consequently, there is a frequently recurring struggle for existence, if follows that any being, if it vary however slightly in any manner profitable to itself, under the complex and sometimes varying conditions of life, will have a better chance of surviving, and thus be *naturally selected*. From the strong principle of inheritance, any selected variety will tend to propagate its new and modified form. (3)

I would suggest, then, that it is no coincidence that these three characters are at the core of social transformation and adaptation in the text. There is also a sense of mobility in Thornton that resonates with Margaret's, although not to the same extent. Patricia Ingham observes that Thornton focuses on "the 'intra-species' struggle," which is more Malthusian than Darwinian (xxi), when he talks of employers being "trampled down by his fellows in their haste to get rich" (151); yet a significant part of Thornton's development in the novel is the way in which he begins to look across classes to recognize and empathize with his workers. Nicholas shows his willingness to be mobile by planning to move to the South in order to find work, although Margaret talks him out of it, as well as in his determination to find equal footing with Thornton. As hybrid characters who are willing to be mobile, Margaret, Thornton and Nicholas are at the center of adaptation and modernity.

The biological metaphor can be brought back to ideas of language and its ties to cultural progress. Margaret shows her capacity to adapt early on in the text, from the moment she returns to Helstone: "She took pride in her forest. Its people were her people. She made hearty friends with them" (19). Yet what is really crucial within this idea of ownership and belonging is that she "learned and delighted in using their peculiar words" (19). Language is tied to identity, and by speaking like the other inhabitants, Margaret adapts and begins to belong. Yet Margaret's belonging to a place is never pure, as she brings together the languages and cultures of the different environments she has lived within; in that sense, she embodies cultural mediation. In Milton, she begins to adopt words from the North, which her mother protests against because it is "factory slang" (233). Margaret responds: "if I live in a factory town, I must speak factory language when I want it" (233). She actively seeks to understand, as can be seen in her many conversations with the Higginses, as well as her important conversation with Mr. Thornton in which they discuss their different understandings of the words "man" and "gentleman" (162–3). These conversations mark an encounter of both language and cultural understanding. As Nicholas says to Margaret, "North and South has both met and made kind o' friends in this big smoky place" (73).

Margaret's ability to adapt in this sense, to learn to speak the language of the North, enables her to mediate between North and South. This is seen when she defends the North to Mr. Bell, when she has so adamantly spoken against it to Mr. Thornton earlier in the text. Yet she is also able to mediate between different classes in the North, for not only does she exist between North and South, because of the different class system, she belongs neither to the class of the masters, nor to that of the workers. Her in-betweenness is as evident in this social aspect as in her geographical positioning, and enables her to mediate between the masters and the workers. Margaret's role in this regard ties together Darwin's emphasis on species survival and Smith's stress on interdependence between classes. Through Margaret's influence, Thornton and Nicholas begin to recognize their mutual need to work together is instrumental for the survival of their respective classes. Therefore Margaret is the necessary variation to bring about cultural adaptation. This is seen most evidently in the way she is central to Mr. Thornton taking on Nicholas as a worker after the strike, a relationship that speaks to the idea of cross-cultural interdependence—in this case, class culture—strengthening the species.

In Margaret's social mediation, cultural signs—as an unspoken part of language—are crucial to developing mutual understanding between characters and, ultimately, social progress. In *North and South*, one of the most significant cultural markers is the handshake. The handshake is a visual and physical sign of connection, of mutual respect and understanding, as well as of agreement. The moments where handshakes take place in the text—or, significantly, do not take place—are crucial to the narrative in terms of revealing levels of alliance and understanding between characters. The first time Mr. Thornton offers his hand to Margaret, she notices the gesture too late—she is not used to the custom. Yet this social awkwardness causes offense to Mr. Thornton, particularly because it follows their first disagreement, when Margaret tells him he does not understand the South, defending its seeming lack of progress, industry, and energy. Place, culture, and character converge in this moment of misunderstanding. Mr. Thornton assesses Margaret as proud, disagreeable, and scornful because of her attitude, sealed by her apparent refusal of his handshake. The first time they do shake hands comes after a conversation where they discuss their different perspectives on civilization, labor, and progress: they begin to understand each other through their willingness to communicate. Although Margaret is oblivious to the significance of the moment, Thornton is very aware that this is the first time their hands have touched. This is partly because of the sexual attraction, but also, I argue, his recognition that Margaret is beginning to understand and adapt to Northern ways. He is no longer offended by her. This handshake precedes the conversation in which they discuss more explicitly their different cultural understandings of the words "man" and "gentleman." The relationship they begin to build breaks down, though, after Mr. Thornton offers his hand in a marital sense and Margaret refuses. At the conclusion of this heated exchange it is Margaret who offers her hand to shake his, but Thornton refuses to take it. It is evident that his refusal is a matter of pride, which provides a counterpoint in his image of "a man," which is one of "endurance ... strength ... [and] faith" (163). Yet his examples of true men include Robinson Crusoe, a prisoner in a dungeon, and Saint John on the island of Patmos: characters isolated from the world. Thornton's man, then, sees social performance as an inauthentic display of character; he acts with honesty, consistency, and integrity regardless of his audience. As the handshake is a symbol of connection, understanding, and respect, for Thornton to take Margaret's offer at this point would be an inauthentic display of cultural mores.

Another key moment of handshaking centers again on Thornton's definition of "man" as a superior accolade to "gentleman"—when he shakes Nicholas's hand after offering him work. Their earlier exchange had been fueled by animosity and the disdain of the other's respective class, yet when Thornton hears of Nicholas's determination to see him, his humility, and his resolve to care for Boucher's children, he gains respect for Nicholas. He recognizes his own spirit of determination in Nicholas, and it is through relating to him, by beginning to recognize sameness, that cross-cultural understanding and appreciation begins. Neither of them can be "gentlemen" in the Southern sense of the word, but they are both "men" according to Thornton's definition. For Thornton, manliness is to do with character—endurance, strength, and faith—rather than appearance, reputation, or social position. In this sense, it is possible for one of any class to be a man; manliness is based more on merit and personal achievement than on heredity. He recognizes this kind of manliness in Nicholas. Thornton and Nicholas are, therefore, equal, which marks the changing times within England's social structure. Their handshake is a sign of mutual understanding, of mutual respect, as they make their agreement between men, rather than as master and worker.

By bringing together Thornton and Higgins, Margaret effectively mediates the animosity between the two classes in the North. By articulating their own positions to Margaret, and then listening to the other side through her, both learn to understand each other before eventually meeting together without need of mediation. In this sense, Margaret's personal cultural adaptation is crucial to the progress of the entire community. From the moment of their handshake, Thornton and Higgins's relationship only grows in respect and appreciation, which is apparent when Thornton has to close his mill and Nicholas is at the forefront of getting the names of the men who would be willing to work for him, should he at any stage be a master again. The importance of their relationship to the progress of the entire community is shown when together they come up with the idea of the dining room co-op for the factory workers so that they have better quality food. Thornton himself eats with the workers in the dining room, which reinforces the sense of communion and equality between them. He gets to know them as men, rather than as enemies. As Mr. Bell states, there's "nothing like the act of eating for equalizing men" (354). While possibly seen as a breakdown of social structure, which could be chaotic, this communion is necessary to social progress. Separation had led to misunderstanding and animosity, strikes, and starvation, while communion leads to understanding and productivity. Yet the encounter is not only important for economic productivity; the sense of humanity, of human interest—of the individual amid the mass—is brought to the fore, through the change in both Thornton and his workers:

> He and they had led parallel lives—very close, but never touching—till the accident (or so it seemed) of his acquaintance with Higgins. Once brought face to face, man to man, with an individual of the masses around him, and (take notice) out of the character of master and workman, in the first instance, they had each begun to recognize that "we have all of us one human heart." (409)

The slight reference here to the seeming accident of their meeting does resonate with ideas of evolution and adaptation in the social or cultural sense—it is this adaptation that is necessary for the survival of the manufacturing species in the North.

Margaret's willingness to adapt to life in the North speaks to her recognition of the spirit of the age. She resonates with Thornton's attitude that those in the North "do not look upon life as a time for enjoyment, but as a time for action and exertion" (326). When she returns to London with her aunt after the death of her father, life seems particularly vacuous. Everything is "languid," "dim" in its "eventless ease," and Margaret fears she will "become sleepily deadened into forgetfulness of anything beyond the life which was lapping her round with luxury" (364). She embodies the notion earlier referred to that "stasis equates with death" (Parkins 513). The monotony of luxury and idleness, of inactivity and complacency lead to depletion—Margaret is "wearied" by it and has "depressed spirits and delicate health" (365). This state is one leading to extinction—if not physical death, at least of her spirit. To be standing (or lying) still leads to extinction; thus the drive for progress is necessary to survival.

Margaret, therefore, uses her wealth literally to buy into the North—she buys into progress and survival by investing in Thornton's mill. At the same time, this move invigorates the flailing North: Mr. Thornton needs the injection of Margaret's wealth for his business to survive. Margaret's multidirectional movement "from south to north, country to city, seaside to metropolis—and back again," and to a lesser extent Thornton's mobility, creates a "sense of dislocatedness ... [that] captures the cultural experience of modernity" (Parkins 508). Rather than a monstrosity, the suggested result is one of "the steady accumulation, through natural selection, of such difference, when beneficial to the individual ... by which the innumerable beings on the face of this earth are enabled to struggle with each other, and the best adapted to survive" (Darwin 107). In this sense, their marriage is a procreative marriage of the North to the South, a picture of cultural fluidity and adaptation that is necessary to speak to the modern nation.

Works Cited

Arnold, Matthew. "The Literary Influence of Academies." 1864. *Lectures and Essays in Criticism*, vol. 3. Ed. R.H. Super. Ann Arbor, MI: U of Michigan P, 1986. Print.

Bigelow, Gordon. *Fiction, Famine, and the Rise of Economics in Victorian Britain and Ireland*. Cambridge: Cambridge UP, 2003. Print.

Darwin, Charles. *On the Origin of Species By Means of Natural Selection*. 1859. Mineola, NY: Dover, 2006. Print.

Gagnier, Regenia. *The Insatiability of Human Wants: Economics and Aesthetics in Market Society*. Chicago and London: U of Chicago P, 2000. Print.

Gaskell, Elizabeth. *The Letters of Mrs Gaskell*. Ed. J.A.V. Chapple and Arthur Pollard. Manchester: Manchester UP, 1966. Print.

———. *North and South*. 1854–1855. London: Penguin, 1995. Print.

Hall, Stuart. "New Cultures for Old." *A Place in the World? Places, Cultures and Globalization*. Ed. Doreen Massey and Pat Jess. Oxford: Oxford UP, 1995. 175–213. Print.

Ingham, Patricia. Introduction. *North and South*. London: Penguin, 1995. xii–xxviii. Print.

Markovits, Stefanie. "North and South, East and West: Elizabeth Gaskell, the Crimean War, and the Condition of England." *Nineteenth Century Literature* 59.4 (2005): 463–93. Print.

Matus, Jill. "*Mary Barton* and *North and South*." *The Cambridge Companion to Elizabeth Gaskell*. Ed. Jill Matus. Cambridge: Cambridge UP, 2007. 27–45. Print.

———. *Shock, Memory and the Unconscious in Victorian Fiction*. Cambridge: Cambridge UP, 2009. Print.

Mullen, Mary. "In Search of Shared Time: National Imaginings in Elizabeth Gaskell's *North and South*." *Place and Progress in the Works of Elizabeth Gaskell*. Ed. Lesa Scholl, Emily Morris, and Sarina Gruver Moore. Burlington, VT: Ashgate, 2015. 107–20. Print.

Parkins, Wendy. "Women, Mobility and Modernity in Elizabeth Gaskell's *North and South*." *Women's Studies International Forum* 27 (2004): 507–19. Print.

Chapter 8
In Search of Shared Time:
National Imaginings in Elizabeth Gaskell's
North and South

Mary Mullen

Elizabeth Gaskell's *North and South* (1854–1855) is a novel about the present. Part social-problem novel, part Bildungsroman, the novel tells the story of Margaret Hale's development and maturation as she confronts the changing relations between masters and men, the public sphere and private domestic space, and culture and capital in industrial England. Beginning in London on the eve of her cousin Edith's marriage, the story follows Margaret as she returns to her childhood home in rural Helstone and then moves to Milton-Northern, a fictional Manchester, where she meets the man she eventually marries, the mill owner, John Thornton. Margaret's ability to use the present to develop—avoiding becoming overwhelmed by either the nostalgic pull of the past or the threat of an unknown future—is as important as the novel's contribution to many ongoing public discussions about the rights of workers, the responsibilities of their employers, and how to unify the nation in a time of increasing inequality and intensified difference. In this way, the rapidly changing industrial present is not simply a setting or problem within the story, but a central medium through which Margaret is able to learn, grow, and act.

Yet, despite its concern with the present historical moment, *North and South* actively rejects a shared present tense—the "empty, homogenous time" that Benedict Anderson associates with the imagined nation (24–6). Anderson famously argues that the abstract, quantifiable time of clock and calendar—often represented in nineteenth-century novels—allows people to imagine themselves moving through time together as a nation. In his account, time's apparent neutrality transcends regional and class differences, thereby unifying the disparate people of the nation. By contrast, Gaskell's *North and South* demonstrates how capitalism threatens shared national time and insists that local culture, habit, and routine are more entrenched than any national imagining. Each region experiences a distinctive approach to time: in London "everything went on with the regularity of clockwork" (50) producing a "well-ordered, monotonous life" for its inhabitants (329); the North's "haste and bustle and speed of everything" (301) makes it a place of "rapid development" (83); Oxford evokes the medieval and the antiquarian; and the South's "slow days of careless ease" (81) make it a place to enjoy the pleasures of the present, but it is also relatively stagnant. Moreover, the novel's characters have different temporal orientations, often at odds with what E.P. Thompson calls capitalist time-discipline. While the workers and Irish "hands" are figures of arrested development who accumulate time in a perpetual present, characters like Margaret, Mr. Thornton, and Nicholas Higgins learn how to navigate the multiple temporalities of the nation to develop towards a future. For the figures of arrested development, the passage of time does not lead to progress, maturation, or change, but rather ensures the continuance of stagnant, habitual routines. Unable to use time to change, their present constantly expands without leading to a different future. Thus, the novel's characters do not travel through time together, but rather some characters progress, becoming active agents of time, while others remain stagnant, passive subjects of time. Describing difference and discordance within the nation, *North and South* supports Irene Tucker's contention that contemporary scholars retrospectively impose "spatial homogeneity" onto Victorian realism (696). In the novel, England and Englishness is hardly unitary—regional and class identities prevent such homogeneity. As Lesa Scholl suggests in her contribution to this volume, regional identity has such purchase that the term "foreigner" applies to English characters traveling within England as well as the "Irish knobsticks" that, however marginal within the novel, are central to the novel's national imaginings (95).

But Gaskell does ultimately embrace a shared national time: what she suggests, specifically, is that a national, temporal consensus is one of the ends of the novel rather than an organizing principle within the narrative. Synchronizing capital and culture, North and South, through an imagined shared future, the novel's resolution reinstates homogeneous, empty time not as historical time—even by the end of the novel, the nation's disparate cultural locations and classes have not integrated into a shared present tense—but as an assumed horizon for national imagining. The tension between the novel's representation of a heterogeneous present and its imagined homogeneous future provides yet another vector through which to understand the novel's disappointing resolution to the social problem plotline. For the novel does not simply move from social problems to private actions or depend on what Raymond Williams calls "money from elsewhere"—a solution external to the social structures Gaskell depicts—to achieve resolution; it suggests that the future the novel gestures towards but does not represent will secure the capitalist time-discipline and shared national time that the novel's present so productively rejects (92). Futurity ultimately determines the limits of the nation's capacity to incorporate difference by actively excluding the throwaway Irish characters—minor characters that keep the narrative moving without being incorporated into its future-oriented development—from the novel's image of the nation.

In our own historical moment, Lee Edelman, Lauren Berlant, and Dipesh Chakrabarty have taught us to be skeptical of futurity. Arguing against "the constraining mandate of futurism," Edelman shows how politics reproduce rather than resist the social order by fetishizing the figure of the child (4). In turn, Berlant identifies "cruel optimism" as an affective structure at work in the contemporary United States, suggesting that the optimism that propels people beyond the impasses of everyday life—that enable them to think in terms of a future—end up being cruel—binding them to structures that prevent this future from being realized (1–2). Similarly, Chakrabarty suggests that futurity constrains historical narratives and explanations, suggesting that in order to rethink historicism in radical ways we must stop thinking of history "as a developmental process in which [it] is possible to become actual by tending to a future that is singular" (249). Arguing that futurity secures heteronormative, neoliberal, and imperial structures, these approaches, however different, suggest that futurity closes down the possibilities of lives lived at odds with the established social order and intensifies inequality.

Reading Gaskell's novel through the lenses of these contemporary theories demonstrates how in the Victorian period, the nation—as a political form, affective structure, and historical entity—depends on an imagined future. Showing that the shared time of the nation does not necessarily emerge from the past (as Romantic nationalists claim) or from representations of the present (as Anderson suggests) but rather from an image of a homogeneous future, *North and South* reveals how an assumed futurity delimits the possibilities of the present. Thus, the novel prompts three important revisions to Anderson's account of shared time. First, characters may not, in fact, share a temporality even when they share a nation, and even when the novel is deeply concerned with the problem of nation-formation. Second, a future-oriented image of the nation emphasizes the instrumentality of time—the capacity of the nation to put time to use—and thus synchronizes national and capitalist time. And third, as Chakrabarty implies, homogeneous, empty time ultimately depends upon restriction and exclusion—in this instance, the exclusion of the Irish as at odds with but constitutive of England's national imagining.

Disrupting the Time of the Nation: Chronotopes, Anachronistic Space, and Encounter

Critics tend to overlook the importance of temporality and history within *North and South* in favor of its representations of space.[1] Only very recently Sue Zemka has argued that Gaskell uses space to illustrate time, adopting M.M. Bakhtin's concept of the chronotope—or visible space-time—to argue that the urban street produces "a pattern of expansion (out into the many) followed by reduction (back into the few)" (794). For Zemka, *North and South*'s temporal expansion in public

---

[1] W.A. Craik argues that the novel "uses geographical setting as an element of its organization" and creates "a design of departures and returns, with the ending a balanced coming-together of the aspects of life that each place presents and explores" (112). More recent critics have dwelled on the ways in which the novel establishes a relationship between public and private spaces. Susan Johnston suggests that the novel depends upon the interpenetration of public and domestic spaces (129); Catherine Gallagher argues that Gaskell relates public and private spaces metonymically (168); and Barbara Leah Harman claims that Gaskell reduces the public to the private in order to focus on gender conflicts rather than class conflicts (53).

spaces ultimately does not subvert the novel's "mandated velocity," which she argues functions as "railroad time"—relentlessly moving forward without any regard for difference (808).

Like Zemka, I suggest that the novel follows a pattern of expansion and reduction organized through time, but I argue that this expansion and reduction actually unsettles the uniformity of railroad time and, along with it, the assumptions of shared national time. The urban street, the chronotope that Zemka identifies, is one of many chronotopes that structure the novel. For Bakhtin, chronotopes suggest genre: historical and gothic novels rely on the castle, the realist novel depends on the parlor or salon, and novels that emphasize chance encounters or episodic adventures turn to the road. Yet, Gaskell's novel is particularly interesting because it fosters movement among a variety of chronotopes. Domestic space features prominently in each region of the novel, yet the temporal valence of each domestic space varies from location to location. For instance, in Helstone the domestic space suggests age, wear and the traditional—"The carpet was far from new; the chintz had been often washed" (23)—while in Milton-Northern the vulgar "over-loading [of] such a house with colour and such heavy cornices" suggests the tastelessness of the new (61). Other spaces within each location also represent temporal differences—"New Street" is Milton's principal street (59) while on the Helstone road, "every turn and every familiar tree [was] so precisely the same in its summer glory as it had been in former years" (385). Oscillating between domestic spaces and public streets with different temporal valences, the novel does not allow a single chronotope to structure the narrative. Instead, the novel's chronotopes embrace the logic of both habit—repetitive, monotonous routines associated with habitations—and chance—contingencies of timing, often in the public street, that disrupt routines. These diverse chronotopes reveal the contradictions at the heart of industrial modernity: despite the increasing drive to standardize and regulate time and space, temporal discordance proliferates.

Importantly, none of these chronotopes represents the nation or the time of the nation. Instead, they draw attention to how the disparate paces within the nation prevent the establishment of shared, national time. According to Anderson, depictions of characters simultaneously moving through homogeneous, empty time help readers to conceive of the nation "as a solid community moving steadily down (or up) history" (26). Yet, in Gaskell's novel, simultaneity only reinforces the often incommensurable paces of distinct cultural locations, social classes, and gender. On the eve of her departure from Helstone, Margaret asks herself, "Where was [Henry Lennox] now?" (53) and imagines him "going through the old round" (53) in London while everything was "falling and fading, and turning to decay around her" (54). This scene depicts simultaneous action in a moment, a shared "now," but only to reinforce their different relationships to time: while Margaret is learning how to deal with the abrupt changes associated with her imminent move to Milton-Northern, Henry Lennox lives a life of continuity. Imagining Henry's simultaneous actions thus reinforces Margaret's sense not only of spatial distance but also of temporal difference: London is far away from the life in Milton-Northern she is preparing for but, importantly, London is "old." Difference and distance also emerge when Margaret learns that she is the same age as the worker, Bessy Higgins. Margaret "thought, more sorrowfully than Bessy did, of the contrast between them. She could not speak for a moment or two for the emotion she was trying to keep down" (103). Their shared age quantifies the accelerated pace of Bessy's life, showing that Bessy is contemplating death at the same time that Margaret is just beginning to think of herself as approaching the proper age for marriage. Rather than fostering a shared sense of time, their shared age reinforces the different paces that have governed their experiences of time.

If, on the one hand, this lack of simultaneity articulates the problem at the heart of the social problem plotline—how to integrate a nation progressing through time at discordant rates—it also creates a more expansive and capacious sense of who defines and participates in the nation. Disrupting assumed hierarchies of progress that might suggest that the North is a site of growth and development while the South is an anachronistic pastoral ideal, Gaskell suggests that the definition of progress is contingent on one's particular, situated knowledge and experience. Anne McClintock's concept of "anachronistic space" is helpful here, articulating how nineteenth-century colonialism mapped historical time and space to suggest that "colonized people—like women and the working class in the metropolis—do not inhabit history proper but exist in a permanently anterior time within the geographic space of the modern empire as anachronistic humans, atavistic, irrational, bereft of human agency" (30). The inhabitants of Helstone or workers like Bessy Higgins might initially seem consigned to anachronistic space outside of history: part of a "picturesque" landscape slowing falling into decay (25), or figures immersed in a perpetual present, "endless bits o' time" (89). But the novel actually legitimates these characters and cultural spaces as part of a heterogeneous historical time, showing the contingency of progress. Instead of mapping historical time to shore up the boundaries of English imperial culture, the novel maps temporal difference to disrupt the assumed differences between anachronisms and agents, sites of progress and sites of tradition.

Take, for example, Margaret's second trip to Helstone, where she, a supposed bearer of progress, begins to think of herself as an anachronism. She visits the local school hoping that she will be able to instruct the children as she has done in the past. But she soon finds that she is unable to teach her "old favourites ... They were growing out of children into great girls; passing out of her recollection in their rapid development, as she, by her three years' absence, was vanishing from theirs" (392). Here, the verbs "passing" and "vanishing" reinforce the extent to which anachronisms emerge from mutual, contingent relationships—not only does Margaret's nostalgic vision fail to account for the girls' "rapid development," but it also does not consider the extent to which she has "vanished" from the girls' lives, and consequently, her very presence at the school is anachronistic. Moreover, the Helstone school itself emerges as a site of advancement. After trying to help the students with a lesson, Margaret thinks that "the children knew more than she did" for while she calls "a" an "indefinite article," the children understand it as "an adjective absolute" (392). Instead of being outside of historical time, these children are the bearers of historical time, revealing that although Margaret is the center of the Bildungsroman plot, she is not necessarily the center of historical progress.

Within Gaskell's depiction of a heterogeneous present, development and knowledge emerge from movement between multiple times and spaces rather than through characters' linear progression through homogeneous, empty time. As Susan Stanford Friedman suggests, this may be true of many Bildungsromane, for she argues that we should approach the genre with a greater emphasis on space and spatial location, writing, "The growth or development—the Bildung—of a character might be seen not so much as a consequence of the play of desire but rather the result of changing cultural interactions and locations" (138). Yet, reading the Bildungsroman through its spatial locations—specifically the temporal dimension of these spatial locations—is particularly important to *North and South* precisely because Gaskell does not allow a single space or cultural location to represent the nation. She adopts what James Buzard calls a participant-observer model where a person self-consciously moves between being inside and outside of a culture—and, as this novel suggests, inside and outside of a time (10–11). Although Margaret decides to return to Milton at the end of the novel to share a future with Mr. Thornton, this does not necessarily suggest that Milton is the future of the nation. Instead, Margaret's numerous encounters with different temporalities and constant movement between being the bearer of enlightenment and an anachronistic remnant of a previous time reinforces the extent to which the nation, like the individual, must develop through encountering difference.

In this way, unlike Susan Johnston who argues that Margaret moves between subcultures "because Margaret's Bildung requires her to choose for herself, and from among a variety of alternatives, both the proper ends of life and the means to those ends" (105), I suggest that Margaret moves between the disparate cultures of the nation to reinforce the extent to which development—both individual and social—requires constant movement and encounters with temporal and spatial difference. Moving between rather than choosing between disparate cultures and times emphasizes the nation's capacity to accommodate different temporalities and cultural identities. Ruptures with the past are easily reincorporated into the nation and uneven development, which might initially threaten to divide the nation, can be overcome. For instance, Milton's rapid development initially leads Mr. Thornton to reject the traditional legislative authority of Parliament and scholarly authority of Oxford because, grounded in custom and tradition, these institutions remain ignorant of "new circumstances" under which the mill owners operate (334). But as soon as he acquaints Mr. Colthurst with "all the facts he wanted coaching in," we are to assume that parliament's authority is restored (430). Similarly, slow-moving cultural locations, such as Oxford and Helstone, do not threaten national unity, but rather aid in the process of "learning from the past" and "shaping out the future," in part by emphasizing the value of culture, beauty, and leisure (330–31).

The nation can accommodate these differences because the future—the horizon for this movement between and integration of disparate temporalities—assumes the establishment of homogeneous, empty time. Thus, I suggest that what Josie Billington calls Gaskell's "immersion in prosaic ordinariness"—an embedded temporality tied to the rhythms of individual lives and open to heterogeneity and difference—ultimately depends upon the acceptance of the future as "an urgent summons and claim" (170). By this I mean that not only did Gaskell, the writer, need to embrace futurity as a way of maintaining constant forward momentum in both her writing and her domestic responsibilities, as Billington so clearly demonstrates, but also that the political logic of Gaskell's novels depend upon an assumed futurity. Collapsing the expansive potential of a nation grounded in temporal and social difference, the future imposes a singular end for discordant cultural temporalities and uneven capitalist growth: development. The generalizing maxim, "But the future must be met, however stern and iron it be," reveals that the nation depends upon the assumption that the future will "be met" (59). Time will be put to use—even in the rural Helstone and the leisurely Oxford—because however much each cultural location differs in pace, rhythm, and temporal orientation, they all assume that the work of history is to use the past to shape the future.

No Future: Irish Time and the Limits of the Nation

The Irish hands and Irish characters appearing on the margins of the novel reveal the limits of the nation's capacity to incorporate difference by demonstrating that nineteenth-century English nationalism ultimately depends upon racial exclusion. While the Irish hands that Mr. Thornton brings to Milton to end the strike fail to develop over time, John Boucher, a weak member of the Union with "Irish blood" and "tones," more actively resists futurity by committing suicide (308). Their exclusion from the nation's developmental time exhibits familiar Victorian prejudice against the Irish. But, more importantly, it suggests that establishing the future as a horizon for national imagining allows the nation to exclude individuals, ethnicities, and behaviors at odds with this imagined future, defining itself through the people and practices it actively rejects. This exclusion merges culture and capital in ways that make visible the imperial politics of developmental time and its narrow conception of futurity. Gaskell celebrates the integration of class and regional difference within England only to imply that the Irish must be excluded in order to achieve the nation's imagined future.

Before turning to the novel's representations of the Irish, it is important to consider Irish presence in England, and Manchester specifically, at the time. Although there was steady Irish migration to Manchester in the late eighteenth century, the most concentrated migration occurred between 1845 and 1852, roughly the period of the famine in Ireland and just before the publication of *North and South*. In the 1851 census, Irish-born people made up 15.2 percent of Manchester's total population (Busteed 99). As Christine Kinealy suggests, "Despite the Act of Union, the Irish in Britain were still regarded as a threat to the political stability and economic prosperity of the metropole" (91). In 1854, J.R. Mulloch described the negative effects of the "floating bridges between Dublin and Liverpool, Belfast and Glasgow, Waterford and Bristol," suggesting that they threatened "to entail very pernicious consequences on the people of England and Scotland" (39). Indeed, many English people feared the consequences of Irish migration. They worried that this would lead to lower wages, a reduced standard of living, riots, worker unrest, and the spread of Catholicism, crime, pauperism, and Irish contagion or "famine fever" (Busteed 107). Irish presence was marked on the landscape, for not only were there the "distinctly Irish quarters" that social reformers found deplorable; there was also an Irish presence within the newspapers (Busteed and Hodgson 141). In addition to frequent news about Irish crime, from August 1845 to March 1850 the *Manchester Guardian* included reports of the Manchester union poor law meetings that divided the people who received aid into the resident poor, casual poor (those who lived in Manchester for less than five years), and Irish poor (Boot 217). Clearly, Irish immigration and Irishness was an active concern for England.

Within this period of increased Irish immigration, the Irish were seen as a threat to England and English national development precisely because they resisted futurity. James Phillips Kay's 1832 study of the cholera epidemic in Manchester vocalizes such an understanding of the Irish, pathologizing them as a "contagious example of ignorance and a barbarous disregard of forethought and economy" (22). Opposing the negative influence of the Irish, Kay argues that English workers "have discovered, with the savage, what is the minimum of the means of life, upon which existence may be prolonged" (21). For Kay, not only are the Irish "savages"—anachronistic embodiments of a lower stage of civilization—they are outside of developmental time, irreconcilable with the healthy virtues of "forethought and economy." Unable and unwilling to put time to use, the Irish are "reckless of the future" in Kay's account because they assume that the poor law will take care of them during hardship (47). As a result, Mary Poovey claims that Kay's study exemplifies how the English nation coheres through a process of "differentiation and displacement"—it differentiates itself from other ethnic and cultural identities (the "savage" Irish) and displaces forms of identity that might cut across national boundaries, such as class or gender (55).

Thomas Carlyle's *Chartism* (1839) presents a similar depiction of the Irish as an anachronistic and arrested race as he suggests that the Irish population is integral to the condition of England question. He associates Irishness with disorder and savagery, writing: "The Irish national character is degraded, disordered; till this recover itself, nothing is yet recovered. Immethodic, headlong, violent, mendacious: what can you make of the wretched Irishman?" (Carlyle 26). Like Kay, Carlyle argues that Irish presence lowers the quality of life of English workers, going so far as to suggest that it ultimately threatens to transform them from reasoning men to unthinking animals, or "from decent manhood to squalid apehood" (28). In his words, "the condition of the lower multitude of English labourers approximates more and more to that of the Irish competing with them in all the markets" (Carlyle 31). Thus, although he, like Gaskell, is at odds with a purely capitalist framework—he laments that "Cash Payment [is] the sole nexus between man and man"—he nevertheless uses this nexus to articulate the threat of Irish presence within England (Carlyle 66). Identifying the Irish as regressive, animalistic, and disorderly, Carlyle argues that their presence impedes one of the few possible solutions to the current condition of England: education. While education encourages progress, or to use one of Carlyle's metaphors, "swimming"; the Irish encourage stagnant subsistence, living on despite the fact that they are "sunk" (Carlyle 29). In this way, Irish backwardness not only degrades the nation in Carlyle's account, but it also actively impedes the progress and improvement needed to address England's social problems.

Each of these texts clarifies the connection between capitalism and English national time. Infusing the market with cheap labor while being willing to subsist on the "minimum," Irish workers enable capitalist growth that undermines rather than contributes to national development. For this reason, Roy Foster claims that "anti-Irish prejudice owed more to class than to race" (288). Bad capitalists content with subsistence rather than growth, willing to accumulate time rather than use it, the Irish lowered the standard of living of English workers.[2] But finding the origin of anti-Irish prejudice is not as simple as Foster suggests, for Gaskell's novel, as well as these earlier texts, reveals the difficulty of differentiating economic, ethnic, and social explanations for anti-Irish prejudice. As David Lloyd suggests, one of the effects of British colonization of the Irish was the destruction of Irish culture so that their "specific and unreproducible orientation towards the future" no longer had legitimacy (40). Dislodged from traditional political and cultural forms through colonial violence, Irish understandings of futurity could only appear recalcitrant to development, at odds with both English and capitalist conceptions of modernity. Thus, capital and culture work together to relegate the Irish outside of a national time defined through development.

Building on these earlier accounts, Gaskell specifically identifies the strike-breakers as Irish in order to attribute their poor workmanship to their race rather than their inexperience. The English workers take "pleasure at the idea of the bungling way in which they [the Irish hands] would set to work, and perplex their new masters with their ignorance and stupidity, strange exaggerated stories of which were already spreading through the town" (228). Gaskell justifies these "strange exaggerated stories" by describing the necessity of training them as "a daily annoyance" (318), and suggesting that even after much time has passed, the Irish remain in need of training. The narrator explains that Thornton's failure "was owing in some degree to the utter want of skill on the part of the Irish hands whom he had imported; much of their work was damaged and unfit to be sent forth by a house which prided itself on turning out nothing but first-rate articles" (420). As Peter Gaskell suggests in an 1833 account, most newly hired hands lack training and thus negatively affect the quality of the work:

---

[2] For more on how the Irish were associated with the accumulation of time, see Gregory Dobbins, *Lazy Idle Schemers: Irish Modernism and the Cultural Politics of Idleness* (2010).

> During turn-outs great numbers of new hands come into the town or district
> where it exists, generally hand-loom weavers, or operatives from other classes
> of manufacturers, or individuals from the mining districts ... but then they are
> ignorant of the details of spinning or weaving; much has to be taught them; a
> great deal of the work is spoiled. (40)

But in *North and South*, Gaskell attributes the ignorance of the new hands not
to a lack of training but to their Irishness. She legitimates the hands' "contempt
for 'them Irishers,'" implying that the Irish workers are unable to do the hands'
labor (228). Always specifying that these new hands are "Irish"—they are "Irish
blackguards" (178), "Irish hands" (209), "Irish 'knobsticks'" (318), but never
simply "the new hands" or the knobsticks—Gaskell insists that their inability to
learn the necessary skills results from their inherent Irish ignorance. At the end of
the novel, the Irish are in precisely the same position they were in at the beginning
of the novel: ignorant and in need of training.

Naturalizing differences between the English and the Irish, Gaskell suggests
that the Irish are meant to do unskilled labor. Frustrated by his inability to get work
at the mills, Higgins tells Thornton that if it were summer, "I'd take to Paddy's
work and go as a navvy, or haymaking, or summut" and Thornton responds,
"Why, you couldn't do half a day's work at digging against an Irishman" (320).
Thornton's response reinforces the distinction between "Paddy's work" and work
in the mill by promoting the inherent superiority of "an Irishman" at digging.
Writing in 1845, Engels makes the implications of Gaskell's concept of "Paddy's
work" explicit, writing:

> But that [the Irishman's lower level of civilization] does not hinder the
> Irishman's competing with the Englishman, and gradually forcing the rate of
> wages, and with it the Englishman's level of civilization, down to the Irishman's
> level. Certain kinds of work require a certain grade of civilization, and to these
> belong almost all forms of industrial occupation (89).

Although Engels's text was not translated into English until after Gaskell's death,
it helps articulate how *North and South* resists the integration of difference through
the logic of occupation. Lacking foresight and a desire for futurity, the Irish are
relegated to the mundane, physical work of unskilled labor. They are allowed to
contribute to the nation, but are excluded from national imagining.

Boucher's suicide confirms the inability of the Irish to meet the future. Before
the reader learns of Boucher's "Irish blood" and "tones," his difficulties show the
harsh material conditions of the workers' lives: his children are hungry and not
yet old enough to work for themselves; his wife exerts continuous pressure on
him; and the Union exercises a "slow, lingering torture" that prevents him from
making his own decisions (232). In the face of these hardships, Boucher drowns
himself in a brook where "there's not water enough to drown him," showing that
he was "a determined chap. He lay with his face downwards. He was sick enough
o' living, choose what cause he had for it" (294). Yet, Gaskell ultimately does not
allow the reader to "choose what cause he had for it" and instead blames his weak

Irish character. After describing the "granite in all these northern people," Margaret explains the Bouchers' weakness by saying, "I should guess from their tones that they had Irish blood in them" (308). As Deirdre David suggests, naturalizing his Irishness is a convenient way for accounting for his suicide, for it deflects attention from the many social conditions that have led to his hopelessness (44).

While Boucher's six children indicate that he is hardly at odds with the reproductive futurity that Edelman argues shores up constructions of the social, his suicide reveals that national imagining depends upon the refusal of alternative futures or the resistance to futurity itself. Although his death leads Margaret to lament that both industrial workers and country laborers "must find it hard to realize a future of any kind," it ultimately secures the English nation as the primary social form that will reduce such difficulties for other workers (301). Tellingly, Boucher's suicide encourages Nicholas Higgins to temper his class antagonism and ask for work from the masters that he opposed in the strike. He does so both to take responsibility for mistakenly incorporating Boucher into the union's politics, saying "I set him off o' th' road, and so I mun answer for him," and to guarantee the future of Boucher's children, knowing now that Mrs. Boucher is incapable of such responsibility (305). In the process, Higgins shifts from the class-based social logics of the union, which includes every worker, to the more narrow, cultural logics of the nation, which includes those workers willing to put time to use. Thus, Boucher's determination for an alternative future confirms the inability of the Irish to be incorporated into England's developmental time. It reveals the possibilities of alternative temporalities only to legitimate the narrow version of futurity embraced by the nation.

Ultimately, Gaskell's depictions of the Irish indicate that a narrow conception of futurity underlies national imagining as they show how a sense of a shared future delimits the extent to which the nation can accommodate difference. *North and South* celebrates characters that subordinate alternative futures and synthesize multiple cultural times, while the throwaway Irish characters become figures for the dangers of arrested development and anachronism. Producing a distinctly Victorian form of "cruel optimism," the novel locates the solution to social problems not in the expansive potential of the heterogeneous present but in a homogeneous future that unifies the nation through capitalist time-discipline and the exclusion of the Irish. This narrow construction of futurity highlights the extent to which English nationalism depends upon racial exclusion—for although English class and regional difference is easily integrated into the nation, Irish difference must be excluded in the name of development. National belonging, presented as an alternative to the uneven development described in *North and South*, actually synchronizes culture and capital in ways that intensify inequality and legitimate imperialism.

Works Cited

Anderson, Benedict. *Imagined Communities: Reflections on the Origin and Spread of Nationalism*. London and New York: Verso, 1993. Print.

Bahktin, M.M. *The Dialogic Imagination: Four Essays.* Trans. Caryl Emerson and Michael Holquist. Ed. Michael Holquist. Austin, TX: U of Texas P, 1981. Print.

Berlant, Lauren. *Cruel Optimism.* Durham, NC: Duke UP, 2011. Print.

Billington, Josie. "Gaskell's 'Rooted' Prose Realism." *Place and Progress in the Works of Elizabeth Gaskell.* Ed. Lesa Scholl, Emily Morris, and Sarina Gruver Moore. Burlington, VT: Ashgate, 2015. 159–72. Print.

Boot, H.M. "Unemployment and Poor Law Relief in Manchester, 1845–50." *Social History.* 15.2 (1990): 217–28. Print.

Busteed, M.A. and R.I. Hodgson. "Irish Migrant Responses to Urban Life in Early Nineteenth-Century Manchester." *The Geographical Journal*, 162.2 (1996): 139–53. Print.

Busteed, Mervyn. "Little Islands of Erin's: Irish Settlement and Identity in Mid-Nineteenth-Century Manchester." *The Great Famine and Beyond: Irish Migrants in Britain in the Nineteenth and Twentieth Centuries.* Ed. Donald M. MacRaid. Dublin and Portland, OR: Irish Academic P, 2000. 94–127. Print.

Buzard, James. *Disorienting Fiction: The Autoethnographic Work of Nineteenth-Century British Novels.* Princeton, NJ: Princeton UP, 2005. Print.

Carlyle, Thomas. *Chartism.* London: Chapman and Hall, Strand, 1842. Print.

Chakrabarty, Dipesh. *Provincializing Europe: Postcolonial Thought and Historical Difference.* Princeton, NJ: Princeton UP, 2000. Print.

Craik, W.A. *Elizabeth Gaskell and the English Provincial Novel.* London: Methuen, 1975. Print.

David, Deirdre. *Fictions of Resolution in Three Victorian Novels:* North and South, Our Mutual Friend, *and* Daniel Deronda. London and Basingstoke: Macmillian, 1981. Print.

Dobbins, Gregory. *Lazy Idle Schemers: Irish Modernism and the Cultural Politics of Idleness.* Dublin: Field Day Publications, 2010. Print.

Edelman, Lee. *No Future: Queer Theory and the Death Drive.* Durham, NC: Duke UP, 2004. Print.

Engels, Friederic. *The Condition of the Working Class in England.* 1844. Ed. David McLellan. Oxford: Oxford UP, 1993. Print.

Foster, R.F. *Paddy and Mr Punch: Connections in Irish and English History.* London: Penguin, 1993. Print.

Friedman, Susan Stanford. *Mappings: Feminism and the Cultural Geographies of Encounter.* Princeton, NJ: Princeton UP, 1998. Print.

Gallagher, Catherine. *The Industrial Reformation of English Fiction: Social Discourse and Narrative Form 1832–1867.* Chicago and London: U of Chicago P, 1985. Print.

Gaskell, Elizabeth. *North and South.* 1854–1855. Oxford: Oxford UP, 1998. Print.

Gaskell, Peter. "The Manufacturing Population of England, its Moral, Social, and Physical Conditions, and the changes which have arisen from the use of Steam Machinery, with an Examination of Infant Labour." *The Victorian Novelist: Social Problems and Social Change.* Ed. Kate Flint. London: Croom Helm, 1987. Print.

Harman, Barbara Leah. *The Feminine Political Novel in Victorian England.* Charlottesville and London: UP of Virginia, 1998. Print.

Johnston, Susan. *Women and Domestic Experience in Victorian Political Fiction.* Westport, CT and London: Greenwood, 2001. Print.

Kay, James. "The Moral and Physical Condition of the Working Classes Employed in the Cotton Manufacture in Manchester." London: J. Ridgway, 1832. Print.

Kinealy, Christine. "At Home with the Empire: the example of Ireland." *At Home in Empire: Metropolitan Culture and the Imperial World.* Ed. Catherine Hall and Sonya O. Rose. Cambridge: Cambridge UP, 2007. Print.

Lloyd, David. *Irish Times: Temporalities of Modernity.* Dublin: Field Day Publications, 2008. Print.

McClintock, Anne. *Imperial Leather: Race, Gender and Sexuality in the Colonial Contest.* New York: Routledge, 1995. Print.

Mulloch, J.R. "Account of the British Empire." 1854. *Irish Migrants in Britain, 1815–1914: A Documentary History.* Ed. Roger Swift. Cork: Cork UP, 2002. 395. Print.

Poovey, Mary. *Making a Social Body: British Cultural Formation, 1830–1864.* Chicago: U of Chicago P, 1995. Print.

Scholl, Lesa. "Moving Between North and South: Cultural Signs and the Progress of Modernity in Elizabeth Gaskell's Novel." *Place and Progress in the Works of Elizabeth Gaskell.* Ed. Lesa Scholl, Emily Morris, and Sarina Gruver Moore. Burlington, VT: Ashgate, 2015. 95–106. Print.

Thompson, E.P. "Time, Work-Discipline, and Industrial Capitalism." *Past and Present* 38 (1967): 56–97. Print.

Tucker, Irene. "International Whiggery." *Victorian Studies* 45:4 (2003): 687–97. Print.

Williams, Raymond. *Culture and Society: Coleridge to Orwell.* London: Hogarth, 1990. Print.

Zemka, Sue. "Brief Encounters: Street Scenes in Gaskell's Manchester." *ELH* 76.3 (2009): 793–819. Print.

PART III
Literary and Imagined Spaces

Chapter 9
Catching the Post:
Elizabeth Gaskell as Traveler and
Letter-Writer

Kathrin Levitan

While on holiday in Auchencairn, Scotland, in 1859, Elizabeth Gaskell told a correspondent, "Please write to us,—an old man whistles at the end of the field, if he has any letters for us, and some one races down for them, holding them up in triumph, if there are many. But suppose the day should arrive when there is no whistle!" (*The Letters of Mrs Gaskell* 434). Gaskell, an avid traveler both in Britain and abroad, was also deeply reliant on and committed to her close relationships with friends and family. While traveling she continued to correspond with her friends, her relations, and her publishers, and as this quotation shows she was often particularly anxious for mail while away from home. This essay will survey the role that letters played in Gaskell's life as a traveler and will explore the sense of place that her letters express.

Gaskell's adult life coincided with a period of dramatic technological changes both in transportation and communication. The first passenger railway in Britain was built between Manchester and Liverpool in 1830, two years before Gaskell moved to Manchester. Then, in the early 1840s, the British Post Office underwent major reforms that resulted in the "Penny Post," which standardized payment and delivery procedures across the country. By the 1850s, railway services across Britain and the rest of Europe were extensive, and a new form of communication, the telegraph, also had become available. Travel and tourism were a sought-after form of leisure for a growing proportion of the British population after the expansion of the railroad. But while travelers may have wanted a break from the everyday work of writing letters, especially business ones, they also were missing out on gossip and news, and letters were lifelines to the outside world. Sending and receiving mail, therefore, was critical to travelers' sense of well-being, and they were often anxious to "catch the post."[1]

Gaskell's travels (on which she was often accompanied by one or more of her daughters) included extended visits to friends and family as well as annual holidays at the seaside and touristic expeditions to continental Europe. Gaskell was a self-conscious traveler, very aware of the speed with which the railroad

---

[1] As Alan Shelston points out, letters "record absences; after all, the call for a letter only arises when one of the parties involved is separated from the other" (49).

could move her from city to country or from region to region, and explicit about the relation between her location and her state of mind. Gaskell was also very aware of the changing technologies of the postal system itself, and of the ways in which sending and receiving mail were different in rural and urban areas, or in Britain and on the Continent. We learn from her about what time the post comes and goes, how long the walk to the post office is, and how these contingencies affected the course of people's days. Scholars certainly have been aware both of Gaskell's love for travel and of the role that technologies such as the railroad played in her fiction.[2] Gaskell's views of the postal service, however, are a bit more obscure.[3] We take it for granted that educated Victorians, especially those with professional and social circles as wide as Gaskell's, spent a large portion of every day writing letters and that letters were central both to career advancement and to personal expression.[4] But Gaskell's letters demonstrate that letter-writing was not only an activity or a task but a self-reflexive process. Gaskell explicitly understood correspondence as bridging geographic distances while she traveled, and she also described writing and receiving letters as essential to her daily life. The emphasis in this study, therefore, will be on those letters that engage explicitly with the letter-writing process itself. These letters address a number of themes of interest both to Gaskell scholars and to scholars of industrialization and nineteenth-century life more broadly: the relationship between rural and urban, the "opportunities and anxieties," in Alan Shelston's words, that travel provided, everyday responses to changing technologies, and the question of how family relationships changed in the context of increasing geographic mobility (91). Ultimately Gaskell, like others of her generation, worked to reconcile her excitement about and reliance on new technologies with her nostalgia for rural, pre-industrial life.

---

[2]   For an analysis of Gaskell's use of the railroad in her fiction, see Alan Shelston, "Opportunity and Anxiety: Elizabeth Gaskell and the Development of the Railway System." For travel in Victorian Britain see Marjorie Morgan, *National Identities and Travel in Victorian Britain* (2001). Also see Jenny Uglow, *Elizabeth Gaskell: A Habit of Stories* (1993) for general biographical information, including details of all of Gaskell's major journeys.

[3]   For postal reform, see Rowland Hill, *Post Office Reform: Its Importance and Practicability* (1837). Also see Catherine Golden, *Posting It: The Victorian Revolution in Letter-Writing* (2010), and Kate Thomas, *Postal Pleasures: Sex, Scandal, and Victorian Letters* (2011). While my study does not look at the role of letters in Gaskell's fiction, it is worth noting Thomas's argument about the "postal plot" in Victorian fiction, in which the eighteenth-century epistolary plot was replaced by plots that relied on the technicalities of the postal system itself. Also see Costantini, Marroni, and Soccio, Preface, for a similar discussion.

[4]   Deirdre d'Albertis has detailed the importance of correspondence in Gaskell's assertion of her own public and private personas. Deirdre d'Albertis, "The Life and Letters of E.C. Gaskell."

Rural Escape and Postal Isolation

Gaskell was accustomed to highly populous as well as rural places. She adored Rome and was usually happy to make an excursion to London as well. But for her, the allure of travel most often lay in its promise of isolation and natural beauty. Gaskell led a busy work and social life as a novelist and a minister's wife in Manchester. Like many of her contemporaries she believed that country air, and in particular sea air, was a rejuvenating remedy for months of tiring work or the everyday business of household and family. In fact, Gaskell, who was very sensitive about the critical reception of her work, sometimes planned her travel in order to get away from home when she knew reviews were about to appear or controversy might be looming. Whether the travel was for health or holiday, therefore, it provided an escape from the everyday. And while Gaskell's connection to Manchester was central to her fiction as well as to her identity, it is worth keeping in mind that she was also a chronicler of rural and small town life, and her own hunger for rural escape was essential to her career. As Josie Billington points out in this volume (159–72), Gaskell's success as a novelist was closely tied to her ability to describe domestic, everyday life in rural England, and in fact to her "provincialism." When we remember that Gaskell sometimes planned her travel for the specific purpose of preparing her novels (as when she went to Whitby to conduct research for *Sylvia's Lovers*) we again can see how Gaskell's journeys of "escape" took on both professional and personal valences.

Gaskell tended to be far more explicit about the technicalities of the postal service when she was on holiday in out-of-the-way places than when she was in London or other cities. When by the coast in North Wales, Gaskell explained to one correspondent that she and her hosts would spend the morning talking until they:

> suddenly remember the post comes in and whisks out again any time between 12 and 2, so hurry away to write letters for the bag; … till the bag comes in; tumble over each other in our haste to get our letters; speak crossly to anyone who speaks to us till we've read, and if possible answered, our letters – then comes a calm in which we can draw deep breaths, for the event of the day is over – the bag is gone off again. (*Letters* 29)

In Silverdale in Lancashire, where Gaskell and her family made "an annual migration to the sea-side" (*Letters* 72a), she writes "in great haste to catch the post in this out-of-the-way place" (*Letters* 264b), and "it is a long hot walk to the post office and it is so disappointing to find no letters there when we get there" (*Letters* 394).

As the quotation that I opened with suggests, Gaskell also noticed, sometimes with humor and sometimes with frustration, the more primitive types of postal services available in the countryside. Such services could be experienced as an extreme inconvenience when waiting for news, but they could also be experienced as a nostalgic return to a pre-industrial rural society. As Gaskell explained to one correspondent:

> You don't know what a broken reed you trusted to in relying on the Silverdale postman. There is a railroad from Lancaster to Silverdale, twelve miles; but there is so much respect shown for vested interests that the post continues to be managed as it has been for dozens of years for above thirty by the same man. He lives at Yealand about four miles from here, and nine from Lancaster. He rides a pony almost as old as himself over to Lancaster every morning to fetch the letters; delivers them in Yealand, walks here; *gets thirsty on the road*, drops his letters, or forgets in which of his various pockets he has put them, – but as it is his and his wife's sole dependence for a livelihood, and they have been honest hard-working people, no one likes to complain, and we submit in as much patience as we can. (*Letters* 492)

This type of postal service was perhaps not very convenient, but it was certainly part of the charm of country life. We get a glimpse here of some of the potential class tensions arising in situations where middle-class urban visitors were dependent on the services of locals whose livelihoods depended on tourism, tensions that can be seen in popular tourist destinations all over the world today. There is also the notion here that Silverdale had not adopted the most up-to-date postal technologies that were available. Rowland Hill's post office reforms of the 1840s had aimed to make delivery procedures more efficient, especially in rural areas. But these reforms clearly had not become a reality in every place. It is through the comparative perspective a frequent traveler like Gaskell provides that such local variations become clear.

Another aspect that is clear is that letters were especially welcome in isolated spots. As Gaskell wrote from Auchencairn, thanking a friend for sending some new books:

> Books are books here,—where potatoes have to be sent for from Castle Douglas, nine miles off—where we are uncertain what King or Queen reigns in England,—where we are far away from newspapers or railways or shops, or any sign of the world: where we go to bed by daylight, and get up because the cocks crow, and cows low to be milked, and we can't sleep any longer. (*Letters* 434)

She then went on "Besides we know nothing out here" (*Letters* 434) "and books and news of any kind are if possible still greater rarities [than potatoes]" (*Further Letters of Mrs Gaskell* 199). This is a generally merry request for letters; Gaskell was certainly enjoying her isolation. In Scotland, where "letters will be so very acceptable," "the air is delicious, and most invigorating" and "we are all in the dark about sophisticated life" (*Letters* 436). Isolation and primitivism were positive aspects of being away from home. Similarly, Gaskell wrote in 1856 to a friend that she had not had time to write:

> till now that I am staying for a few days in the deep quiet of an old Hall, far removed from railways and post offices and all such new-fangled inventions where nothing more interesting than the adventures of the rooks in building their nests ever happens to disturb the deep serene. (*Further Letters* 154)

From another rural spot she wrote, "here is Sue, who has ridden over, to bring us news of the civilized world—in the shape of letters &c &c." (*Letters* 4). The idea that letters represented civilization, and that both railways and post offices were "new-fangled inventions," suggests the ways in which the post was connected to other developing technologies. It also alerts us to a paradox: travel relied on the technologies of the railroad and the post office, yet one of Gaskell's purposes in traveling was to remove herself from such symbols of modern life.[5] We can perhaps view this paradox as representative of a larger ambivalence about industrialization that is familiar to historians of the nineteenth century. Cities, railroads, and factories were exciting and impressive, but they were also a threat to rural life and to pre-industrial modes of interaction.

Yet if being isolated from "civilization" could be a delightful escape, being on holiday also could be boring, and the strangeness or foreignness of a place could be lonely. While in Whitby with two of her children, Gaskell wrote to a friend, "Do please remember our utter isolation from all the usual sources of gossip and we don't know a creature here and the evenings are very long,—and send us PLEASE a long account of what she is like etc. etc. etc...." (*Letters* 446). In a description of her first visit to Charlotte Brontë's household, she explained, "Breakfast over, the letters come; not many, sometimes for days none at all" (*Further Letters* 102), and this point contributes to her overall portrayal of Charlotte's life as solitary and depressed.

Even worse than being isolated from news and gossip was the possibility that by traveling Gaskell may have been missing some more serious intelligence, particularly about the health of her family. She wrote to her daughter Marianne in 1854, "*Do* write. Only think! It will be *Tuesday* before we can even hear from home; and certainly Thursday before we can hear from you, darling. But do write us a long letter, we seem so very far away from you. & I shan't begin to enjoy myself till I hear from you" (*Letters* 209). Letters like this one, expressing anxiety about being out of touch, are extremely common. When Marianne was 30 years old, Gaskell fretted to her, "I do hope you will sometime learn to understand how a *mother* may crave to have a line or two, twice a week or so" (*Letters* 580). The extent to which discussions of receiving letters sometimes dominated the letters themselves is worth emphasizing. In a single letter to Marianne from Heidelberg, Gaskell made the following statements: "We *hope* for letters but I am afraid none will come." "I do so look forward to your letters from home." "Now I must end my

---

5   Jenny Uglow points out that Gaskell tended to exaggerate the isolated nature of some of her vacation spots, and that Auchencairn was not quite so removed from "civilization" as Gaskell suggested it was. Uglow also points out that Gaskell used her address itself to express her isolation, heading her letter from Auchencairn "Mr. Trumbull's, Auchencairn, *By* (i.e. 22 miles off) Dumfries" (457). Other scholars have suggested that street addresses, a requirement after the Post Office reforms, could influence people's very identity through the sense of permanence and place that they provided. See Rebecca Earle, ed. *Epistolary Selves: Letters and Letter-Writers, 1600–1945* (1999), 10. The connection between one's mailing address and one's identity is evident in this example from Auchencairn.

letter unless indeed we hear from you before the English post goes out, a chance for which it is worth while keeping my letter open till afternoon." "Oh how I do want your next letter, my child! I cannot think how I am to get over the days till Wednesday" (*Letters* 404a).

Catching the Post

Gaskell's travel plans were often tentative and open to change. In many cases, she stayed away from home for an extended period, traveling from visit to visit, meeting friends or family along the way. This meant that she was reliant on letters while she traveled in order to make arrangements for her next stop. Accounts from home also influenced her travel plans; for example, a letter that told of a family member recovering from an illness allowed her to stay away longer, while bad news of some kind might compel her to return home sooner than expected. Because of this uncertainty and the often complicated nature of her travel arrangements, Gaskell frequently gave very specific instructions to her family about how and when to write. A typical example is the following: "Do you understand that I am stopping here till Saturday morning 11 o'clock and I shall be *very* glad of a letter *here* on Saturday morning which I can receive if you write to-morrow" (*Letters* 472).

Arriving at a new place also meant learning how the mail worked there, since despite the relative standardization of the postal service after the 1840s reform, different households continued to receive mail at different times. We hear in Whitby that by going to the Post Office, "we get our letters two hours sooner than if we wait for the delivery; so write to Post Office...." [We then] "come home close upon post time 1/2 past 4 (so if we don't get our letters done before we go out we can't send them that day ... We want letters my darling ... with news ...)" (*Letters* 447). There are numerous examples like this. While visiting her friends the Gregs, she wrote to her daughters "I find the post does not go out until 1/2 past 5 ... I am afraid you won't get this till tomorrow morning, & then I can't hear till Thursday morning; letters have just come at breakfast time for Mr. & Mrs. Greg; so I suppose that's the time they come in ... be sure & write *directly* at any rate, & send it down to the *town* post" (*Letters* 21).

Traveling abroad made such procedures even more complicated. From Heidelberg Gaskell wrote to Marianne: "English letters, arriving in the afternoon, are not distributed on *Sunday* afternoon, not till *Monday* morning—so avoid sending letters that come on a Sunday" (*Letters* 405) and "(Notice & tell me when you receive this letter, as I want to know how long letters take in getting home)" (*Letters* 404a). She also told Marianne before a trip to France "*we shall stay to receive morning post on that day* before going to Paris ... I hope you will understand it all? If not ask and fully understand before we go abroad for we *may* be difficult to catch by post afterwards" (*Letters* 506a). Writing in 1861 to Marianne, who was staying in Rome, Gaskell said:

> TODAY (notice the date) came your letter to me last TUESDAY'S (Decr 7) and your letter to *Julia*, dated SATURday Decr 21, showing that your *Tuesday's*

letter had not been sent out that day—And before then one of your *Saturday's* letters did not reach us till the Thursday *week* following. We are not anxious about you, darling, so it is only because of the delays that (we think) must take place at your end of the world in *sending* letters. (*Letters* 496)

We can see here how the distinction between efficient and primitive postal services within Britain could also be applied to a comparison between Britain and other, less industrialized countries.

These examples suggest the extent to which the technicalities of the post were topics of letters, and beyond that the extent to which Gaskell relied on her correspondence while she was traveling, for both practical and emotional reasons. Certainly, the most recurrent letter-writing challenge that Gaskell faced when traveling was being late for the post. Sentences like "*In a great hurry* – just come for letters before we expected" (*Letters* 376a), and letters that end in mid-sentence with "here's post" (*Letters* 2) are extremely frequent, and accentuate both the uncertainty that came from a lack of familiarity with local postal procedures and the very great importance of sending and receiving letters on a particular day. It is true that Gaskell often ended her letters from home in a hurry too. But while "here's post" may have served as an accepted, easy way to end a letter written from home, or as an excuse for a hastily written rather than an elegant letter (see *Letters* 347a), when used while traveling it seems to have suggested a more genuine anxiety about making sure that her letters got sent.

Interestingly, being on holiday could either increase or decrease Gaskell's time for writing, and it is not the case that all of her letters from away were written in haste. From her childhood home of Knutsford, which served for her as an important country escape from Manchester, she wrote "I shall be so outrageously busy when I get home (whither I am going tomorrow morning) that I shall employ this gap of spare time by writing to thank you for your kind letter" (*Letters* 15). Yet it was sometimes the opposite—traveling could leave little time for writing. In 1852 she wrote to Marianne, "This is a short bad note, but I write with no end of people in the room, all talking about things that interest me,—I shall write when I get home" (*Letters* 144). And paradoxically, it was sometimes rural isolation itself that prohibited her from finding the time to write (or at least provided an excuse for not writing). From her summer retreat of Silverdale Gaskell wrote that because of the difficulty of housekeeping for her own family and her guests in a place with no shops, "I have been too busy to write a line beyond necessary letters, and not always even them" (*Letters* 267). Finally, while in most cases traveling meant that there were lots of activities about which to write, Gaskell also sometimes expressed the notion that in quiet places there was not much to say. She apologized to a friend that, "We are so very retired here that unless I told you, how the hay crops &c were going on, & what show of fruit there is, I could send you little interesting news," and "I fear you have thought this a most dull letter, but as I told you before we are very very retired" (*Further Letters* 3–4).

Other challenges involved the physical accoutrements of writing letters. Gaskell frequently complained about or apologized for the bad quality of her pens and paper in places where new ones were not readily available. When staying by herself at the Nightingale family home in Derbyshire, she said "I am very much ashamed of my paper; but I am 3 miles from any kind of shop" (*Letters* 216). And most humorously, having run out of paper she told her correspondent, "Don't frame my letter though it is a rarity. How long is it since you had a crossed letter before?" (*Letters* 214); this is a reference to the old custom of writing in two directions on a single paper in order to save the cost of an additional enclosure. Of course, there was also the possibility that travel could bring unusually luxurious letter-writing materials. When visiting the Duke of Devonshire's extravagant estate of Chatsworth, Gaskell and her daughter were unexpectedly asked to stay the night at the house itself instead of at the nearby inn. She wrote the next morning to another daughter, "Such a delicious pen! It is quite a pity I have not a book to write instead of a letter!" (*Letters* 372).

Changing Technologies and Postal Mishaps

Living as she had through such technological changes in modes of travel and communication, Gaskell was herself very aware of the recent history of postal services, as her reference to the crossed paper suggests. Gaskell, after spending time in the Lake District and meeting William Wordsworth's widow, relayed several stories about the young Wordsworth, who would walk for miles "to get news of the French Revolution ... in stormy winter evenings to meet the mail" (*Letters* 139). Wordsworth's village of Grasmere had no post office, and they were "5 or 6 miles away from Ambleside, the nearest post town" (*Further Letters* 200). She several times repeated a variation of the following story:

> one day a proof came of one of the Lyrical ballads,—postage to be paid back,— & postage from Ambleside to London 13d. In the afternoon the three walked to Ambleside to post & pay for the proof.—then they walked home, & at tea Wordsworth who had been silent for some time culminated into an exclamation of how bad some one word in the sent-off ballad was,—did not answer to his meaning a bit. So he & Miss Wordsworth set off *again* to Ambleside, got in after the Post Mistress had gone to bed, for they keep early hours there,—stated the case,—they are good friendly people those Lake country folk,—got the letter out of the post box,—for you see they could not afford a second 13d; had a candle lighted, sent the Post Mistress to bed,—sate up till the mail went out at 4 am,—& as the guard was blowing his horn, *the* word came into Wordsworth's head—(or Dora's,) and it was written down, sent off, candle put out, and they trudged back to breakfast at Grasmere with merry hearts. (*Further Letters* 200)

In those days, she quotes Mrs. Wordsworth saying, "postage was very heavy, and we were obliged to be very prudent" (*Letters* 139). Gaskell again seems to have had a complex response to changing technologies; she was certainly aware of the much greater convenience and accessibility of postal procedures in her own day, yet she was also a touch nostalgic for pre-industrial modes of communication.

What strikes the modern reader most of all is how efficient the post was in mid-nineteenth-century Britain. The speed with which Gaskell could expect to receive a reply to a letter written from London to Manchester is to us astounding. There were multiple pick-ups and deliveries per day, even in some rural areas. Yet despite Gaskell and her contemporaries' great reliance on the post, and what seems from a twenty-first century perspective like an extremely efficient and rapid system, there was plenty of room for error and uncertainty, especially while traveling. Gaskell was aware of that uncertainty, which is part of the reason that she gave such explicit instructions to her correspondents about when and where to write. She also can be found explaining to a correspondent that she had never received a letter she knew had been sent but had somehow missed her on her travels (*Letters* 15), or suggesting that she may have missed one because some particular piece of news had not arrived (*Letters* 524). She was also aware that sometimes addresses were uncertain, and wrote to a friend in 1855, "I will write you a long letter if you will let me know if this reaches you safely, for I don't know your exact address, and feel rather as if I was sending a letter into the wilderness" (*Letters* 231). Here we understand that writing even a single long letter was a serious exertion of time and labor, and that Gaskell valued her own time and her own letters enough that she was not willing to send one "into the wilderness." On another occasion she explained to her children, "I am very very glad to have heard from you today; only in future direct your letters (*be sure*) to *Crix Chelmsford Essex*, they reach me a whole day sooner; *don't* put in either Hatfield or Witham … we did not hear until today (owing to the mistake in the direction which made me rather uneasy)" (*Letters* 19).

One of the results of the 1840s postal reforms was a greater standardization of street addresses, yet we can see from Gaskell's correspondence that this standardization happened gradually and haphazardly, and many addresses remained vague by later standards. At the same time, knowledge of addresses was a way to maintain control over one's own correspondence. In the midst of an exchange with John Stuart Mill addressing his unhappiness with references that Gaskell had made in *The Life of Charlotte Brontë* (1857), Gaskell ended a letter with the statement "I will not even give you my address for I do not want you to answer this [letter]" (*Letters* 435). Whether Gaskell was reluctant to give Mill the trouble of replying, or whether she in fact did not wish to hear from him because she was tired of or uneasy about the dispute, is not completely clear. But whatever the reason for Gaskell's attempt to end the correspondence, her plan backfired, for Mill did in fact write back and was still angry with Gaskell (*Letters* 439). Addresses, apparently, were not so difficult to find.

Gaskell also was aware that a missed letter might be due to human error or mischief beyond the post office, as when she suggested that missing letters sent from a particular destination "makes me strongly suspect the tipsy Crewe butler" (*Letters* 585). On occasion, both these individual and institutional errors could result in real frustration:

> I wrote *one* letter (& I had before posted *2* by the butler's directions) all to tell Papa by Monday evening's post that the children will not be coming till to-day.

> Well he never got them! Lady C. heard the Exhibition was *not* open on Monday so the children never went; while all the time it *was* open & they might have gone & to-day came 2 letters from Papa; one posted on Sunday desiring an immediate acknowledgement of enclosure, & another last night, miserable about children. Oh! I am *so* sorry. (*Letters* 286a)

While mishaps with personal letters could result in frustration and anxiety, Gaskell also experienced professional anxiety because of the mail. On several occasions a manuscript went missing, once because she was traveling and her instructions to her publisher about where to send it resulted in confusion. Upon discovering the error she wrote:

> But where *is* the MSS—Oh! If it is lost, I shall have to hang myself! I thought it *might* be gone to Miss Shaen's … where I shall meet Marianne *tomorrow*; but this morning came my dear Cornhill, all safely *here*; so please, where *did* I tell you to send the MSS? for of course it is my fault … Oh dear! Please where *is* the MSS. (*Letters* 472a)

After another incident she wrote gratefully, "My story is found! and is going to bring me in a good price! … Where it wandered to I can't tell; but, after being sent off from Manchester by Passenger train on the Wednesday it did not reach London till Monday" (*Letters* 505). The fact that she understood a five-day delivery as extremely unusual and alarming demonstrates how rapid Gaskell expected the post to be. She also described an amusing episode that emphasized the need for certain addresses: "The funniest little event of late has been the arrival of a letter directed to Madame Gaskell l'illustre auteur Angleterre which had been two months travelling about England in search of my illustriousness; the mocking commentary on which was an envelope *covered* with '*Not Knowns*'; a sight to be seen!" (*Letters* 623).

After the Post Office reforms, postage had become cheap within Great Britain. Yet payment of postage continued to be a topic of discussion. Sometimes Gaskell sent postage stamps as a form of allowance to her daughters, the assumption being that this was one of their major expenditures. She occasionally joked that she would send a letter back "unpaid" if it was not a good letter or did not include certain wanted information (*Letters* 103); this referred to the pre-1840s procedure where the recipient would pay instead of the sender. In 1863 she wrote to Marianne from Italy, "Hearn … takes this letter to the post. Does not know enough Italian to pay for it, so you will have to pay double which serves you right for not writing, you little monkey" (*Letters* 523a). Of course, letters abroad followed different payment systems, and this was sometimes a cause for confusion as well, as when she wrote to Marianne from France, "We have just got your letter (*over-charge 1 franc 20 c from not being sufficiently affranchie -*)" (*Letters* 585). In another instance Gaskell reprimanded Marianne, who was visiting Rome: "Your December 7th letter had to be paid pretty heavily for at this end, although I could see you had paid for it at Rome. It was *2* foreign sheets and *a half*, besides the envelope, so remember that is too much" (*Letters* 496).

Gaskell's sense of the geographical distance between herself and her correspondents is also evident in the topics and style of her letters. This was most immediately true because the frequency of the post differed depending on the distance the letter was being sent. Gaskell's correspondence with her American friend Charles Eliot Norton was affected by the fact that the post to America only went once a week, so she and her family could work on a letter all week. She said in one letter to Norton:

> When I think how long it is since I have written to you I am vexed & ashamed; but one always fancies one ought to put on one's best clothes & one's diamond ring ... before writing to America. The little daily notes, almost without beginning and without end, that one talks out on paper seem impossibilities when they have to go across the Atlantic ... I should so often have written to you had it not been for this. (*Letters* 546)

From France she also expressed the notion that letters from afar should be about serious or interesting things. Responding to her daughter's letter about a plumbing problem at home in Manchester, she theorized about its cause then changed the topic with, "However one does not expect to write about *drains* from Dieppe, does one?" (*Letters* 585).

During Gaskell's lifetime, the electric telegraph gradually came to be an accessible form of communication. Gaskell made an early reference to the telegraph in 1847, when she wrote to her two oldest daughters, thirteen and ten at the time, "Tell Aunt Anne to send a message *by the electric telegraph*, if you are both drowned, or burnt, &c." (*Letters* 18). This is a somewhat humorous, or at least not completely serious reference to the telegraph. But by the late 1850s, she was more seriously considering the use of the telegraph as a possible way to circumvent the uncertainty of the mail.[6] This was particularly useful when it came to making travel plans, as when Gaskell wrote to Marianne from Heidelberg: "I am going to telegraph to you, for I cant bear to think of your having the fatigue of going to Bingen, & am so afraid my letters won't reach in time to stop your setting off" (*Letters* 473). It was also useful for dealing with the anxiety connected to her family's health, as when Gaskell wrote to Marianne also from abroad, "Remember *telegraphs*—I calculate we shan't have your letter till *Wednesday* next & it seems a long time to wait" (*Letters* 404a). Yet interestingly, Gaskell ultimately did not see the telegraph as fundamentally different from any other form of long-distance communication, as a note to her friend whose son was leaving for India makes clear. She wrote, "I do not think he has an idea (when had children ever!) of how much you suffer at the prospect of separation,—he spoke of 'telegrams' as 'diminishing the distance';—which showed me how little he understood what the

---

6   Gaskell also made reference to the telegraph in a letter about the art of novel-writing. She advised Herbert Grey that the novelist ought to be "an Electric telegraph something or other," presumably implying that the novelist had the ability to communicate ideas directly and instantaneously by setting "*objects* not *feelings*" before the reader (*Letters* 420). Also see Uglow (211) for analysis of this passage.

pain of absence *really* is" (*Further Letters* 210). This raises the question, salient in our own time, about the extent to which changing technologies actually change people's interactions and experiences. Is there something fundamentally different in the experience of communicating by letter or by telephone, by text message or email? Is anxiety about our loved ones actually reduced by the knowledge that we can communicate with them instantly, or does the anxiety simply take on a different form because of the different expectations we have about how quickly we are likely to hear from someone?

Conclusion

Gaskell, who had the means and the motivation to travel extensively, was not necessarily representative of all or most nineteenth-century travelers. Furthermore, while letters were clearly very welcome to Gaskell when she traveled, receiving the post may have been different for certain kinds of people, travel, or letters. At one point Gaskell explained to one of her husband's correspondents that William was away on vacation and did not want any letters: "Mr. Gaskell gone from home for Xmas holidays—does not come back till the end of next week—& I am 'not to forward any letters except on *indispensable* business', that he may have the *complete* rest he needs so very much. He does not *wish to have to be writing a letter to any one*" (*Further Letters* 220). Gaskell herself toured northern Italy with her daughters for five weeks in 1857 without receiving any forwarded letters, and although she did not know it at the time, this isolation from news left her blissfully ignorant of the terrible controversy brewing at home over her *The Life of Charlotte Brontë* (Uglow 425).

Gaskell's letters, while they do not answer all of our questions about the relationship between communication and travel, do illuminate the ways in which she experienced her own geographic mobility, and they bring insight into her notions of the relationship between urban and rural, home and away, tourist and local. As holidays became accessible to more and more British people during the nineteenth century, letter-writing was also becoming more accessible. Literacy was increasing, paper was cheap, and the Post Office was entering its most efficient and rapid phase. Yet this story of increasing access is complicated by the ways in which industrialization and tourism created new kinds of interactions. Places were linked to one another by the railroad and the postal service, and the economy of certain places became more dependent on tourism. Yet as Gaskell suggests, the attraction of many holiday spots lay at least partly in their unindustrialized, out-of-the-way characteristics. The contradiction was that in order to attract tourists, places needed infrastructure, including a modern functioning postal system. Yet in order to attract tourists they also needed to remain secluded and idyllic. Tourists wanted an escape from industrial society, yet they depended on industrialization to get to their holiday destinations and they did not want their escape to be so total as to completely isolate them from the rest of the world.

Letters, unlike many other forms of descriptive writing, give insight into the mundane and everyday, and they suggest that traveling could be boring and lonely as well as pleasurable. This in itself suggests that it is fruitful to examine letter-writing and travel in tandem. I also have tried to demonstrate the mutual reliance of travel technologies and postal technologies: one could not travel far from family without a means to stay in touch, and one could not stay in touch without new modes of transportation like the railway. Gaskell, while undeniably nostalgic for rural ways of life, was certainly not a Luddite. She embraced technologies like the railroad and the Penny Post with enthusiasm, and used them to enhance her professional, personal, and social life. Her letters about letter-writing demonstrate the importance of letter-writing to Gaskell's sense of place in an industrializing society.

Works Cited

d'Albertis, Deirdre. "The Life and Letters of E.C. Gaskell." *The Cambridge Companion to Elizabeth Gaskell*. Ed. Jill L. Matus. Cambridge: Cambridge UP, 2007. Print.

Billington, Josie. "Gaskell's 'Rooted' Prose Realism." *Place and Progress in the Works of Elizabeth Gaskell*. Ed. Lesa Scholl, Emily Morris, and Sarina Gruver Moore. Burlington, VT: Ashgate, 2015. 159–72. Print.

Earle, Rebecca, ed. *Epistolary Selves: Letters and Letter-Writers, 1600–1945*. Aldershot: Ashgate, 1999. Print.

Gaskell, Elizabeth. *The Letters of Mrs Gaskell*. Ed. J.A.V. Chapple and Arthur Pollard. Manchester: Manchester UP, 1966. Print.

———. *Further Letters of Mrs Gaskell*. Ed. J. Chapple and A. Shelston. Manchester: Manchester UP, 2000. Print.

Golden, Catherine. *Posting It: The Victorian Revolution in Letter-Writing*. Gainesville, FL: UP of Florida, 2010. Print.

Hill, Rowland. *Post Office Reform: Its Importance and Practicability*. London: Charles Knight and Co., 1837. Print.

Morgan, Marjorie. *National Identities and Travel in Victorian Britain*. Basingstoke: Palgrave Macmillan, 2001. Print.

Shelston, Alan. "Opportunity and Anxiety: Elizabeth Gaskell and the Development of the Railway System." *The Gaskell Society Journal* 20 (2006): 91–101. Print.

Thomas, Kate. *Postal Pleasures: Sex, Scandal, and Victorian Letters*. Oxford: Oxford UP, 2011. Print.

Uglow, Jenny. *Elizabeth Gaskell: A Habit of Stories*. New York: Farrar, Straus, Giroux, 1993. Print.

Chapter 10
Gaskell the Ethnographer:
The Case of "Modern Greek Songs"

Anna Koustinoudi and Charalampos Passalis

> Reading any good ballad is like eating game; and almost everything else seems
> poor and tasteless after it.
>
> —Elizabeth Gaskell, "Modern Greek Songs"

On 18 February 1854, Charles Dickens wrote to Elizabeth Gaskell: "Such has been the distraction of my mind in my story that I have twice forgotten to tell you how much I liked the 'Modern Greek Songs.' The article is printed and at press for the next number as ever is" (Dickens 329). A week later, "Modern Greek Songs" appeared in the 25 February issue of *Household Words* as part of Elizabeth Gaskell's regular contribution to Dickens's weekly journal, together with works by such writers as Henry Morley, William Duthie, James Henry Leigh Hunt, and William Blanchard Jerrold.

Elizabeth Gaskell's active interest in popular traditions, customs, and folklore was well known, and her interest was not confined to the traditions of her native England, or even to those of Scotland, Wales, and Ireland, but was wide enough to include a variety of folkloric traditions of other, often distant lands and their people.[1] This, coupled with the fact that her sense of place and space (either real or imaginative), which subscribed to a life of frequent travel and almost constant mobility within her native country and abroad, testify to her perception of personhood and identity as informed by notions of spatial and cultural diversity and/or hybridity, a fact also reflected in her own diverse domestic, social, cultural, and literary pursuits. Thus, Gaskell's interest in folklore of all kinds, including that of cultures other than her own, naturally becomes manifest in her literary works, especially as part of the plot in her Gothic pieces, where along with her exploration of the supernatural, she also displays an interest in local lore and traditions.[2]

---

[1] As A.W. Ward notes in his introduction to the Knutsford edition of *The Works of Mrs. Gaskell*, "Her books and her letters are full of observation of such relics and reminiscences of the past among her own conservative neighbours at Lancashire and Cheshire; and they attracted her in the course of her wonderings home and abroad her readings about distant lands and their inhabitants" (qtd. in Sharps 196).

[2] It was often the case that Gaskell quoted epigraphs from a variety of popular sources following in a tradition initiated by Sir Walter Scott in the Waverly novels. These would be commonly attributed to popular folk material such as old songs or old plays, parts of the so-called popular wisdom. A characteristic example of this practice is her use of the oral

Gaskell's ethnographic strategies, rhetoric, and role as mediator between cultures, especially regarding class specificity and socio-cultural space(s), have been duly discussed by scholars, mainly in terms of what has come to be known as "cultural mapping" in works like *Cranford, Mary Barton*, and *North and South*. With her "Modern Greek Songs," however, Gaskell embarks further on a comparative exploration of (inter)nationally diverse cultures that nonetheless seem to bear similarities despite their geographical distinctness and distance, thus celebrating cultural diversity as a valuable universal given.

Through "Modern Greek Songs" Gaskell intended to present to her English readership a review of Claude Fauriel's *Chants Populaires de la Grèce Moderne* (1824–1825) in the form of a general survey of the whole work, including summaries of certain parts she particularly liked. Almost all the information regarding Greek traditions, customs, and folksong in Gaskell's article is drawn from the introduction of volume I of the original French edition of Fauriel's work (*Discours preliminaire*, vii–cxliv). However, Gaskell seems to be familiar with both volumes of Fauriel's study, for she does not hesitate to re-arrange Fauriel's introduction (from the first part onwards), using at the same time material from the second volume of the book in an attempt to unify, by summarizing, her material so as to support her own text, while imparting to her reader as much information as she can on Fauriel's work in its entirety.

The material she uses in her article is not, of course, exclusively drawn from Fauriel, but also from personal experience and anecdote through which she draws parallels between the Greek and other cultures, including her own. The essay covers a wide spectrum of Greek provincial life as this is lived through a series of seasonal feasts and celebrations, along with all those ceremonial performative acts that underlie life and death, such as customs related to farewell rituals, as well as betrothal, wedding, and funeral ceremonials. Special mention is also made of the folksongs and ballads that occasionally accompany these events, while a large part of her article is devoted to the Greek armed warriors, the Klephts (free-booters) and Armatolians,[3] who were unofficially involved in the struggle for independence and who are likened to such heroic English outlaws as Robin Hood. This was the time when Greece had been under Turkish rule, for almost four hundred years, as part

---

traditional "Oldham Weaver," a Lancashire ballad, in chapter four of *Mary Barton* (1848) as well as her quoting, in the same chapter, from another well-known ancient ballad, "The Demon Lover."

[3] The description of the Klephts and the Armatoloi are also presented in Sheridan's translation: "The Klephtai (or Plundereres) are either Greeks, who originally never submitted to the Turkish yoke, but sacrificed the possession of more fertile lands to the love of liberty, established their home and country in the wild and extensive mountain tracks of Epirus and Acarnania, and from thence kept a desultory, but still renewed, warfare against the usurpers of their possessions; or they are Armatoloi, subsequently pillaged and outraged into rebellion" (Sheridan 2). For an extensive presentation of their role, lifestyle, and deeds, see Charles-Brinsley Sheridan, *The Songs of Greece, from the Romaic Text, Edited by M.C. Fauriel, with Additions. Translated into English Verse* (1825).

of the Ottoman Empire since 1453 (the year of the fall of Constantinople), during which an extended guerrilla war against their oppressors was systematically fought by these armed warriors. Their daily habits and living conditions, characterized by their laborious struggle for survival, occasional battles with the conquerors of their country, strict code of honor, and their patriotism are duly emphasized: "These are," Gaskell tells us, following Fauriel, "the Adam Bells, and Clyne o' the Cloughs, or perhaps, still more the Robin Hoods of Greece" ("Modern Greek Songs" 6), while she draws explicit parallels between their habits and lifestyle:

> These mountain peasantry came down in armed bands upon the fertile plains and the luxurious towns, and stripped the Turks and those who had quietly submitted to their sway, whenever they could; it was from those who were thus robbed, that the mountaineers received the name of Klephts. But our Saxon ancestors did the same to the Normans; Robin Hood was an English Klepht, taking only what he thought was unjustly acquired, and unfairly held. The Turks found it rather difficult to make war against these guerrillas; they fled to wild and rocky recesses of the mountains when pursued. (8)

By being particularly defensive of the Klephts, comparing their acts to those of her own Saxon ancestors, Gaskell seems to be making an indirect comment about the same practices followed by the people of her own culture when it comes to celebrating similar heroic deeds by native heroes. She thus sets in contrast the way readers might tend to judge and think of their own history, in an attempt to soften their judgment of Greek folk narratives.

Gaskell often re-arranges the information that is scattered in various parts of Fauriel's nine-part introduction, thus smoothly introducing her reader to this type of Greek popular lore, tradition, folksong, and custom. The origin of the songs, ballads, and dances that accompany the victories and the feasts of these outlaws, usually chanted and performed after victorious battles, is also given special attention as part of the blind poets tradition, the so-called local minstrelship: "All these songs are chanted to particular airs. The poet must be also his own musician: if he can also improvise he is a fully-accomplished minstrel" (6). Gaskell notes, while providing a detailed account of the origins of the creators ("the little Homers of the day" as she calls them), the songs themselves, and the dances that often accompanied their performance. She writes:

> These minstrels are divided into two sets; those who merely remember what they have learnt from others, and those who compose ballads of their own, in addition to their stores of memory. These latter, in their long and quiet walks through country which they know to be wild and grand, although they never more may see it, "turn inward," and recall all that they have heard that has excited their curiosity, or stirred their imagination either in the traditional history of their native land, or in the village accounts of some local hero. Some of the minstrels spread the fame of men whose deeds would have been unknown beyond the immediate mountain neighbourhood of each, from shore to shore. In fact these blind beggars are the novelists and the historians of modern Greece. (6)

Gaskell probably got to know Fauriel and his work through her close association with her Paris-based friend, Madam Mohl (born Mary Clarke), wife of the German orientalist Julius Mohl. Besides being an influential literary patron and art connoisseur, Madam Mohl was one of the best-known salonists of the Parisian intellectual circles, whose drawing rooms were frequented by some of the most sophisticated intellectuals and literary celebrities of the time including Stendhal, Chataubriand and, of course, Claude Fauriel himself.[4] Jenny Uglow remarks that Mary Clarke-Mohl was a "woman of genius, but a genius for people, not on the page" and that she "wore an air of freedom that seemed unattainable for women in the British society" (347). Mary Clarke had been in love with Fauriel for some years, but he would not respond to her attentions, even if he shared her life as a regular member of her salon, and it was four years after he died, according to Uglow, that Mary Clarke finally married Julius Mohl, Fauriel's younger friend (348).

It was also through Felicia Hemans's version of "The Message to the Dead," which Gaskell mentions in the article itself, that she developed an interest in Fauriel's text. Hemans's poetry often refers to the contemporary Hellenic reality, and it is thus not only Fauriel's work that provides Gaskell with a link to the Greek folkloric background, but also a whole body of contemporary poetry that dealt with things Greek, both the ancient glorious past and also the less fortunate present, characterized by the Greek struggle for independence against the Ottoman empire. In her article, Gaskell also mentions an occasional encounter with a Greek family and their traditions during the festive Easter period, of significant importance in the Greek Orthodox tradition—a personal connection that must have gone far to pique her interest in the folkloric background.

Claude-Charles Fauriel (1772–1844) himself was a remarkable scholar of excellent reputation, a prolific writer, and well-versed in comparative literature—a man with an eye for alternate generic forms, especially those springing from the oral tradition. His book was widely read in France and was obviously inspired by the Greek struggle for independence, which was already well under way as he was writing, and which reached its zenith in 1824, the year when his work was published. As is evident from the introduction (*Preliminaire*) of the book, Fauriel displays an unusual familiarity with the Greek language, traditions, and customs, which might partly account for Gaskell's mistaken belief that he was Greek "inspite of his French name" ("Modern Greek Songs" 1). It was, however, common knowledge that he was French and a native of Saint Etienne, having spent his childhood in Vivarais.[5] Although Sheridan's English translation (an abbreviated version of the

---

4   As Pamela Law notes, "the *salons* in their diversity were still functioning in the nineteenth century as complex 'public spheres' useful in the formation of opinion, taste, manners and morals" (61) especially when conducted by such connoisseurs as Madame Récamiere and Mary Clarke, the latter having been a regular attendant of Madame Recmiere's circle and salon before starting her very own.

5   According to Michael Hertzfeld, European scholars such as the French Claude Fauriel and the German Werner von Haxthausen never visited Greece, despite their active interest in and extensive research about its folkloric tradition.

original two-volume text) of *Chants Populaires de la Grèce Moderne* appeared in 1825, that is, shortly after the original French text, Gaskell seems to be unaware of its publication, for all of her references are to the French original without avoiding, however, some inaccuracies as she quotes from it.[6]

What were the reasons, one might wonder, behind Gaskell's decision to present to her English reading audience an account of Fauriel's book? She provides a couple of them in the introduction of her article, the main one pertaining to the exceptional interest this particular work presented to its French readers upon publication and the hope that it will be equally interesting to the readers of *Household Words*, since it deals with "the manners and peculiar character of the people among whom these ballads circulate and the history of whose ancestors and popular heroes they commemorate" (1). She also claims, rather enigmatically, and in contradiction to her previous statement, that the work is no longer in circulation and for this reason is largely unknown to the majority of her English readers; she does not mention, however, Sheridan's own statement in his English translation of Fauriel's work that the original text had been widely known among the scholarly circles of London for quite some time after it was originally published: "I have lately met with a French book which has interested me much; and, as it is now out of print, and was never very extensively known, I imagine some account of it may not be displeasing to the readers of *Household Words*" (1). Fauriel's text, writes Gaskell, deals with "the habits and customs of a people whom we are apt to moan over, as having fallen low from the high estate of the civilization of their [polished] ancestors" and "it becomes worth one's while to learn something of their present state" (1).

What was Gaskell's relation to the Greek civilization, both ancient and contemporary? Gaskell demonstrates a familiarity with the history and mythology of ancient Greece—place names like Thessaly (referring to the central municipal division of Greece), and various forms and deities, such as Oreads, Satyrs, Graces, Hamdryads, Nymphs, and Neriads are mentioned in "Modern Greek Songs," thus proving a certain familiarity with ancient Greek mythology. But Gaskell also appears to be informed, up to a point, on contemporary Greek reality, as her account of her visit to the Manchester Greek family during the festive period of Easter shows. However, Gaskell's interest in and even admiration for a most glorious ancient Hellenic past must be seen in light of the influence of Romanticism on her, as well as her love for all sorts of genuinely popular verse and folksong endorsed by such celebrated poets as William Wordsworth, Gaskell's own favorite poet. Popular verse and poetry constitute for her, "real ballads—poems springing out

---

[6]   While, for instance, Fauriel explicitly mentions that the population of Greece at the time was between seven and eight million (Quant aux sept ou huit millions d'hommes, *Discours Preliminaire* vii), Gaskell restricts it to four million ("Modern Greek Songs" 1). She also records the name of the Greek klepht Niko Tsaras as Niko Isaras. The former error could be attributed to haste (it is well known that she was always under pressure with her writings amidst her numerous daily duties and responsibilities), and the latter is probably a typographical error.

from the heart of the nation whenever it is deeply stirred, and circulating from man to man with the rapidity of flame never written down, but never forgotten" (7), since these cultural products, springing from the very center of human existence and experience, never cease to accompany almost all aspects of human activity. Gaskell shows a lively interest in the indisputable artistic and literary value of folksongs ("very poetical, and full of meaning in themselves," as she claims), drawing parallels with those of the Scottish tradition, thus attempting a comparative approach of the two cultures, while drawing an analogy between these orally transmitted songs, certain customs, and superstitions common to various cultures.[7]

Gaskell's fascination with local lore, popular custom, and folksong becomes manifest in the beginning of the article when she draws a parallel between Fauriel's study and Sir Walter Scott's three-volume set of collected ballads, titled *Minstrelsy of the Scottish Border* (1802–1803), which displays a structure similar to that of Fauriel's work, comprising an extensive, annotated introduction. There are, moreover, references to other scholars, such as to the Scottish geologist, writer, and folklorist Hugh Miller (1802–1856), which further testify to Gaskell's lively interest in various forms of folklore. Also of note is Gaskell's use of comparative comments to complement and expand those of Fauriel's text, a fact that testifies to her ability to trace and display the similarities between traditions and customs that are in other ways diverse.

A parallelism between feasts and customs in Scotland and Greece that occur throughout the annual cycle constitutes her initial object of comparison. The New Year's Day celebrations of the Greeks are compared to those of the Scottish tradition as they were collected and recorded by Sir Walter Scott in his *Minstrelsy*. "In both cases," Gaskell tells us, there is a preliminary discourse explaining the manners and peculiar character of these people among whom these ballads circulate" (1) as well as certain similarities, but also differences in the ways their customs are practiced:

> Let us take the household songs. There are two feasts which are celebrated in every house. The first is on New Year's Day, the feast of St. Basil in the Greek Church. The account which M. Fauriel gives reminds me much of a Scottish New Year's Day. The young men pass from one house to another until all their friends have been visited; bringing with them presents, and going, in glad procession, to salute all their acquaintances. But, instead of our "I wish you a happy new year and many of them", the young Greeks, on entering each house, sing some verses in honour of the master or head of the family; others in honour of the mistress; the sons of the house have each their song, nor are the daughters forgotten. Those who are absent or dead receive this compliment last of all. (1)

Similarly, the celebrations and festivities performed in connection with the reception and/or welcoming of Spring, which in Greece customarily coincides with

---

[7] She writes: "Many ballads are composed expressly for these occasions; nor can there be a surer mode of securing their popularity. One sung for the first time at a paneghyri is circulated the next day through eight or ten villages. Some of these songs are literally ballads in the old Provençal sense of the word" (7).

the first of March of each year, are compared to those performed in celebration of the same event on the first of May in England:

> In Greece this is held on the first of March; the first of May would often be early greeting to the spring in England. At this pretty holiday, the children in their spring of human life join the young men, and go singing about the streets, and asking for small presents in honour of the soft and budding time; and every one gives them an egg, or some cheese, or some other simple produce of the country. The song they sing is one which, for its grace and the breath of spring and flowers which perfumes it, is known in many countries, as well as in Greece, under the name of the Song of the Swallow. The children carry about with them the figure of a swallow rudely cut in wood, and fastened to a kind of little windmill, which is turned by a piece of string fastened to a cylinder. (2)[8]

Another interesting comparison relates to the similarities, "and slight differences" (7) between the so-called Greek Paneghyris, "feasts in honour of the patron saint of some one hamlet" (7) and English wakes:

> They must bear a close resemblance to the wakes in England; for they are always held on the Sunday after the saint's day to whom the parish church is dedicated. But there are some slight differences between a Greek paneghyri and English wakes; the Eastern festival is gayer and more simple in character. (7)

Comparisons, however, are not restricted to customs and rituals within the time cycle. Gaskell is also interested in betrothal and marriage as well as funeral rituals and folksong, the latter known as "myriologia" all of which have constituted an integral part of provincial everyday life in Greece, particularly during the years when Greece was under Ottoman rule and occupation. "At every one of the ceremonials ... a song appropriate to the occasion is chanted; they explain the motive of each particular act—of what event in human life is to be considered a type" (4), she tells us. What is also of interest to the reader of "Modern Greek Songs" is the fact that although Gaskell is intent upon giving a strictly descriptive account of how these ceremonies are performed, she also alludes to the cultural norms, conventions, and stereotypes governing the social bonds and relations of those inhabiting these rural communities. The bride's position as an object of display, as well as one of exchange and as agent of servitude in her husband's family is not to pass unnoticed here. She will remain symbolically veiled and unseen until the middle of the banquet and throughout her married life living in the shadowy margins of her newly acquired patriarchal family under the rule of her in-laws and husband, which is from now intent upon replacing that of her father:

> [A]fter the *cortège* has borne the bride to the house of her husband, the whole party adjourn to church, where the religious ceremony is performed. Then they return to the dwelling of the bridegroom, where they all sit down and feast;

---

[8]   The Song of the Swallow is a custom that still revives in many parts of Greece on the 1st of March of each year.

except the bride, who remains veiled, standing alone, until the middle of the banquet, when the paranymph draws near, unlooses the veil, which falls down, and she stands blushing, exposed to the eyes of all the guests. The next day is given up to the performance of dances peculiar to a wedding. The third day the relations and friends meet all together, and lead the bride to the fountain, from the waters of which she fills a new earthen vessel; and into which she throws various provisions. They afterwards dance in circles round the fountain. (4)

Within the same context, Gaskell pays particular attention to the death and funeral rituals performed once a beloved person has died. Following Fauriel's paradigm, the myriologia, funeral folksongs chanted in mournful sadness exclusively by women who sit around the coffin, receive Gaskell's attention as a universal cultural phenomenon accordingly practiced not just by the Greeks, but also by her contemporary Irish as well as by the ancient Hebrews:

When any one dies, his wife, his mother, and his sisters, all come up to the poor motionless body, and softly close the eyes and the mouth ... Other women are busy with the corpse while they change their dress in a neighbour's house; the body is dressed in the best clothes the dead possessed; and it is then laid on a low bed ... leaving the door open, so that all who wish once more to gaze on the face of the departed may enter in. All who come range themselves around the bed, and weep and cry aloud without restraint. As soon as they are a little calmer some one begins to chant the myriologia—a custom common to the ancient Hebrews, as well as to the more modern Irish - with their keenness and their plaintive enumeration of the goods, and blessings, and love which the deceased possessed in this world which he has left. In the mountains of Greece, the nearest and dearest among the female relations first lifts up her voice in the myriologia; she is followed by others, either sisters or friends. (4)

Special mention is also made of the habit of the mourners to use the dead person as a medium to send messages to their dead relatives, a custom widely practiced also in the Highlands of England, Lancashire in particular:

Occasionally there is some one among the assemblage of mourners who has also lately lost a beloved one, and whose full hearts yet yearn for the sympathy in their griefs or joys which the dead were ever ready to give, while they were yet living. They take up the strain; and, in a form of song used from time immemorial, they conjure the dead lying before them to be the messenger of the intelligence they wish to send to him, who is gone away for ever. A similar superstition is prevalent in the Highlands. (5)

The article concludes with an extensive reference to a number of Greek pagan traditions and superstitions, drawn from the fifth part of Fauriel's introduction. As these have survived from ancient times, many of them constitute remnants of the Greek antiquity intermingled with a later Christian tradition. Although "the Greeks would shudder if they thought they preserved any of the old Pagan superstitions," Gaskell notes, "without their knowing it, much of the heathen belief is mingled with their traditional observances" (10), and shortly after that "[m]any of the superstitions derived from their ancestors are common to all nations" (10). Interestingly, it is this sense of universality viewed, perhaps, through the prism of Gaskell's own Unitarian background that permeates Gaskell's text throughout. It hints, somehow, at a belief in faiths older, larger, more universal and encompassing than Christianity alone.

An analogy is finally drawn between the way plague is personified "as a blind woman, going from house to house giving death to all whom she touches" (10); in a similar way, both in Scotland and Greece, folk traditions resort to euphemism in order to refer to evil, disease, and even death itself:

> The Furies are no longer known; but every one remembers how the attempt was made to propitiate them by calling them the Eumenides; just as in Scotland the fairies, who stole children and performed all manner of small mischief, were called "the good people" … The small-pox is personified as a woman scowling on children, but who may be mollified by calling her, and invoking her under a Greek name which means "she who mercifully spares;" the small-pox indeed is universally spoken of as Eulogia—the "well spoken-of", she whom all are bound under pain of terrible penalties to name with respect … Death is personified under the form of a stern old man, who comes to summon the living to leave the light of day. He is called Charon, although his office is more properly that of Mercury. (11)

Through her "Modern Greek Songs," Gaskell succeeded in presenting the readers of the immensely popular *Household Words* with some interesting aspects of the life of the people inhabiting the Greek provinces of the time, through her own perception of imaginative, geographical spaces. At the same time, along with many other literary intellectuals of her country, Lord Byron being the most prominent among them, she further contributed to the development of a philhellenic spirit towards the cause of the Greek liberation that was already under way within the scholarly circles of England, and she did so in a most pleasant way by incorporating into her work "something she had herself observed, and in such way as to grace it with a touch of poetry and romance" (Sharps 195).

Works Cited

Dickens, Charles. *The Letters of Charles Dickens*. Ed. Georgiana Hogarth and Mary Dickens. Cambridge: Cambridge UP, 2011. Print.

Fauriel, Claude-Charles. *Chants Populaires de la Grèce Moderne, Recueillis et Publiés, avec une Traduction Française, des Eclaircissements et des Notes*, 2 vols. Paris: Firmin Didot, Père et Fils (and Dondey-Dupré, Père et Fils), 1824–1825. Print.

Gaskell, Elizabeth. "Modern Greek Songs" (1854). *The Gaskell Web*. Web. 16 September 1997. <https://www.lang.nagoya-u.ac.jp/~matsuoka/EG-Modern.html>.

Herzfeld Michael. *Ours Once More: Folklore Ideology, and the Making of Modern Greece*. Austin, TX: U of Texas P, 1982. Print.

Law, Pamela. "Mary Clarke and the Nineteenth-Century Salon." *Sydney Studies in English* 11 (1985–1986): 51–68. Print.

Sharps, John-Geoffrey. *Mrs. Gaskell's Observation and Invention: A Study of her Non-Biographic Works*. Sussex: Linden Press, 1970. Print.

Sheridan, Charles-Brinsley. *The Songs of Greece, from the Romaic Text, Edited by M.C. Fauriel, with Additions. Translated into English Verse*. London: Longman, 1825. Print.

Uglow, Jenny. *Elizabeth Gaskell*. London: Faber & Faber, 1993. Print.

Chapter 11
Reading "An Every-Day Story" Through Bifocals: Seriality and the Limits of Realism in Elizabeth Gaskell's *Wives and Daughters*

Julia M. Chavez

Wives and Daughters (1864–1866), Elizabeth Gaskell's sprawling novel about a young girl's struggle to find her place in the social structures of the provincial English countryside of the 1830s, has been widely praised as a realist masterpiece, second in Gaskell's *oeuvre* only to the comic *Cranford* (1851). Henry James, critical of so many long Victorian novels, praised Gaskell's last novel as creating "a world … complete in every particular, from the divine blue of the summer sky to the June-bugs in the roses." It is so real, James contends, that "the hours given to its perusal seem like hours actually spent, in the flesh as well as the spirit, among the scenes and people described" (Review in the *Nation*, 22 February 1866). For James, it would seem, *Wives and Daughters* embodies the "reality effect" that Roland Barthes so famously theorizes in relation to nineteenth-century literature (148), creating a hermetically sealed version of reality into which one can escape.

While Gaskell surely deserves praise for her realism, her last (and unfinished) novel can also be interpreted from a radically different perspective—as a text that systematically reveals the limits of Victorian realism by acknowledging, even drawing our attention to, fissures in its well-constructed provincial world. Rather than allowing an illusion of totality to persist, *Wives and Daughters* invites readers to consider the larger context of empire and imperial conquest through the travels of the scientific explorer, Roger Hamley. The specter of a world beyond the provincial village of Hollingford, which enters the narrative via Roger's correspondence, invites complacent, nostalgic readers to refocus attention on the larger world beyond England. The result is an imperative for bifocal reading, as the novel encourages movement between a myopic vision of rural England and a far-sighted vision of empire.

Serialization of the novel within the *Cornhill Magazine* from August 1864 to January 1866 similarly demands a bifocal reading strategy, for the dissemination of the novel within the surrounding periodical content destabilizes any totalizing perspective. Although Gaskell the author develops a narrative authority, as Hughes and Lund persuasively demonstrate in their work on Victorian publishing practices (16), the novel is placed—instalment by instalment—within competing voices. Read as a serial within a periodical that embraced a cosmopolitan ethos, *Wives and Daughters* reconfigures the relationship between England and the rest of the world, implicitly challenging the hegemony of Victorian imperialism.

View 1: English Provincial Society under a Microscope

Life in Gaskell's fictional Hollingford is certainly depicted with the layers of detail that create a self-referential reality (Barthes 148). From the first chapter, the material objects surrounding the heroine, Molly Gibson, are described in meticulous detail, from the "little white dimity bed" in which she lay to the

> primitive kind of bonnet-stand on which was hung a bonnet, carefully covered over from any chance of dust with a large cotton handkerchief; of so heavy and serviceable a texture that if the thing underneath it had been a flimsy fabric of gauze and lace and flowers, it would have been altogether "scomfished." (1)

This faithful representation of the details of domestic life that contextualize the characters—a realism bordering on ethnographic[1]—carries through to the last paragraph of the novel completed before Gaskell's death, in which Molly's stepmother, Hyacinth Gibson, longs to possess the "figured silk at Brown's" (683). Through these details, Gaskell creates a realist masterpiece—what James calls "a new and arbitrary world ... complete in every particular" (246). The chosen details are not necessarily symbolic or didactic; instead, they work to create a convincing sense of coherence. Following Ian Watt's suggestion in *The Rise of the Novel*, the realism of Gaskell's novel "does not reside in the kind of life it presents, but in the way it presents it" (11).

Josie Billington reveals another important layer of Gaskell's realist aesthetic in her book, *Faithful Realism*. According to Billington, Gaskell's "close reading of life" produced a prose style that is characterized by revisions that produce "a density of possible meanings in place of a single or settled one" (42–3). In other words, it is not just what Gaskell writes, but the way she writes that approaches lived experience. As Billington eloquently concludes:

> Gaskell's achievement was precisely to loosen the "strict limits" of prose, leaving "empty spaces" so as to redeem life's ordinary messiness and restore to realist interest the apparently inconsequential and incomplete—the subtle odds and ends of life which spill over time and category. (74)

In this reading, Gaskell's prose is realistic because it is fluid rather than stable, active rather than static.

Even a cursory look at contemporary reviews of the novel suggests that readers did indeed find themselves transported by Gaskell's realist vision. Echoing James's

---

[1]   James Buzard has written extensively on ethnographic and autoethnographic discourse in mid-nineteenth-century novels in his book, *Disorienting Fiction*. Borislav Knezevic has written specifically of ethnographic discourse in Gaskell's *Cranford*.

sentiments, a reviewer for the *Contemporary Review* describes the experience of being engrossed in a nostalgic, Gaskellian world without agendas: "[Gaskell] writes for the delight of writing, of drawing soft pictures, and tracing loveable characters," the reviewer asserts, and "[t]hese are at once the means and end with her; nothing lies beyond them to take the fancy off from the page before it … We lounge along the book as through some wood on a lazy autumn day" (292). In this novel, the reviewer concludes, Gaskell has created a provincial paradise that is not artistically arranged to bring out a didactic message. "Perhaps we have little reason to give for our delight," the reviewer asserts; "we cannot produce one fact learned on our ramble; it is enough for us to have been filled with dreamy thoughts, and come home refreshed in heart. And so it is with 'Wives and Daughters;' its plot is nothing grand and startling; the delight of it is its gentle, even progress" (293). From this description, *Wives and Daughters* stands as an oasis in the midst of modern life—one enters and experiences an alternative reality that is slow, gentle, and reassuring. Moreover, the reality one enters is unmistakably a world of childhood. The nursery-rhyme opening, as Hughes and Lund note, creates an "entrée … through the childish, the domestic, the particular" (18). That the novel is set in the 1830s reinforces a nostalgic quality, for this is the "childhood" of the 1860s.

Such nostalgia, according to Marie E. Warmbold, characterizes the *Cornhill Magazine* more generally. In its entirety, she argues, this periodical promoted a sense of nostalgia in its readers, who consisted of "the cosmopolitan gentleman, who may have had to earn his money in the city but enjoyed thinking of himself as a country gentleman, and his family" (138). It is perhaps the strong sense of nostalgia in Gaskell's last novel that prompted another reviewer (this time from the London Review) to liken *Wives and Daughters* to George Eliot's realist masterpiece, *Adam Bede* (*London Review* 456).[2]

The realistic mode of Gaskell's last novel within this nostalgia-filled magazine is particularly striking when contrasted with popular sensation novels such as Wilkie Collins's *Armadale*, which was published alongside Gaskell's text in the *Cornhill Magazine*. The reviewer from *The British Quarterly Review* notes, in amazement, that Gaskell:

> has constructed no intricate plot, described no startling incidents, neither elopement, crime, murder, nor suicide has been introduced into her story; only the births, deaths, and marriages of an ordinary village chronicle; we are permitted to see how the people live, and to hear how they talk; and without any very intense curiosity about what comes next, and, indeed, scarcely knowing why, we feel the greatest interest in all that they say and do. (579)

---

[2]　According to Knezevic, Gaskell created a similar kind of distance in her early serial, *Cranford*, which appeared in Charles Dickens's periodical *Household Words*. In this novel "quaintness [is] generated by an assumed contrast between the provincial world of Cranford and the metropolitan world of London readers" (406).

The *Athenaeum* similarly acknowledges Gaskell's great achievement in competing head-to-head with sensation:

> Yet "Wives and Daughters" constrained many to take up the periodical in which the quiet tale month by month unwound itself,—in contrast with fictitious matter to all appearance far more artful, and certainly, in regard to spicery of incident, far more "sensational" (as the word runs). (295)[3]

It would seem from these accounts that *Wives and Daughters* creates a perfect parallel world for modern readers to enter—and in that way it might legitimately be hailed as a model of the realist aesthetic, an aesthetic that has often been criticized (especially by postcolonial critics) as attempting "the representation of a single authenticated experience" (Moss, para. 1) at the expense of competing perspectives.

The Jamesian reading of *Wives and Daughters* as a seamless depiction of English country life under a microscope is problematic, however, for it does not actually account for all that Gaskell includes in the novel. More importantly, the reviewers' romanticization of a country idyll negates the progressive elements of the novel—most significantly in the subplot involving the naturalist Roger Hamley. As the acknowledged suitor of Cynthia, and the unacknowledged beloved of Molly, Roger infuses the mundane everyday existence of Gaskell's young female characters with energy and acts as a hinge joining the realist and sensational threads of the plot. In addition, as a Darwinian figure, he disrupts any notion of a self-contained provincial space by both traveling abroad in search of scientific knowledge and periodically piercing the monotonous life of Hollingford through his letters and ultimate reappearance.

View 2: British Imperialism in the Distance

For all of the talk of the perfection with which Gaskell draws "English town-life" in her representation of Hollingford (Reader 349), Gaskell's plot also includes elements that cannot be contained within that narrow frame. Knezevic has argued of Gaskell's earlier work, *Cranford*, that "the world outside … is seldom directly represented in the novel, but it hovers on the edges of representation as an immense field of forces affecting the town in many ways" (407). The same could be argued of *Wives and Daughters*. Roger Hamley's scientific expedition to Africa, sketched in hazy detail through fragmentary correspondence, for example, challenges the perceived totality of Gaskell's provincial realist vision. Periodic references to the African expedition cause readers to shift focus from the contained foreground

---

[3]   Of course, as Lisa Surridge and Mary Elizabeth Leighton argue in "The Plot Thickens," any distinction between realism and sensation becomes less apparent when the illustrations for the novel are brought into the mix. Indeed, the exchange of letters between Cynthia and Preston could be read through the lens of familiar sensation tropes, although Molly is ultimately able to remedy the situation in a practical, realistic, and non-sensational way.

of Hollingford to the uncontained background of the global canvas. In these moments, Gaskell's fictional village becomes a small point on the globe and the illusion of monolithic realism shows itself.

When a letter from Roger arrives for an affianced but distanced Cynthia, and is then read by the faithful Molly, the rural English countryside is suddenly touched by events a world away—in Abyssinia (433–4). Gaskell does not brush this global contact under the rug, but instead highlights it:

> Molly took the letter, the thought crossing her mind that he had touched it, had had his hands upon it, in those far-distant desert lands, where he might be lost to sight and to any human knowledge of his fate; even now her pretty brown fingers almost caressed the flimsy paper with their delicacy of touch as she read. She saw references made to books, which, with a little trouble, would be accessible to her here in Hollingford. Perhaps the details and the references would make the letter dull and dry to some people, but not to her, thanks to his former teaching and the interest he had excited in her for his pursuits. But, as he said in apology, what had he to write about in that savage land, but his love, and his researches, and travels? There was no society, no gaiety, no new books to write about, no gossip in Abyssinian wilds. (434)

There is no detail to attach to this foreign space, as Roger's last series of negatives underscores, but the very existence of the "wilds" beyond Hollingford cautions against a myopic reading of the world. While it might be tempting to escape into the idea of village life that is blissfully ignorant of anything beyond the horizon, the novel persists in bursting such idealistic bubbles.

The outside world breaks through once more (and again in the form of a written account) in chapter 41, when Molly receives a pamphlet mentioning Roger's work abroad:

> [I]t was an account of an annual gathering of the Geographical Society, and Lord Hollingford had read a letter he had received from Roger Hamley, dated from Arracuoba, a district in Africa, hitherto unvisited by any intelligent European traveler; and about which, Mr. Hamley sent many curious particulars. (473)

Again, details of Roger's experiences are fuzzy at best, but the presence of a world beyond the English countryside, a world that ruptures the vision of completeness that Henry James found to be so attractive, is painfully evident. Deirdre d'Albertis has encouraged us to see Roger's African reports as the specter of British imperialism. In her words, "[t]he continent is figured in the novel as a blank wilderness upon which Roger Hamley exercises his 'great natural powers of comparison, and classification of facts'" (146, quoting *WD* 410).

The juxtaposition of the domestic world of Hollingford and Roger Hamley's African expedition sets up an inside/outside dichotomy that is not new in Gaskell's work. Rather, it is reminiscent of Gaskell's much earlier novel, *Cranford*. In *Cranford*, women stay safely at home and are only indirectly influenced by "the outside world in which men travel" (Cass 424). As Hilary Schor argues, "men in

Gaskell's world represent flashy voyaging and empire building while the women initially resist the world of dangerous wealth, exotic opulence, and mysterious danger because they will never see it" (116–17). Although *Wives and Daughters* creates a nostalgic rural paradise, to be sure, the African subplot suggests that provincial life is not untouched by Britain's imperialism.

We might see *Wives and Daughters*, therefore, as demonstrating the limitations of a realism that attempts to ignore empire. Historian Eric Hobsbawm has characterized the period from 1848 to 1875 as a period in which the globe was "transformed from a geographical expression into a constant operational reality. History from now on became world history" (47). Similarly, James Buzard has linked the consecration of "global capitalism" to the Crystal Palace Exhibition of 1851 ("Then on the Shore of the Wide World" 441). This global turn is perhaps the message that Gaskell's novel makes manifest. The English country novel can create a parallel reality, but that reality is always illusory at heart given the narratives that it must exclude to remain coherent. In this way, Gaskell ultimately refuses to "indulge the audience's nostalgia completely" (142), as Warmbold so eloquently put it. English life—even provincial life—cannot be extracted from England's global presence. This is a point that Mary Mullen illuminates in her essay in this volume on shared time in Gaskell's *North and South*.

Extending this reading of the novel, Mary Elizabeth Leighton and Lisa Surridge have noted the ways in which the illustrations accompanying the initial serialization of the novel draw attention to the unassimilated portions of the plot. Illustrated chapter initials, such as the one for chapter 37, which depicts Roger in Africa, create extradiegetic effects, Leighton and Surridge argue, reminding readers of scenes that are not represented in the verbal text, and that do not occur in the same temporal register (94). At these moments, the novel indicates to readers that the seamless provincial world of Hollingford is only a coherent realist vision to the extent that the world beyond is suppressed through practices of "spatial homogeneity" (Mullen 108). Once it is acknowledged, the "reality effect" that seems so seductive to Henry James is lost. Perhaps this is one reason why some contemporary readers, such as the writer for the *London Review* who had praised Gaskell's realism, reacted so negatively to the illustrations. "We should have been heartily glad if the publishers had not thought it worth while to reproduce the eighteen caricatures which disfigured the pages of the Cornhill" (456) he concludes. Apparently, this was one reader who was not prepared to investigate the extradiegetic effects that Leighton and Surridge encourage us to consider.

When extradiegetic effects are considered, as I think they should be, we see that the novel, as published in the Cornhill, does not create a totalizing view of reality—society laid under a microscope—as James suggests. In fact, this approach seems to be in keeping with much of the scholarship on Gaskell's *oeuvre*. Emily Blair has argued, for example, that *Wives and Daughters* is essentially a novel that "tells its story through narrative indirection" (585). In her analysis, Gaskell's novel is always working in opposing directions. Domestic detail in the novel "does the ideological work of creating the proper English middle class," Blair argues, but "background details in the narrative subvert this ideological work," drawing our attention to the "incomplete and unnarrated plots of *Wives and Daughters*" (585). For Blair, the repressed story has to do with desire. Extending Blair's insights, I want to suggest that another unnarrated story is the story of empire.

Billington also brings attention to the open qualities of Gaskell's realism through her detailed analysis of manuscript revisions and syntax. Gaskell's talent, Billington argues, is her "reluctance to name things finally and definitively" (41). According to Billington, Gaskell's novel captures the experience of living in time, and not just because of serial publication. Instead:

> the apparent successiveness of Gaskell's prose offers an image or approximation of temporal experience itself. Her sentences move fluidly on down the page while moving between co-existing minds and levels, as if in representation of the fact that a life lived in time is densely simultaneous even as it is linear. (68)

Visual metaphors are particularly useful in Billington's analysis of Gaskell's "faithful realism." Thus she writes of *Wives and Daughters*, "The picture will not stay still even within a single sentence. Nothing remains causally final or separately fixed, even temporarily" (59). Adopting and extending this visual metaphor, I contend that *Wives and Daughters* invites a bifocal reading practice, which requires an oscillation between near and distant focal points.[4]

View 3: Bifocal Reading and the Material Limits of Realism

The simultaneous presence of a near-sighted view of English provincial society and a far-sighted view of the world beyond Hollingford creates in *Wives and Daughters* what Knezevic has described (in the context of *Cranford*) as "two coexisting narrative spaces whose relationship is problematic. On the one hand, there is the synchrony of the ethnographic report; on the other, there is the eventful diachrony of the town's implication in trade and empire" (417). This structure, in turn, calls for a bifocal reading that oscillates between a microscopic and internally coherent treatment of Hollingford society and the present absence of global history implicated in Roger Hamley's African journey. When the materiality of Gaskell's novel, as originally published in the *Cornhill Magazine*, is considered, this feature of the text is even more apparent. The serialization of *Wives and Daughters* over a two-year period compounds the bifocal effect. Monthly publication fragments Gaskell's fictional world and disseminates pieces of that reality into a larger network of competing realities. Each instalment becomes like the "crumbs and

---

[4]   Bifocal eyeglasses were an established ocular technology by the time Gaskell completed *Wives and Daughters*, having been invented in the 1760s (Levene 148). Benjamin Franklin refers specifically to "double" spectacles in a letter dated 21 August 1784, writing: "I cannot distinguish a Letter even of Large Print; but am happy in the invention of Double Spectacles, which serving for distant objects as well as near ones, make my Eyes as useful to me as ever they were...." (Levene 141–2).

scraps of daily news" that reach the Hollingford book club (which prove to be so often erroneous), or the individual letters that circulate throughout the novel between Hollingford, Africa, and London.

In addition to the general fragmentation of the text, which seems inherently hostile to a sustained realism, the specifically cosmopolitan content of the *Cornhill Magazine* further highlights all that a monolithic provincial vision leaves out. Hughes and Lund have discussed the significance of an "editorial principle ... at work in each month's layout, an index to the editor's sense of how fiction, nonfiction, and poetry related to each other" (21). The editorial decision to include articles profiling exotic locations like the interior of China and the Sandwich Islands, or "exotic" peoples like the Maori of New Zealand, shifts the reader's focus so as to highlight England's existence within a global context. These accompanying periodical articles break up any hegemony inherent in the realism of *Wives and Daughters* by countering it with global voices.[5]

The articles I have mentioned are particularly convincing in this regard because they are not historical, so as to be placed in a different temporal register from the reader, but rather contemporary accounts of foreign locales and people. The article "A Midsummer's Ride in China" from the March 1865 issue of the *Cornhill* fills in some of the blank space created through the African subplot of *Wives and Daughters* by chronicling a British soldier's ride through the desolate regions of China in July 1861. This, the narrator explains, is one of "those ever-fewer regions where pathless solitudes still exist" (307). Unlike the sketchy version of Africa that we get through Roger Hamley's letters, however, this narrator describes the villages he visits with all of the detail of an ethnographer. Reminiscent, perhaps, of Gaskell's initial description of Molly's bonnet, the narrator of this article on China describes the clothing of local residents in great detail:

> The mandarins, in their long tunics of blue silk gauze, belted at the waist, and buckled in with costly morsels of sculptured jade—their handsomely embroidered facings indicative of rank, their neat accoutrements of fan, pipe, and watch-cases dependent from their belts—were in striking contrast to their attendants, who, dirty in clothing, unwashed, and foul-smelling, crowded eagerly behind their masters to witness our reception. (317)

Although the narrator emphasizes the remoteness of the region, as one "never before explored by Europeans" (319), his account fills this unknown space with humans and their activities. In this way, it provides the human narrative that Roger Hamley's letters do not.

The voice of the colonial "other" comes out directly in another article appearing in the *Cornhill* alongside *Wives and Daughters*. In the piece "Maori Sketches" from the October 1865 issue of the magazine, the narrator profiles what

---

5   Here, *Wives and Daughters* again reminds one of Gaskell's earlier *Cranford*. Also published serially within a periodical, "the installments of the novel would have resembled field reports from a provincial town ... the novel blended quite easily in style and tone with nonfictional contributions to the Dickens journal" (Knezevic 409).

he calls the struggle between "the advancing civilizers and the retreating savages" in New Zealand, which English citizens learn about through "telegrams," as well as "missionary reports, state papers, and pamphlets" (498). Here, the narrator provides the reaction to a charter by a local Maori chief in his own voice:

> One thing we understood well, however, for he told us plainly that if we wrote on the Governor's paper, one of the consequences would be that great numbers of Pakehas would come to this country and trade with us, and that we would have abundance of valuable goods … After the speaker of Maori had ceased, then Te Tao Nui and some other chiefs came forward and wrote on the Governor's paper, and Te Tao Nui went up to the Governor and took the Governor's hand in his and licked it! We did not much like this, we all thought it so undignified. (506–7)

Although this article exoticizes the Maori chief in a way that may make us cringe, particularly in the wake of Gayatri Spivak's foundational theoretical writing on subaltern voices,[6] the article does simultaneously undermine the idea that the world is a blank space for British imperialists by giving a voice to a native people who inhabit colonial space. Unlike Roger Hamley's conclusion that there was nothing to write about in a "savage land"—"no society, no gaiety, no new books … no gossip" (434), this article confirms that there were indeed local perspectives.

The interconnectedness of global history is reinforced yet again by an article called "Politics in the Sandwich Islands" in the January 1865 issue of the Cornhill. This report of a political crisis involving the king of Hawaii and a new constitution reinforces the links between England and, from the British perspective, a relatively obscure kingdom in the North Pacific. "Such is the little passage of history which has been in progress during the last few months in Hawaii," the narrator writes. "It is 'distinct,' though 'distant;' and interesting when we recollect that the English nation also had its childhood" (117). While Gaskell's novel introduces British imperialism at a hazy distance, amidst the nostalgia of provincial childhood, the accompanying articles in the cosmopolitan Cornhill render it "distinct." For those reading the novel in its periodical context, this kind of framing highlights the limits of *Wives and Daughters* as a monolithic realist novel, limits which Gaskell the novelist weaves into the texture of her novel through the blank spaces of Roger's African journey.

Conclusion

These limits are underscored, at least for *Cornhill* readers, in a final article entitled "An Australian's Impressions of England" from the January 1866 issue, for here empire speaks back directly. Narrated by a colonist who has supposedly been absent from the "motherland" since childhood, this article provides a critique of England through a series of contrasts between the wide spaces and open opportunities of the sparsely populated colony and the crowded, hierarchical, and

---

6   See "Can the Subaltern Speak?"

stagnant society of England. Speaking from the outside world that Gaskell's novel merely gestures toward, this narrator concludes: "the careful cultivation of Britain, the utilization of every little bit of land … the rarity of commons or waste land, gives us a painful impression. We feel cribbed and cabined and confined" (118). This is a charge that might be launched equally effectively against the provincial society of Hollingford, a society in which Molly Gibson sits at home reading and waiting for the return of the manly explorer, Roger Hamley. It is perhaps a charge that Gaskell herself weaves into her novel when she conspicuously raises the specter of a world beyond the minutely depicted Hollingford.

When considered in its full context, we have in the end a novel that turns in against itself in profound ways. *Wives and Daughters*, especially in its serial form, demonstrates the impossibility of maintaining a seamless reality from a single vantage point, a conclusion that is painfully punctuated by Gaskell's own untimely death before completing the final instalment. In offering a "bifocal" plot within a serialized realist novel, one that reinforces the "wonderfully ordinary many-mindedness of her prose" (Billington 62), Gaskell challenges the monolithic vision of realism as much as she adopts it. Moreover, by staging this challenge through Roger's journey to Africa, Gaskell obliquely reveals the dual consciousness of Victorian imperialism. Empire funds the protected existences of village enclaves—the quaint village of Hollingford, as well as Gaskell's earlier *Cranford*—and Gaskell's novel refuses to allow readers to overlook that key detail. However strong the nostalgic desire for a monolithic illusion originating in the textual effects of realism, *Wives and Daughters* requires its readers to continually adjust their vision and perspective so as to acknowledge global history.

Works Cited

"An Australian's Impressions of England." *Cornhill* 13 (January 1866): 110–20. Print.

Barthes, Roland. "The Reality Effect." *The Rustle of Language*. Trans. Richard Howard. Oxford: Blackwell, 1986. 141–8. Print.

Billington, Josie. *Faithful Realism: Elizabeth Gaskell and Leo Tolstoy: a Comparative Study*. Lewisburg, PA: Bucknell UP, 2002. Print.

Blair, Emily. "'The Wrong Side of the Tapestry': Elizabeth Gaskell's *Wives and Daughters*." *Victorian Literature and Culture* 33 (2005): 585–97. Print.

Buzard, James. *Disorienting Fiction: The Autoethnographic Work of Nineteenth-Century British Novels*. Princeton, NJ: Princeton UP, 2005. Print.

———. "'Then on the Shore of the Wide World': The Victorian Nation and its Others." *A Companion to Victorian Literature and Culture*. Ed. Herbert Tucker. Oxford: Blackwell, 1999. 438–55. Print.

Cass, Jeffrey. "Scraps, Patches, and Rags of Daily Life: Gaskell's Oriental Other and the Conservation of Cranford." *Papers on Language and Literature* 35.4 (1999): 417–33. Print.

d'Albertis, Deirdre. *Dissembling Fictions: Elizabeth Gaskell and the Victorian Social Text*. New York: St. Martin's P, 1997. Print.

Gaskell, Elizabeth. *Cranford*. 1851. Oxford: Oxford UP, 1998. Print.

———. *Wives and Daughters*. 1864–1866. Oxford: Oxford UP, 2000. Print.

Hobsbawm, Eric. *The Age of Capital 1848–1875*. New York: Vintage, 1975. Print.

Hughes, Linda K. and Michael Lund. *Victorian Publishing and Mrs. Gaskell's Work*. Charlottesville, VA: UP of Virginia, 1999. Print.

James, Henry. "Wives and Daughters." *Nation* 2 (22 February 1866): 246–7. Print.

Leighton, Mary Elizabeth and Lisa Surridge. "The Plot Thickens: Towards a Narratological Analysis of Illustrated Serial Fiction in the 1860s." *Victorian Studies* 51.1 (2008): 65–101. Print.

Levene, John R. "Benjamin Franklin, F.R.S., Sir Joshua Reynolds, F.R.S., P.R.A., Benjamin West, P.R.A. and the Invention of Bifocals." *Notes and Records of the Royal Society of London* 27.1 (August 1972): 141–63. Print.

"Maori Sketches." *Cornhill* 12 (October 1865): 498–512. Print.

"A Midsummer Ride in China." *Cornhill* 11 (March 1865): 307–19. Print.

Moss, Laura. "'The Plague of Normality': Reconfiguring Realism in Postcolonial Theory." *Jouvert* 5.1 (2000). n.pag. Web. 23 January 2015.

Mullen, Mary. "In Search of Shared Time: National Imaginings in Elizabeth Gaskell's *North and South*." *Place and Progress in the Works of Elizabeth Gaskell*. Ed. Lesa Scholl, Emily Morris, and Sarina Gruver Moore. Burlington, VT: Ashgate, 2015. 107–20. Print.

"Politics in the Sandwich Islands." *Cornhill* 11 (January 1865): 109–17. Print.

[Review of *Wives and Daughters*.] *Athenaeum* (3 March 1866): 295. Print.

[Review of *Wives and Daughters*.] *British Quarterly Review* 43 (2 April 1866): 579–80. Print.

[Review of *Wives and Daughters*.] *Contemporary Review* 2 (May–August 1866): 292–3. Print.

[Review of *Wives and Daughters*.] *London Review* (21 April 1866): 455–6. Print.

Schor, Hilary. *Scheherazade in the Marketplace: Elizabeth Gaskell and the Victorian Novel*. New York: Oxford UP, 1992. Print.

Spivak, Gayatri. "Can the Subaltern Speak?" *Marxism and the Interpretation of Culture*. Ed. Cary Nelson and Lawrence Grossburg. London: Macmillan, 1988. 271–313. Print.

Warmbold, Marie E. "Gaskell in Cornhill Country." *Victorian Periodicals Review* 33.2 (2000): 138–49. Print.

Watt, Ian. *The Rise of the Novel: Studies in Defoe, Richardson, and Fielding*. London: Chatto & Windus, 1957. Print.

Chapter 12
Gaskell's "Rooted" Prose Realism

Josie Billington

When Thomas Hardy wrote in 1880 "a certain provincialism of feeling is invaluable" (*Early Life* 189), he was in part defending the singularly non-metropolitan orientation of his own writing within a male nineteenth-century tradition of fiction (represented by Charles Dickens, Anthony Trollope, William Makepeace Thackeray) that was overwhelmingly London-centric. The dominant tendency of Victorian fiction by women, on the contrary—from the publication of Charlotte Brontë's *Jane Eyre* in 1847 and Elizabeth Gaskell's *Mary Barton* in 1848 through to George Eliot's *Middlemarch* in 1872—had been robustly to establish provincialism, on the one hand, as the basis for the literary re-imagining of parochial England as a quasi-mythic landscape in the work of the Brontës or, on the other hand, as the foundation of high Victorian realism in the fiction of George Eliot. In fact, while Hardy defensively regarded himself as part of a minority, only in the case of Elizabeth Gaskell did association with a provincial fictional mode contribute to her reputation as a minor novelist. Gaskell's work has suffered in critical esteem by its being closely identified with the related spatial-social categories (and often pejorative terms) "provincial" and "domestic" at once. Rather than seeking to rescue Gaskell from these categories, this essay argues that it is impossible to separate the distinctive achievement of this writer's work in the realist mode from the very rootedness, domestically and regionally, which, paradoxically, has tended to deny Gaskell status as a great realist writer. But as with Hardy's provincialism, "domestic," as used in this chapter, stands for something bigger than itself—an artistic disposition, worldview, and metaphysic that constitutes the implicit dynamic of Gaskell's prose realism. This essay is concerned to disclose Gaskell's customary novelistic mode by contrast with the reciprocally illuminating work of her female contemporaries, George Eliot and Charlotte Brontë.

Memory and the Present: George Eliot and Elizabeth Gaskell

The distinctive quality of Gaskell's rootedness is most immediately evident in her correspondence, especially where she invites comparison with the life writing of her sister novelists. Gaskell and George Eliot, at equivalent stages in their literary careers—established, successful writers, both about to produce their best and most mature work—write of a sense of failure in relation to their own work. First, Gaskell, in 1859, writing to her friend Charles Eliot Norton, recounts visits to

London and Auchencairn in Scotland. The commissioned novel to which Gaskell refers is *Sylvia's Lovers* (1863):

> I once thought of writing a paper for the Atlantic about our dear Scotch village (in Kirkcudbrightshire), but time failed me first and now we find that the Atlantic has failed. (N.B. Smith & Elder have offered me 1000£ for a three vol. novel, including the American rights &c, which I believe they disposed of to Mr. Field, whom I never saw—Not a line of the book is written yet,—I think I have a feeling that it is not worth while trying to write, while there are such books as Adam Bede and Scenes of Clerical Life—I set "Janet's Repentance" above all, still.—) Now to go back to Auchencairn. Mr. Gaskell joined us for a fortnight. (*Letters* 581)

George Eliot herself, 10 years later, having completed three chapters, the first 50 pages, of *Middlemarch* (1871–1872) wrote in her journal:

> I do not feel very confident that I can make anything satisfactory of "Middlemarch". I have need to remember that other things which have been accomplished by me, were begun under this same cloud. G. [George Henry Lewes] has been reading "Romola" again, and expresses profound admiration. This is encouraging. (138)

The first contrast of note is that, in Gaskell's case, expressions of insecurity of her worth as a writer, and even references to her métier as a novelist, are exceptional. Gaskell's abundant and generously open correspondence is overwhelmingly concerned with her role as wife and mother, and as Kathrin Levitan points out in this volume, letters themselves served to bridge geographical distance and re-connect Gaskell to domestic concerns (124). At every practical level, the writing was subordinate to the life. It was not, in fact, doubt of its worth that had held up the writing of *Sylvia's Lovers* but preoccupation with her daughters' health and education (Uglow 491–3). By contrast, George Eliot's ambiguous social position as the unmarried partner of the nominally married George Henry Lewes isolated her at once from the usual society enjoyed by a London literary woman and from her own family. The importance of the value of her work became more acute in proportion to the personal value of the life she had sacrificed to pursue it, and thus increased the anxiety and depression incurred in part by that loss. "Shall I ever write another book as true as 'Adam Bede,'" she wrote, when starting on her second novel, *The Mill on the Floss*; "The *weight* of the future presses on me" (*Journal* 300). And when writing *Daniel Deronda*, almost two decades later:

> Each part as I see it before me *in werden* seems less likely to be anything else than a failure; but I see on looking back this morning ... that I really was in worse health and suffered equal depression about "Romola" and so far as I have recorded, the same thing seems to be true of "Middlemarch". (*Journal* 145)

In order to look forward and keep going with her novel, George Eliot wills herself to look back. Her journal is the objectification of an inner life put compulsively into words, a form of external memory. One of the central tenets of secular

Victorian social, psychological, and fictional discourse, says Sally Shuttleworth in her study of "embodied memory" in the Victorian novel, was that memory functions as the ground of a continuous, coherent personal identity through time (Shuttleworth 47–8). Identity is evolved through repetition and, crucially, through *recognition* of reproduced states of consciousness. "Without this recognition we should live in the present alone" (Carpenter 454), devoid not only of a sense of past continuities, but also of a future imaginatively constructed *on the basis* of the memory of unified consciousness. In fact, memory in George Eliot creates a future *in despite* of the present and its disabling sense of failure. Her volitional act of remembering previous failures which had been overcome is a psycho-moral exercise of the *"recollective faculty* of the will … [the] single power of furnishing voluntary combinations in place of those which come unbidden and vaguely into the mind" (Holland 155). Yet the very call to life which is deliberately and often desperately summoned thus *outside* of George Eliot, *by* George Eliot, is, even so, always involuntarily and animately *inside* her. Written in the midst of the struggle to write, the journal is a vital internal stimulus, more resonantly close to the present recurrence of despondency, than fixedly past. In the terms of contemporary cognitive science, such memories "are not possessions that you have or do not have" but mental constructions created in the moment, according to pressing inward demands, and thus "about the present as much as about the past" (Fernyhough 8).

The dynamic and temporal-cognitive direction is entirely different in Gaskell's letter. The expression of doubt, while not itself casual, *happens* casually—*en passant* and in parenthesis—amid a letter. The letter is mostly travelogue, which moves fluently along, with brisk generosity. But a shaft is suddenly opened to disclose a potentially profound area of authorial anxiety, and, just as suddenly, it is closed over as life's surfaces and the onward pull of time reassert themselves as the priorities: "Now to go back to Auchencairn." Paradoxically, the writing simply flows on past its own second thoughts about the worthwhileness of *trying* to write. There is no time to worry about failure, no time certainly to write a journal about it, no time even to write the very things which, had she got around to writing them all, might have forestalled that (albeit balked) sense of failure in relation to herself as an author. "Time failed me," she says of the piece on Scotland she had wanted to write for the Atlantic. But the very swiftness of ongoing time propels even the syntax of failure *behind* her, urgently and impatiently into a future *ahead*: "not a line of the new book is written *yet*." This novel *will* get written under the pressure of its having to be written. The future is not a weight but an urgent summons and claim. Where George Eliot needed to be pulled backward and inward to the "live" continuities provided by the accumulated memory of her private journal, Gaskell, by contrast, is pulled forward by the insistent demands of a busy outer life.

These contrasting dynamics were contingent upon differences in temperament and situation which were at once mutually reinforcing and which proceeded from the life to the work. Their fiction shows a consciousness in both writers of the determinants that shaped a female life in the Victorian period, the expression of which is itself shaped by the distinct female configurations which George Eliot and Gaskell represent. Interrupting work on her third novel, *Romola* (1862–1863), to write the parable *Silas Marner* (1861), George Eliot described the married, childless Nancy Cass thus:

> She filled the vacant moments by living inwardly, again and again, through all her remembered experience, especially through the fifteen years of her married time, in which her life and its significance had been doubled ... This excessive rumination and self-questioning is perhaps a morbid habit inevitable to a mind of much moral sensibility when shut out from its due share of outward activity and of practical claims on its affections—inevitable to a noble-hearted, childless woman, when her lot is narrow. "I can do so little—have I done it all well?" is the perpetually recurring thought; and there are no voices calling her away from that soliloquy, no peremptory demands to divert energy from vain regret or superfluous scruple. (214–15)

Resuming her work on *Romola* after *Silas Marner* was published, George Eliot found herself again "without any confidence in my ability to do what I want" (*Journal* 102). Sixty pages into *Romola*, she wrote: "Will it ever be finished? – ever be worth anything?" (*Journal* 110). This has the very cadence of "I can do so little – have I done it all well?" Reading the journal alongside the novels, one senses that the public and authoritative voice of the novels—the witnessing presence and humane language designated by the name "George Eliot"—is a continuation, and itself a kind of memory, of the private and inward cry we hear in George Eliot's journal. That record, I have suggested, substituted, at some level and to some degree, for the continuities of an "outward," "practical" life of "peremptory demands" which manifestly helped save Gaskell from a despairing sense of failure in her own achievements. Though Christopher Ricks might be right to suggest that George Eliot became a novelist when she decided not to have children (217), the novels, as this passage demonstrates, were not therefore an evasion of what had been missed or had failed in her personal life. On the contrary, George Eliot's sympathetic imagining of the vacancy, narrowness, and self-critical excesses of Nancy Cass's childless life were built upon the memory of her own morbid sensitivity to loneliness and failure: "The more intimately I seem to discern your weaknesses, the stronger to me is the proof that I share them. How otherwise could I get the discernment?" (*Theophrastus Such* 4). Novel-writing was a form of creative remembering which allowed George Eliot to look back at her personal struggles and raise them to a psychical level at which they were no longer merely personal (Davis 386–7). The great breadth of vision of George Eliot's masterpiece *Middlemarch* is the result of George Eliot's dispersing her fears and failures among invented characters, thereby releasing memory into an analytic function, which was at once imaginatively intimate and of species significance by virtue of using personal experience without being limited to it. This creative procedure corresponds with the explicit philosophy of her novels in which, from the familial orientation of *The Mill on the Floss* to the Judaic axis of *Daniel Deronda*, memory functions "not simply as a register of personal identity, but actively binds the individual to a shared, biologically grounded history" (Shuttleworth 53).

In the famous letter Gaskell sent to George Eliot on receiving confirmation of the latter's identity, Gaskell wrote generously, and humbly, of her admiration of her sister-author's achievements: "I never read anything so complete, and beautiful in fiction, in my whole life before" (*Letters* 449). She went on to say, apparently adverting to the form of address she uses to open the letter ("My dear Madam"), "I should not be quite true in my ending, if I did not say before I concluded that I wish you *were* Mrs. Lewes" (*Letters* 449). Yet had Mrs. Lewes existed in reality, it is likely that George Eliot, as a specific voice and language, would *not* have existed in the same kind of way. Conversely, Gaskell's own literary achievements proceed to a large degree from the fact of her being "Mrs. Gaskell." Consider how distinct the operation of memory is in Gaskell's work when she herself imaginatively inhabits a susceptibility to disabling self-doubt, now on behalf of a fellow-novelist rather than an invented character. Recording the fate of Charlotte Brontë's first novel, *The Professor* (1857), Gaskell wrote:

> Currer Bell's book found acceptance nowhere, nor any acknowledgement of merit, so that something like the chill of despair began to invade his heart. And remember, it was not the heart of a person who, disappointed in one hope, can turn with redoubled affection to the many certain blessings that remain. (*Life* 305)

Significantly, recollection of the salutary kind so vital to George Eliot, takes place vicariously and unexpectedly here. Gaskell's "remember," while clearly an injunction to the reader at one level and possibly a self-reminder to the woman who sometimes experienced her own "certain blessings" as frustrations of her own purposes, is nonetheless, by comparison with George Eliot's deliberate "I have need to remember," casually additional: "And remember" is unwilled and unpremeditated—a passing afterthought or under-memory, which momentarily pushes its way to the surface and recedes again. In the novels, also, memory comes and goes unbidden—often inconveniently so—amid the temporal exigencies of the ongoing prose. When Mr. Gibson, in *Wives and Daughters,* is about to rebuke the suitor of his adolescent daughter for sending a love-missive to his "baby" (16-year-old Molly), he finds himself involuntarily recalling his own first love, "Poor Jeanie was not so old, and how I did love her!" (48). When the stern Mrs. Thornton is reluctantly called to the dying Mrs. Hale in *North and South* and asked to look kindly on the bereaved daughter, Margaret Hale, she is struck by "a sudden remembrance, suggested by something in the arrangement of the room,—of a little daughter—dead in infancy—long years ago" (241), which inclines her to Margaret Hale against the strong personal disinclination she feels toward her as the woman loved by her only son. The past comes back not as an austere corrective, but thus gently, unpredictably, and indefinitely. It was Margaret Oliphant, who, out of a sense of her own busy absorbedness, made a distinction between realistic married lives and the Romantic intensity of single ones:

> It is curious to note how much more keen is the memory, how much more distinct all the personal details of recollection in the minds of those who have kept themselves intact, so to speak and have never lost their childish individuality. The man, and more especially the woman, who has married, and confused the remembrance of early days with so many recollections more poignant—has a memory of a totally different quality from that of the virginal old age which has never replaced its first impressions with others more important. ("Edward Gibbon" 231–2)

Where George Eliot converted individual memory into its shared or collective equivalent, for Gaskell there was neither the necessity nor the possibility of purposefully *using* memory. Rather, the past characteristically loses specificity, becoming the embedded matter of a life experience which leaves behind the drama or meaning of any single instance of it. The removal of the Gaskell household to Plymouth Grove in 1850 was the occasion of one of the rare mentions of the death of Gaskell's son, William, from scarlet fever in 1845:

> Do come to us soon! I want to get associations about that house; *here* there is the precious perfume lingering of my darling's short presence in this life—I wish I were with him in that "light, where we shall see all light," for I am often sorely puzzled here—but however I must not waste my strength or my time about the never ending sorrow; but which hallows this house. I think that is one evil of this bustling life that one has never time calmly and bravely to face a great grief, and to view it on every side as to bring the harmony out of it. (111)

It is worth our remembering in this context that it was the death of Gaskell's infant son that first propelled her toward fiction (Uglow 153–5). Even as she regretted the disproportion of time's economy ("never ending … never time"), she allowed virtue to be made of that "evil." Her very capacity to move on from her maternal bereavement was one of the great gifts of maternity and wifehood itself. Yet in Gaskell's life and in her art the past is never simply secondary to the forward momentum of prosaic time, but always powerfully implicit within it. The present is dense with the ghosts and echoes of the past, just because the present as mere event—especially the event of death—is too meagre to contain the meanings ("never ending sorrow") which it generates. One great hidden power of Gaskell's fictional prose—so hidden that it requires the evidence of the original manuscript to reveal it (Billington 50–74)—is its capacity to make the present thus thick with the cumulative deposits of the past within a prose movement which is apparently as linear and undiscriminating as time itself. In this example from the original manuscript of *Wives and Daughters* (1864–1866), Squire Hamley, some while after his wife's death and daily more estranged from his eldest son, Osborne, comes "home to dinner weary and sore-hearted":

> It was just six o'clock, and he went hastily into his room on the ground-floor, and feeling as if he were very late, but the room was empty. He came into the drawing room ^ glancinged at the clock on the mantelpiece as he tried to warm his hands by the fire. (*MS* 386)

Death—"but the room was empty"—is written *into* the busy domestic ritual. As time and story simply go on, the present, almost physically (as with "something in the arrangement of the room," "sorrow which hallows this house") seems to hold the past as a thing almost palpably invisible. Gaskell's novels have a dual loyalty to the continuities of time and to its density and richness, carrying forward the hidden amorphousness of the past, holding it just beneath the level of narrative interest, until released as subtle surprise. One evening after Mrs. Hamley's death, Roger joins his father in the study to share a pipe with him:

> "I used to write to her when she was away in London, and tell her the home news. But no letter will reach her now! Nothing reaches her!" Roger started up. "Where's the tobacco-box, father? Let me fill you another pipe!" and when he had done so, he stooped over his father and stroked his cheek. (276)

An event, understated and undramatic, resonates powerfully with an under-event from the past: "When [Roger] caressed his mother, she used laughingly to allude to the fable of the lap-dog and the donkey; so thereafter he left off all personal demonstration of affection" (42). The love that sought the mother now finds the father who misses the woman.

The Syntax of the Real: Charlotte Brontë and Gaskell

These differences between what I have called George Eliot's elevated "species" memory and what might be called the more contingent "under-memory" of Gaskell's prose, proceed from a different relation to, and distinct experience of, time—the ontological outcome, I have argued, of distinct modes of nineteenth-century femalehood. It was Virginia Woolf who first suggested that the structure of female experience materially influenced the "shape" of female writing in the nineteenth century. Even the relatively youthful and "pliable" form of the novel could not allow, Woolf argued, these writers' release into the kind of "natural prose" associated with their male forebears. Woolf finds in Charlotte Brontë's prose, for instance, a distortion of thought and language: "a mind which was slightly pulled from the straight, and made to alter its clear vision in deference to external authority ... The writer was meeting criticism ... admitting she was 'only a woman' or protesting that she was 'as good as a man'" (*A Room of One's Own* 77–8). The defensiveness Woolf identified (specifically in *Jane Eyre*) is exhibited in the characteristically inverted syntax of both Brontë's life-writing and her fiction: "What I am, it is useless to say. Those whom it concerns feel and find it out. To all others I wish only to be an obscure, steady-going private character" (*Life* 324). "Passive as I lived, little as I spoke, cold as I looked," says Lucy Snowe in *Villette*, "I *could* feel" (134). More usually, the assertive "I" emerges only to bury yearning—"Friends, not professing vehement attachment, not offering the tender solace of well-matched and congenial relationship ... but towards whom, my heart softened instinctively and yearned with an importunate gratitude, which I entreated Reason betimes to check" (*Villette* 223). This habitual invertedness, even as it is a symptom of a desire for self-concealment, fear of criticism, and a shame of her own personal need, is also necessarily therefore intensely and self-consciously self-regarding. Here, by contrast, is one of Gaskell's most famous letters, in which she wrote to her friend, Eliza Fox: "I have a great number of 'Mes' and that's the plague":

> One of my mes is, I do believe, a true Christian – (only people call her socialist and communist), another of my mes is a wife and mother, and highly delighted at the delight of everyone else in the house ... Now that's my "social" self I suppose. Then again I've another self with a full taste for beauty and convenience whh [*sic*] is pleased on its account. How am I to reconcile all these warring members? I try to drown myself (my *first* self) by saying it's Wm who is to decide all these things, and his feeling it right ought to be my rule. And so it is—only that does not quite do. (*Letters* 108)

Next to Brontë's un-"straight" sentence shapes, Gaskell's syntax seems wonderfully self-forgetful, without conflict. "My first self" manifestly is *not* Gaskell's priority. The parenthetic phrase is a semantic distinction for her correspondent's sake, not a worried inward-looking self-verification. As a wife and mother, beset by unequal or unequatable considerations, randomly claiming priority at the same time, Gaskell recognizes that there is not and cannot be one right or finally true self. The distinction at issue here is not between a male and female syntax but between a single and a married one. For crucially, this is the characteristically busy, immersed, "natural" syntax of Gaskell's novels, the connectives moving easily in different directions and becoming, even in their apparent casualness, almost semantic signals of the shifts from one dimension of being to another, or between myriad subjectivities and levels. For a representative example: there is a moment very early in *Sylvia's Lovers*, where the heroine returns to her family at their cliff-farm home after a routine visit to neighboring relatives:

> They seemed as if they had never missed Sylvia: no more did her mother for that matter, for she was busy and absorbed in her afternoon dairy-work to all appearance. But Sylvia had noted the watching not three minutes before, and many a time in her after life, when no one cared much for her out-goings and in-comings, the straight upright figure of her mother, fronting the setting sun, but searching through its blinding rays for a sight of her child, rose up like a sudden-seen picture, the remembrance of which smote Sylvia to the heart with a sense of a lost blessing, not duly valued while possessed.

> "Well, feyther, and how's a' wi' you?" asked Sylvia, going to the side of his chair, and laying her hand on his shoulder. (61)

Seamlessly, in the very middle of its own unfolding ("and many a time in her after life"), a sentence slips narrative time and line, crosses a threshold—at "and"—into a new level of meaning which does not belong to the narrated moment, nor even to the novel's story. The Sylvia for whose out-goings and in-comings no-one much cares never features in the novel again. The evocation of that future into which the narrated moment passes as painful memory and a heart's chronic sense of loss, is as inconsequential as it is momentary—something "sudden-seen" and apparently as suddenly forgotten. Compare this moment from the manuscript of *Wives and Daughters*, relating to the selfishly vain Mrs. Kirkpatrick, now Mrs. Gibson:

> She saw she was often in some kind of disfavour with her husband and it made her uneasy. She resembled Cynthia in this; she liked to be liked; and she wanted to regain the esteem which she did not perceive she had lost for ever. ~~Even~~ Molly sometimes took her stepmother's part in secret. (*MS* 606)

The cancellation of "Even" is perhaps a tender second thought, making a tiny gap in time, out of generic regret for having already moved on from the irrevocable loss which the character who suffers it is too limited to see. But not even the manuscript signals the huge shift of level which takes place in the preceding sentence: at that innocuous connective "which," the narrative breaks through to a dimension of oblivion ("for ever") infinitely more troubling than Mrs. Gibson's own. It is at these tiny moments, which strictly do not belong anywhere—less moments, than vividly realized spaces or gaps in time—that a remote story of an eighteenth-century whaling community in Yorkshire, or a tale of Victorian northern industrial life (*Mary Barton*, *North and South*) or the depiction of an outmoded, genteel rural society (*Cranford*, *Wives and Daughters*), acquire sudden importance and intense reality even within their small ordinariness. These instances help to define what is to be valued in "provincialism" aside from the Romantic "individuality" which Hardy prized (*Early Life* 189). Undramatically commonplace, these "lost" events are at the same time powerfully resonant, for quietly giving status to the kind of nebulous or residual life-stuff that is easily ignored or overlooked. It is in such seemingly merely contingent "after" events, or loosenings—the random, amorphous matter given off by a life lived in time, yet which spills out of time and category, and seems hardly to qualify as reality at all—that the most real things happen, even as these happenings are written in amidst a narrative of things going on as usual. "Well, feyther, and how's a' wi' you?" The present reasserts itself with ease as the new paragraph begins; though it's a clue to the hidden complexity of this prose that the present now carries with it a silent remembrance that Sylvia's open affection towards her father ("going to the side of his chair and laying her hand on his shoulder") must in part contribute to that after-sadness in relation to the more taken-for-granted mother.

Gaskell's is a mind so busily married to time, as to be unworriedly used to thinking on many levels at once, as though that were normal. In arguing for this continuity and formal relation between the personal life and the fictional writings, I take my cue from Gaskell herself, who, on the few occasions when she explicitly commented upon her art, attested to the mutually strengthening qualities of her home duties and her writing. "A good writer of fiction," Gaskell wrote to an aspirant female author,

> must have *lived* an active and sympathetic life if she wishes her books to have strength and vitality in them. When you are forty, and if you have a gift for being

an authoress you will write ten times as good a novel as you could do now, just
because you will have gone through so much more of the interests of a wife and
mother. (*Letters* 695)

There has been understandable reluctance in recent decades to take these words
at their conservative face value. But Ferdinand Mount's controversial suggestion
that the apparently conservative institutions of marriage and family are radically
anti-institutional, reminds that values other than mere conventionalism are operant
in Gaskell's "domestic" ethos. Inequality seeped into marriage, from the outside,
the public world, Mount argues: it is *within* marriage and family that notions of
equality and open-heartedness existed long before they became part of a radical
political programme. Old ideals of marriage are opposed not to individual rights,
but to egotism, male or female. These ideals assume a family ethic—duties of nest-
building, nurturing, protecting, teaching—which demand mutual self-sacrifice
(Mount 241). Certainly, what Gaskell the wife and mother (particularly Gaskell the
minister's wife) seems to have given to Gaskell the author, even in her own view,
was a gift for, a kind of apprenticeship in, the energetic absorption in concerns,
modes, and experiences *not* her own, which, for her, moreover, constituted the right
province of the novelist. "Introspection … is not a safe training for a novelist,"
Gaskell wrote emphatically to her daughter in 1859, the same year of the letter to
Norton. "I think you must observe what is *out* of you instead of examining what
is in you" (*Letters* 541). Gaskell's generous, abundant absorption in what was out
of her, other selves and lives, resulted in a form of omniscience which is closer
to Keatsian negative capability—a loss of ego, a dissolving into other selves, a
seeing from below—than to the God-like vision from above, often associated with
the term. The continuity between life and writing in Gaskell's case is between the
prosaic medium in which she lived (both the domestic home and the provincial
one, Manchester) and the prosaic medium—her realist prose—in which she wrote.
Their tendencies, concerns, even tempo are generically related. Ordinariness roots
them both.

    Other writing by contemporary women, Gaskell knew, always ran the risk of
compensating for the *lack* of an ordinary life. In her letter to her daughter warning
against inward examining, Gaskell surely had in mind as a cautionary example
the morbidly introspective tendency which had troubled her in Charlotte Brontë's
work. "The difference between Miss Brontë and me," she wrote in 1853, "is
that she puts all her naughtiness into her books, and I put all my goodness. I
am sure she works off a great deal that is morbid into her writing and *out* of
her life" (*Letters* 228). Gaskell clearly did not endorse Romantic expressionism
as autobiographical relief. Yet she did recognize, long before she came to know
Charlotte Brontë personally, that morbidity in the case of a single woman often
had nowhere else to go. Her reading of the "Passages in the Life of a Daughter
at Home," by Caroline Emilia Stephen, relative of Virginia Woolf, left a "painful
impression" of "the trials of many single women, who waken up some morning
to the sudden feeling of the *purposelessness* of their lives." "I think I see every
day," she writes in this context, "how women deprived of their natural duties as

wives and mothers, must look out for other duties if they wish to be at peace" (*Letters* 117). Writing later in the letter of the restlessness of the age, the "search after the ideal in some, and morbid dread of the ideal in others" she says:

> I am always thankful and glad to Him that I am a wife and a mother and that I am so happy in the performance of those clear and defined duties; for I think there must be a few years of great difficulty in the life of every woman who foresees and calmly accepts a single life. (*Letters* 118)

It is because there is nothing pious or merely formally religious in Gaskell's "I am always thankful and glad" that we have to take seriously the proposition that the difference between being a married and a single woman of the Victorian period might have been as far-reaching and deep-going in its consequences for the individual as the difference between being male and female. Moreover, the Victorian single woman and the Victorian man (single or married) potentially had in common, on this evidence, the pressure of looking out for what to *do* in a world which was increasingly drifting without direction and in which individuals were restlessly in search of ideals to replace lost absolutes. The distinctive achievements of Gaskell's work—her at-homeness in her medium, literal and literary, her adjustedness to a fallen, relative world, the steeped in itself ordinariness that seems not to need the support of a philosophy, George Eliot-style, to tolerate the complexity and difficulty it reveals—might have to have been that of a married person, a literary married person, of course, but a married person of that gender, of that time. Not only was a married woman's role in the Victorian world given, settled, clear, and defined: since successful marriage and motherhood were religiously and socially sanctioned in the Victorian age as representing the summit of fulfilment in the female life, a woman in that era who was a happy wife and mother could be so without conflict. Gaskell's fictional prose, that is to say, might have been the outcome of a situation or set of circumstances historically particular, perhaps unique.

The literary consequences and influence of these circumstantial factors reach further than the implicit dynamic of Gaskell's realist prose. Only *Mrs.* Gaskell perhaps—the writer who could be a writer only by going beyond confessional autobiography—could have made the sympathetically imaginative endeavor of writing *The Life of Charlotte Brontë* (1857): it seems inconceivable that Charlotte Brontë could have written "The Life of Mrs. Gaskell." As Gaskell's biography re-invented the genre of life-writing for the nineteenth-century, so *Mary Barton* and *North and South* are the acknowledged successes in the Victorian era of the provincial social-problem novel. By comparison, Charlotte Brontë's *Shirley* (1849) and George Eliot's *Felix Holt* (1866) have enjoyed only equivocal critical esteem as works which register the upheavals of the Industrial Revolution. Yet the very celebration of *North and South* as an "industrial" novel has tended to obscure the remarkable formal feat which helps make it the most powerfully dynamic example of the genre. The narrative witnesses unprecedented and fluidly unceasing social change, across the myriad disturbances of an entire social-industrial milieu—

from the micro-level of domestic intimacy to the macro-level of economic class conflict—through the perspective of a character who is herself undergoing radical evolution, and whose own singular visionary discovery is that change is a staple of life. As Lesa Scholl reminds in her essay in this volume, Margaret Hale not only focalizes socio-cultural mobility: she embodies it (154). "There was change everywhere," Margaret realizes when she returns south to her childhood home (and place once again summons the past on its own painfully subtle terms): "This slight all-pervading instability had given her greater pain than if all had been too entirely changed for her to recognise it" (*North and South* 394, 400). Only a writer as acceptingly rooted as Gaskell could thus toughly inhabit the instability—minutely tiny, yet "everywhere"—of this particular historical unsettlement. Gaskell's very radicalism, including this novel's multiplicity of class perspectives and its dismantling of political stereotypes and institutionalized perceptions, is inseparable from her capacity for untroubled immersion in prosaic ordinariness.

Works Cited

Billington, Josie. *Faithful Realism: Elizabeth Gaskell and Leo Tolstoy*. Lewisburg, PA: Bucknell UP, 2002. Print.

Brontë, Charlotte. *Villette*. 1853. Ed. Margaret Smith and Herbert Rosengarten. Oxford: Oxford UP, 1984. Print.

Carpenter, William B. *Principles of Mental Physiology*. London: Henry S. King, 1874. Print.

Davis, Philip. *The Victorians*. Oxford: Oxford UP, 2002. Print.

Eliot, George. *Silas Marner*. 1861. Ed. Q.D. Leavis. Harmondsworth: Penguin, 1985. Print.

———. *The Impressions of Theophrastus Such*. 1879. Ed. D.J. Enright. London: J.M. Dent, 1995. Print.

Fernyhough, Charles. *Pieces of Light: The New Science of Memory*. London: Profile Books, 2012. Print.

Gaskell, Elizabeth. *The Letters of Mrs Gaskell*. Ed. J.A.V. Chapple and Arthur Pollard. Manchester: Manchester UP, 1966. Reprint, Manchester: Mandolin, 1997. Print.

———. *The Life of Charlotte Brontë*. 1857. Ed. Angus Easson. Oxford: Oxford UP, 1996. Print.

———. *North and South*. 1855. Ed. Angus Easson. Oxford: Oxford UP, 1982. Print.

———. *Sylvia's Lovers*. 1863. Ed. Andrew Sanders. Oxford: Oxford UP, 1982. Print.

———. *Wives and Daughters*. 1864–1866. Ed. Angus Easson. Oxford: Oxford UP, 1987. Print.

———. *Wives and Daughters*. Gaskell Collection 1877. John Rylands Library, University of Manchester. Print.

Hardy, Florence Emily. *The Early Life of Thomas Hardy 1840–1891*. Cambridge: Cambridge UP, 2011. Print.

Harris, Margaret and Juliet Johnston, eds. *The Journals of George Eliot.* Cambridge: Cambridge UP, 1998. Print.

Holland, Henry. *Chapters on Mental Physiology.* London: Longman, 1852. 155. Print.

Levitan, Kathrin. "Catching the Post: Elizabeth Gaskell as Traveler and Letter-Writer." *Place and Progress in the Works of Elizabeth Gaskell.* Ed. Lesa Scholl, Emily Morris, and Sarina Gruver Moore. Burlington, VT: Ashgate, 2015. 123–36. Print.

Mount, Ferdinand. *The Subversive Family: An Alternative History of Love and Marriage.* London: Cape, 1982. Print.

Oliphant, Margaret. "Edward Gibbon." *Blackwood's Magazine* 130 (August 1881): 229–47. Print.

Ricks, Christopher. "George Eliot: 'She was still young.'" *Essays in Appreciation.* Oxford: Oxford UP, 1998. 206–34. Print.

Shuttleworth, Sally. "'The Malady of Thought': Embodied Memory in Victorian Psychology and the Novel." *Memory and Memorials, 1789–1914.* Ed. Matthew Campbell, Jacqueline M. Labbe, and Sally Shuttleworth. London: Routledge, 2000. 46–59. Print.

Uglow, Jenny. *Elizabeth Gaskell: A Habit of Stories.* London: Faber & Faber, 1993. Print.

Woolf, Virginia. *A Room of One's Own and Other Essays.* Ed. Hermione Lee. London: Vintage, 2001. Print.

PART IV
Cultural Performance and Visual Spaces

Chapter 13
Applied Meteorology:
Scientific Accuracy and Imaginative Writing in Elizabeth Gaskell's "Cousin Phillis" and *Wives and Daughters*

Frances Twinn

After three visits to the Great Exhibition of 1851, that showcase of British achievement in art and science, Elizabeth Gaskell declared emphatically "I'm *not* scientific nor mechanical" (*Letters* 159). This protestation is belied by evidence from and close examination of her later rural fiction "Cousin Phillis" (1864) and *Wives and Daughters* (1865) which display an acute awareness of the physical science of Meteorology. An important and overlooked aspect of her writing is "the near-scientific exactness" (Blythe 470) of her meteorology, as literary critics have focused on the social and economic problems associated with her early fiction, and suggested that she is a "writer of place," a descriptor applied by Burroughs at the outset of his argument in an earlier essay in this volume. In fact, one can search in vain for commentary about the weather in the novel. Whilst Romantics such as Wordsworth became renowned for their poetic appreciation of nature, and Coleridge and Shelley for their "Romantic Weather"[1] apparently little has been written about the weather in fiction. John Mullan, in a volume on Jane Austen's works, poses the question, "Why is the weather important?" He claims that "she is the first novelist to mark small changes in the weather that anyone might notice on any ordinary day" (101).[2] Bentley and Ogden make an unsubstantiated claim for Emily Brontë: "that no writer in English Literature has presented the weather more exactly or more beautifully than Emily Brontë" (66). They merely follow this observation with a brief synopsis of her artistic methodology. Dickens's weather, of course, has been treated more comprehensively. The fog both in *Bleak House* and on the Thames marshes in *Great Expectations* looms large and is an integral part of Dickens's artistry but, on the whole, the critical coverage of the weather is not extensive across the canon of English Literature.

---

[1]   Arden Reed and John Chapple both discuss the weather with reference to these Romantic poets.

[2]   John Mullan engages with an article by Euan Nisbet about *Emma*. Nisbet's contention is that Austen wrote the novel during 1814 which was a year of an anomalously extreme weather. This discussion raises interesting issues which might be followed up.

Meteorology, the science of the atmosphere—that most dynamic and complex of the natural systems—was a fledgling, but blossoming science during Gaskell's lifetime as theoretical advances were being made and daily localized weather reports and then national forecasts were published.[3] It is the intention of this chapter to assess Gaskell's late fiction from the point of view of applied meteorology, by considering Gaskell as both a "landscape meteorologist" (Bonacina "Landscape") and "biometeorologist"[4] and to demonstrate how the weather, which is woven into the structural design and inter-textual woof and weft of these rural narratives, provides a multi-layered text dense with association. Such an approach offers an original and innovative perspective intended to enrich the reading of her work whilst, at the same time, highlighting the discourse about the relationship between science and art. Meteorology is an entirely appropriate vehicle for such a conversation as the sky has been recognized as "a finely tuned paradigm for the alliance between art and science" (Thornes, *Skies* 17) and, as Bonacina observes, "scientific and artistic methods are only different modes of approach of the self-same world … to open up wider vistas of truth" ("Landscape" 485). Bonacina was the first meteorologist to coin the term "landscape meteorologist" which defined the "artistic side of meteorology." It

> comprises those scenic influences of sky, atmosphere, weather and climate which form part of our natural human environment. This study … is one of pictorial impressions, whether the natural scenery is merely received and carefully stored in the memory, or is photographed, painted or described and so in a measure perpetuated, however dimly in comparison with the original scene. (485)

Bonacina's approach to the science was an attempt to demonstrate that much could be learnt and appreciated about the atmosphere from the study of art, as well as science. His ideas provided the inspiration for Thornes's study of Constable's clouds and landscape paintings (*John Constable's Skies*) and it was this source which provoked the ideas for this chapter because it seems to me that both Gaskell and Constable are conscious artists. From my reading of Thornes's original and fascinating research, it became apparent that the landscapes of Hope Farm and Hollingford were the verbal equivalents of some of Constable's canvasses. It seems appropriate, therefore, to consider Gaskell in the light of Bonacina's applied science of landscape meteorology and adapt and apply Thornes's analytical methodology to examination of Gaskell's late fiction. Gaskell can be seen to fit perfectly into Bonacina's definition, as she "described" the landscapes from "memories carefully stored" of her early years. I would argue that the "daily intimate," lived "experience" (Waugh 28) and "felt life" of her first 21 years in the much-loved Cheshire countryside provided her with the equivalent of Constable's "atmospheric laboratory" on Hampstead Heath (Thornes, *Skies* 53) to inform her

---

[3]   Interestingly, the *Manchester Examiner* had been publishing a weather report since 1847, the first newspaper in the country so to do.

[4]   The details can be found on the International Society's web site at biometeorology.org.

late fiction. In a similar way, her two-week stay in Whitby provided the laboratory she required for the landscape, skyscape and waterfront of *Sylvia's Lovers* as discussed by Burroughs.

As an applied meteorologist, Gaskell should also be considered as a proponent of another, even more recently established, branch of that scientific discipline, that of biometeorology. This interdisciplinary field of science is the study of the interactions between the biosphere and the earth's atmosphere. Although now internationally recognized with its own peer-reviewed quarterly journal, biometeorology did not have the same academic respectability at the time Gaskell was writing. It was viewed as a digression in the closing paragraphs on an article about the weather published in the second half of 1860 in the newly introduced but widely read *Cornhill Magazine* ("Weather" 565–79).[5]

The anonymous author writes:

> Who is there that has not felt the influence of climate and weather clearing up or observing his intellectual faculties? We attribute this, perhaps correctly, to an indirect action through the state of our health ... It would not be wise—nor, indeed, is it safe—to carry speculation for in such a matter; but, perhaps, some of those peculiarities of constitution that have puzzled and distressed many persons of high nervous organisation, really owe their origin to a more ready sensibility to these real but definable sources. (579)

He continues in a new concluding paragraph, "We have drawn away in some measure from the immediate subject of the weather in these last remarks" (579). These days this relatively newly established science is probably more easily recognized by the term "weather sensitivity." Contemporary nature writer Richard Mabey recognizes this tendency in himself, writing that he kept "a nature diary" which was constantly interrupted by sulky notes about his "weather malaise"—a reminder that climate is also an influence on, and metaphor for, well-being (44). Gaskell often commented in letters about her sensitivity to the Manchester weather and its detrimental effects on her health and well-being (*Letters*, 597; 607; 745). As Burroughs indicates, she had a "need for a coastal holiday to replenish her [family's] health" (19). Perhaps then, it is not surprising that she is inclined to use weather to reflect state of mind and attributes of character. In her late fiction, there

---

[5]   This article briefly discusses the current knowledge and measurement of the weather. It speculates on, but is somewhat dismissive of, what we now recognize as "biometeorology." Although there is no apparent record that William Gaskell borrowed the *Cornhill Magazine* from the private subscription Portico Library of which he was a member, he did borrow journals such as *Blackwood's*, *Fraser's*, and *Notes and Queries*. One of his most frequent borrowings was *The Gentleman's Magazine* which published a daily weather report for some years during the late 1840s and early 1850s. It is difficult to know whether his wife would have been influenced or gained meteorological knowledge from such sources. I think it unlikely, although of course it is inevitable that the weather would have been a subject of conversation in the Gaskell household as so much decision making would have been weather-determined at that time (as it still is today!).

are several examples of inextricable, inescapable, and deterministic links between the weather, physiology, and the human psyche.

Gaskell as a "Landscape Meteorologist"

Just as an artist must choose a paint medium for his or her canvas, so a writer's choice of words informs his or her work. It is important to point out that whilst Gaskell was aware of some technical meteorological terms, she mostly employed those which would have been well-known to readers constantly living under English skies. Her choice of words informs what I have called her "meteorological lexicon," which is depicted within Thornes's meteorological framework, adapted and applied to Gaskell's writing. This is illustrated in Figure 13.1 as a "word cloud."[6]

In his definitive text, Thornes recognized four essential components of landscape meteorology: the sky; the "*atmosphere*,"[7] the clouds and the weather, and optical effects. Thornes's *modus operandi* acts as a guide for, and serves to illustrate, the following textual analysis and close readings of "Cousin Phillis" and *Wives and Daughters*.

Gaskell's Meteorological Lexicon—Some General Guidance

Unlike Constable, who went "skying" into "his atmospheric laboratory" (Thornes 53) of Hampstead Heath where he observed and recorded the sequential development of the clouds and their attendant weather and then painted the sky *en plein air*,[8] in her rural fiction, Gaskell described using firsthand but carefully stored memories from her early years to make her as much of a landscape meteorologist in Bonacina's terms as Constable. Ruskin, a leading exponent of the link between

---

[6] My thanks to Jordan Kammellard for the design of this illustration. I have adapted Thornes's blueprint a little to reflect Gaskell's skyscapes. For instance, as she does not use optical effects like rainbows, I have moved thunder and lightning from the weather to that criterion to demonstrate her use of the more unusual and extreme elements of the weather. To this, I have added her meteorological lexicon for both clarity and to facilitate discussion.

[7] Readers will note that the word "*atmosphere*" is used in the artistic sense according to Thornes and will be italicized and put in quotation marks. In this case, it carries connotations of mood and tone (Thornes described his sub-sets as "hue" and "tone" 23) as distinct from its meteorological realism connected with the weather in the troposphere, that is, the lower part of the atmosphere which is the region of the weather.

[8] "Skying" meant the artist went out into the landscape to record the sky and its weather and note down changes and developments. This is firsthand fieldwork as the landscape and skyscape becomes effectively a scientific laboratory. It is interesting to note that Gaskell undertook her version of skying when she visited Whitby for two weeks in order to appreciate its wild land and seascapes and to map the topography of town and coastline. Ironically it poured with rain unceasingly and she managed with an umbrella but without a map, consequently, her topographical outcomes were not perfect. Nevertheless it was on the basis of this experience that she was able to evoke the Monkshaven of *Sylvia's Lovers* as discussed by Rob Burroughs in this volume of essays.

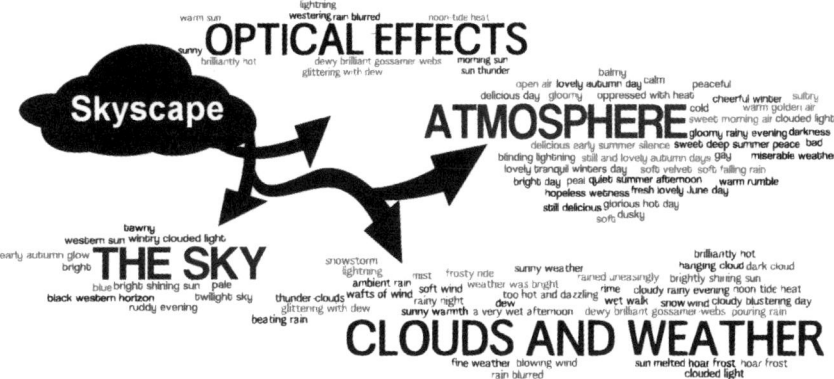

Fig. 13.1 "Word Cloud," designed by contributor, Frances Twinn, for this collection.

art and science at the time Gaskell was writing, exhorted painters "that every class of rock, earth and cloud must be known by the [writer] painter with geologic and meteorological accuracy" (Ruskin xxxviii).[9] Gaskell follows his advice by making "nice" distinctions between the technicalities of hoar-frost and rime in the garden scene at Hamley Hall (*WD* 216) which is also borne out in the use of "thunder-cloud" which, to the modern reader, may appear colloquial; for despite Howard's ground-breaking classification, he had not identified, by name, the towering dark clouds now known as "cumulo-nimbus" (Howard 97). Scientifically accurate, the lexicon includes many words to evoke "*atmosphere*." This somewhat ephemeral and hard to define element of the weather is one of Thornes's criteria, and Gaskell's masterly use of adjectives and adverbs enables her to create tone and mood evocatively on the page, especially when she is conveying a sense of a character's "weather sensitivity." The list of these adjectives and adverbs is long and not only includes words which sprinkle both texts, such as "sultry," "balmy," "sweet," "soft," "gloriously hot," "lovely," and "tranquil," but also includes the activity represented by present participles to denote the atmosphere's dynamism. Winds are "blustering," the "unremitting rain" is "pouring," the lightning "blinding," the clouds are "over-spreading," and the road "crisping." Whilst these verbs or "doing" words are noticeably and consistently employed to convey a sense of the processes at work, in addition they denote Gaskell's attempt at meteorological realism. The lexicon includes several examples of what Ruskin might have abhorred as "pathetic fallacy," but I consider effectively and appropriately indicative of "weather sensitivity." There are instances such as "cheerful winter," "miserable weather," and "hopeless wetness of the day," but they slip in appropriately and unobtrusively without detracting from the mood, tone, and sense of the weather, and neither do they halt the action.

---

[9] Gaskell would take Ruskin's *Modern Painters* to a "desert island" (Uglow 465).

As part of the fabric of the narratives, Gaskell's painterly writing includes careful, accurate observation of skyscape as well as landscape. The weather generates narrative drive, allows the reader to pause and, like the characters portrayed, have time for reflection. It can also be deterministic, control the structure, act as a plot device, create dramatic tension and "*atmosphere*," and highlight character. In Gaskell's late fiction, the weather is not the flat canvas on which the action is superimposed but an intricately woven part of the narrative because she perceived it as an integral part of life. Gaskell is writing from 40-year-old memories. Her purpose is not to write a scientific treatise but an appealing tale in which the much-loved and remembered landscape of Cheshire, which inspired her, is inextricably and, for her, ineluctably connected to the atmosphere. Gaskell's, perhaps slightly romanticized, hot, settled summers, her autumnal "mists of mellow fruitfulness," the deep penetrating frosts of winter and the changeability of unsettled weather are derived from daily, lived experience and her responses to different weather systems.

The structural design of both "Cousin Phillis" and *Wives and Daughters* owes much to Gaskell's skills as both landscape and biometeorologist. The narrative drive of "Cousin Phillis" is predicated on the changing seasons which indicate time passing and the action takes place mostly on the relatively isolated Hope Farm where the livelihood of the Holman family is dependent upon and determined by seasonal rhythms and the weather. To some extent the same is true of *Wives and Daughters*; the changing seasons are recorded faithfully but, true to its thematic content of the development of natural science, the signifiers are not hay, cereal apple, and kitchen garden harvests, but the natural landscape of flowering plants and trees which are evocatively described. In human terms, this theme is manifested in Roger, considered to be modeled on Gaskell's cousin, Charles Darwin, whose rapidly advancing research career as a naturalist takes him to the wilds of Abyssinia (*WD* 433). In fact, both novels have male protagonists whose scientifically oriented careers take them overseas. Their departures, which each leave behind broken hearts, are denoted by meteorological watersheds as the weather shifts from warm and hot settled anticyclonic weather to frontal system changeability, which brings wind and rain. The changing weather is manifest too, in the heroines' emotional and psychological states. For both Phillis's and Molly's hopes and expectations, mirrored in the fine settled weather, are dashed to disappointment and misery as the weather turns. Molly looks out at the "rain-blurred outer landscape"(514) from her home in Hollingford whilst the November winds blow down trees on Hope Farm as Holdsworth sails to Canada.

Weather Systems

Summer Anticyclones

Until Paul's first visit to Hope Farm, in "the soft September air" (*CP* 165), a year after he has arrived to take up his post in Eltham, there is *no* weather in "Cousin Phillis." From that occasion onwards though, the structure of the novella is based on the changing cycle of seasons which is dominated by anticyclonic conditions. These are high pressure systems of a single air mass which vary seasonally. In the summer their provenance is tropical, in the winter, polar. They are often prolonged as they "block" the prevailing westerly Atlantic airstreams and bring settled calm weather with usually sunny skies. The weather changes from summer heat to misty autumn mornings which are followed by the cold and snows of winter. The action takes place over a period of two and half years and can be seen as Gaskell's attempts at a fictionalized meteorological journal. The parallels between a letter to her sister-in-law in 1836 (*Letters* 5–6) and two passages in "Cousin Phillis" (162, 165) which depict Sandlebridge Farm in fact and fiction demonstrate this point. Although not specifically about the weather, the warm sunshine of a summer anticyclone can be "felt" in these evocations. In that letter too she reveals she has "brought Coleridge with me, & am *doing* him and Wordsworth [—] *fit place for the latter!*" (*Letters* 7). This reference to the Romantic poets makes a useful link to their preoccupations with nature and the topography of the sky and the weather. The weather, dominated by seasonal anticyclonic conditions, is depicted with exemplary accuracy as it determines the jobs undertaken on the farm and brings Paul and Phillis into close contact. The characteristic hot and dry weather, with cloudless blue skies and light winds which culminate in thunderstorms, appears in two consecutive summers in "Cousin Phillis" as her first encounter with the opposite sex develops into the loss of innocence and sexual awakening.[10]

The "near-scientific" exact meteorology with which Gaskell paints a picture of the hay-harvest in the first summer initiates the narrative drive and creates dramatic tension. She balances her skill both as writer and landscape meteorologist to fulfill Thornes's four criteria. The evening is "sultry," the weather "oppressive." The two adjectives create that somewhat ethereal, but tangible, sense of the "*atmosphere*" and how it feels as distinct from a visual description of the sky. Gaskell includes words such as sultry and oppressive to imply humidity, deliberately leaving the reader to make the leap imaginatively into the feelings of the characters in the story. In this respect, she contrasts, of course, with Constable, whose topographical skies are *seen* by the viewer rather than imagined by the reader. Gaskell proceeds to paint the *completely* still air via the *tiniest* of unmoving leaves. This utter lack of movement conveys *exactly* the state of the air *immediately before* a thunderstorm and thus highlights Gaskell's skill as a landscape meteorologist. Like an artist who can only paint the wind "indirectly" (Thornes, *Skies* 42), Gaskell's intention is evident. As she builds up to the climax of the thunderstorm, her attention to detail and her desire to create a perfectly accurate image and sense of the "*atmosphere*" at that moment renders the scene both sensually and realistically compelling (*CP* 200).

---

[10] John Constable, *The Cottage in the Cornfield* 1833 (Thornes plates 30 and 31, 111 and 112), depicts a habitation surrounded by arable farmland painted in the stillness of "fierce … cumulus. That lonely cottage by the ripening corn will hardly escape a crashing storm that afternoon" (109). Bonacina's (1937) description appears to exactly echo the scene painted by Gaskell of the hay harvest just before the first thunderstorm.

Having established the "*atmosphere*," the topography of the sky is sparingly described by the visual and poetic use of two words, "clouded light" (*CP* 200). The "gathering dark clouds" (*CP* 201) mask the sun, reduce light levels, and intensify heat to create "*atmospheric oppression*," encapsulating *exactly* what happens as a thunderstorm approaches. The heating of the ground during anticyclones causes the unstable air to rise and eventually the water vapor will condense to form high vertical rain-bearing electrically charged clouds known as thunder-clouds. The storm breaks with "blinding lightning and rumble and quick-following rattling peal of thunder right over our heads" (*CP* 201). Gaskell would have known from both experience and, perhaps, careful observation and teaching as a child in the countryside, that if thunder and lightning, that is, onomatopoeic sound and light, occur simultaneously, it is because the storm is directly overhead. Although not specified in meteorological terms, it is possible to deduce from Gaskell's description is that she is portraying sheet rather than fork lightning (Connelly 56, Pretor-Pinney 65).[11] The "blinding lightning" has probably occurred "within the cloud," which is the most common form of the manifestation of the discharge of electricity as it is redistributed between negatively charged ice crystals and positively charged water droplets, both of which can be found within these towering columns of cloud (Pretor-Pinney 65). As the electricity is discharged, it instantaneously heats the air along its path, initially generating a distant "rumble" of noise and then, as the whole path is heated, the thunder registers as a sharper, more sudden "rattling peal" which is heard by those on the ground "out yonder" (*CP* 201). Without the epic proportions of Virgil, or Turner's "sublime,"[12] Gaskell economically, objectively, accurately, and realistically describes the tumultuous processes taking place so that the thunderstorm assails the senses of the reader both audibly and visually:

> I saw the three ... their heads, joined together in an eager group over Holdsworth's theodolite ... I was wanted to assist, and was quickly set to work to hold the chain ... So we went on, the dark clouds still gathering, for perhaps five minutes

---

[11]   George Eliot and Charlotte Brontë notably employ thunderstorms in their fiction for dramatic purposes. George Eliot's lightning is like Gaskell's within-cloud, sheet lightning (Eliot 760), whereas in *Jane Eyre* the fork lightning splits the tree in two (Brontë 269). Fork lightning is air-to-ground lightning which follows the easiest path to the ground. All these instances are used by their authors to provide dramatic tension between their two protagonists.

[12]   In Wilkinson's translation, Virgil depicts an epic rather than realistic thunderstorm in Book 1 of his *Georgics*. "Clouds roll and roll together an ugly storm / of murky rain. Down headlong falls the sky / in sheets / ... The Father himself in the midmost night of cloud / Wields thunderbolts amain" (Lines 323–5, 329–30). Turner's *Valley of Aosta* depicts a skyscape full of tumult which owes more to Ruskin's description of the topography of Turner's skies when he likens the thunder-clouds to colossal mountains with "edgy summits" and invokes his much-derided use of pathetic fallacy throughout. Gaskell's realistic artistry appears to owe little to either of these possible formative influences on *Cousin Phillis* (Ruskin, vol. 1 251).

after my arrival. Then came the blinding lightning and the rumble and quick-following rattling peal of thunder right over our heads. It came sooner ... than they had looked for: the rain delayed not; it came pouring down; and what were we to do for shelter? Phillis had nothing on but her indoor things-no bonnet, no shawl. (*CP* 201)

Gaskell is masterly in narrating a dramatic moment that operates on several different levels. The artistic intent can be deduced from her use of sheet lightning. It sheds light upon the *whole* scene rather than pinpointing one spot which might not be the shelter of the overhanging sandbank where the characters are in close physical proximity. Here the atmosphere lends a sense of power to the scene. It represents the power that Holdsworth wields over Phillis's emotions and her own empowerment as a rapidly maturing woman who signifies by the absence of bonnet and shawl a radical break from parental over-protection.

Technological scientific innovation is woven into vividly realized skyscape and weather which carries symbolic and metaphorical overtones. Ebenezer, a typically phlegmatic farmer used to judging the weather, seems to be aware of the tumult and the impending rain. However, he hopes that the storm would delay long enough to allow them time to see Holdsworth's demonstration of the practicality of the theodolite. The tension and narrative drive is generated by atmospheric processes as Phillis, conscious of Holdsworth's magnetic attraction, is jolted out of her isolated innocence. The combination of the heat and atmospheric tumult both symbolizes the emotional upheaval within Phillis and provides dramatic tension. It also carries implications of change for small relatively isolated rural communities like Hornby, and its individual families, for Holdsworth represents externally induced technological change through the potentially useful theodolite and engineering innovation in the form of the railway, which is the underpinning *raison d'être* of the story. Such innovation is the context of Burroughs's essay as he seeks to establish how the railway increased the mobility of people and their accessibility to place, especially the coast.

The subsequent onset of "pouring rain" determines the action, at once generating narrative drive and increasing the pace and dramatic tension as the completely unprepared characters "hurry" to seek the inadequate shelter of the sandbank.[13] Gaskell consummately dramatizes this scene, bringing it to a climax when Phillis comes into contact with Holdsworth's wet shirt:

Quick as the darting lightning around us, Holdsworth took off his coat and wrapped it round her neck and shoulders, and, almost without a word, hurried us all into such poor shelter as one of the overhanging sand-banks could give. There we were, cowered down, close together, Phillis innermost, almost too tightly packed to free her arms enough to divest herself of the coat, which she, in her turn, tried to put lightly over Holdsworth's shoulders. In doing so she touched his shirt. (*CP* 201)

---

[13] The inspiration for the sandbank is likely to have been derived from her familiarity with the sandy heath that characterizes Alderley Edge in Cheshire. Twinn, 1999, 372–3.

The touch, intentional or inadvertent—the reader must decide—is mirrored in the sky's electrical discharge as the lightning flashes. As the thunder dies away, Holdsworth "said something gravely, and in a too low a tone for me to hear" (*CP* 201). It could be argued that his tone echoes the thunder. Modern readers, in decoding this scene, would not be in any doubt about Gaskell's understated erotic innuendo as they would note that the scene begins and ends with the use of the word "intercourse." However, for the Victorian reader her intentions might not have been so clear (Little, Fowler, and Coulson 1025).[14] It is likely, however, that the erotic connotations of the light and power of the thunderstorm may have resonated with the Victorian reader. This visual evocation of a summer anticyclone, although sparing in its topographical detail of the skies, is sensual for the realism of its "*atmospheric*," sultry culmination in a thunderstorm.

The interpretation of the term "*atmosphere*" can perhaps be fully appreciated by considering the second spell of anticyclonic weather in "Cousin Phillis." Gaskell unequivocally states her belief in biometeorology here. By juxtaposing the weather with a physiological effect she sees it as a "provoking factor" (Larner 99) in its influence on health and well-being. In fact this is not the only occasion that Mrs. Holman feels unwell due to the oppressive heat but on this occasion she has retreated to bed having succumbed to a headache. "Yes; there is thunder about. Mother has had to go to bed with *one* of her bad headaches," Phillis explains to Paul (*CP* 223, emphasis added).[15] The word "one" is suggestive of a recurrent state. However, not only is the weather responsible for the headache, but it is also a useful plot device, as her absence leaves Paul free to divulge the contents of the letter he has received from Holdsworth, now in Canada, announcing that he has married. This is a turning point in the story for Phillis as her hopes and expectations of his return are dashed. It is clear from the foregoing discussion about Gaskell as a biometeorologist that she integrates imaginative, metaphorical "weather-sensitive" issues ineluctably into her meteorological realism to reinforce the fusion between science and the imaginative life of her characters.

Gaskell's fondness for embedding her artistic aims into anticyclone weather is continued in *Wives and Daughters*. If, as Thornes states, "the atmosphere is an integral part of every landscape" (*Skies* 18), there are no better examples than these two moments of quiet contemplation. Pauses provide Gaskell with an opportunity to slow the narrative and reveal the psychological reality of the character who is center stage. Mr. Gibson is at the heart of two of these pauses. On his journey to Hamley to break the news to Molly of his impending marriage, he stops under an elm tree in the summer heat wave apparently to watch the "early harvest" of oats but really to delay the evil moment of imparting unwelcome news:

> It was a *brilliantly hot* summer's morning; men in their *shirt-sleeves* were in the fields getting in the *early* harvest of oats; as Mr. Gibson rode *slowly* along, he

---

14 The *Shorter Oxford Dictionary* dates the sexual connection originating in 1798.

15 Gaskell herself was susceptible to headaches for which she blamed the weather and the air of Manchester (Larner 99).

could see them over the *tall* hedge-rows, and even hear the *soothing measured* sound of the fall of the *long* swathes, as they were mown. The labourers seemed too hot to talk; the dog, guarding their coats and cans, lay panting *loudly* on the other side of the elm under which Mr. Gibson stopped for an instant to survey the scene. (*WD* 112, emphasis added)

The anticyclonic conditions are realized by the use of the two words "brilliantly hot" as the sun shining out of a clear sky transfers its heat via the ground to the atmosphere. Moreover, the sense of the intense heat is conveyed by its effects on the figures and the dog in the landscape, all of whom are attempting in their own ways to adjust to the high temperature. As a landscape meteorologist, Gaskell creates a deterministically weather-laden scene economically, effectively, and "*atmospherically.*" This is a "moment of being" (Woolf, Title page) for Mr. Gibson. The soft sibilants, the "ly" of the adverbs and the "o" of the vowels soothe Mr. Gibson's senses as he pauses to contemplate the harvest before he has to face his difficult task of telling his much-loved daughter of his impending marriage.

Autumn Anticyclones
It is autumn on the second occasion and the season here is manifest through the detailed description of nature. Once again, Mr. Gibson is riding to Hamley Hall in the knowledge that Osborne is terminally ill and Roger is leaving on a prolonged expedition to Africa. As a doctor, Gibson is in a quandary, because he is uncertain as to how much the squire should be made aware of the truth of Osborne's state of health:

> So he rode on, meditating; his reins slack, his head a little bent. It was one of those still and lovely autumn days when the red and yellow leaves are hanging-pegs to dewy, brilliant gossamer-webs; when the hedges are full of trailing brambles, loaded with ripe blackberries; when the air is full of the farewell whistles and pipes of birds; clear and short – not the long full-throated warbles of spring; when the whirr of the partridge's wing is heard in the stubble-fields, as the sharp hoof-blows fall on the paved lanes; when here and there a leaf floats down and flutters to the ground, although there is not a single breath of wind. (*WD* 382)

Although reluctant to admit his weather sensitivity, Gibson's mood *is* determined by the seasonal weather. Gaskell uses the scene to comment on the underlying humanity and sentient being that lurk beneath the apparently brusque, severe, sarcastic, and business-like exterior of the doctor by remarking,

> The country surgeon felt the beauty of the seasons perhaps more than most men. He saw it at all times of day and night and in all weathers. He never spoke about what he felt on the subject; indeed, he did not put his feelings into words, even to himself. But if his mood ever approached to the sentimental, it was on such days as this. (*WD* 382)

The weight of responsibility that lies upon Gibson's shoulders as a respected clinician and his sense of that responsibility are revealed as the narrative slows.

This pause allows Gaskell to focus on the internalization of her character as well as giving the reader a clue to her own weather sensitivity.

Winter Anticyclones
Gaskell's depiction of an intense winter anticyclone echoes the foregoing autumn in terms of its integration of nature into the scene. Molly, despite the intense cold, escapes into the garden at Hamley Hall prior to her imminent departure after a prolonged stay as Mrs. Hamley's companion (*WD* 216–17). Mrs. Hamley is dying, Osborne and his father are at loggerheads, Roger has returned and is trying to keep the peace, and Molly feels unwanted and "passionately unhappy" (*WD* 216):

> Now, the trees leafless, there was no sweet odour in the keen frosty air; and looking up at the house, there were white sheets of blinds, shutting out the pale winter sky from the invalid's room. Then she thought of the day her father had brought her news of his second marriage: the thicket was tangled with dead weeds and rime and hoar-frost; and the beautiful, fine articulations of branches and boughs and delicate twigs were all intertwined in leafless distinctness against the sky ... The afternoon sun was shining brightly on the windows; and, stirred up to unusual activity by some unknown cause, the housemaids had opened the shutters and windows. (*WD* 216)

The meteorological power of this scene comes from the very carefully observed, pale, winter sky and the frost which adorns the vegetation. The use of technical meteorological terms and the distinction made between hoar frost and rime demonstrate more than a layman's knowledge of such conditions. It is likely that this knowledge is derived both from the "continuing existence" of Gaskell's memories of her Cheshire childhood and a desire to be "an objective recorder" (Uglow 211). Not only do they form as a result of different processes, but there is a subtle difference in texture between hoar frost and rime.[16] In this case the frost was part of "the thicket tangled with dead weeds." Whilst accurate and realistic, the frosted, uncared for, decaying vegetation also symbolizes Molly's confusion about being needed, her own dying hopes, and Mrs. Hamley's impending death. The pale winter sky is an accurate reflection of such seasonal skies when the afternoon sun reflects all wave lengths to create almost white skies.

As a landscape meteorologist, Gaskell repeats the pattern of accuracy alongside the imaginative and metaphorical to slow the narrative and reflect the

---

[16]   Hoar-frost forms on clear nights with little wind when the temperature falls below freezing. The temperature of objects, like vegetation, is less than $0°$ C. It may occur due to the freezing of water droplets or sublimation that is when water vapor turns directly to ice. Rime is the result of below-freezing air in which super-cooled droplets of water are suspended. When they come into contact with surfaces the temperature of which are also below freezing point, they freeze to form white deposit. The texture is denser than that of hoar frost and is an index of intense, prolonged cold. The blanketing effect of the rime may signify Molly's imperative to supress her true feelings as she returns home to her father and new stepmother.

psychological realism of Molly. Interestingly, despite the fact that Constable went to great pains to depict accurate skies, Thornes detects that he also included an imaginative element in his paintings and was not above adding optical effects like rainbows when it suited his composition (Thornes, "Skies" 200). Perhaps Ruskin would have been delighted with both writer and painter for portraying the "truth about skies" which included an imaginative dimension. A moment of tranquillity in the garden identifiable by the weather represents not only a narrative pause as Molly confronts the reality of her situation but is, also, a prelude to a dramatic moment when Molly, on returning to the house, learns that Osborne has secretly married. At this point the narrative increases in pace.

Frontal Weather

It has been established in the foregoing discussion that the meteorological watershed that appears in Gaskell's final works focus on the change from anticyclonic to frontal systems. The latter, like anticyclones, are ineluctably linked to mood psyche and emotions. Frontal weather, described by Richard Mabey as "insidious rain and grey skies" (8), brings a range of unsettled conditions from prolonged unceasing rain, to sunshine and showers but, so often, it brings cloudy, windy days. Like thunderstorms, wind represents atmospheric disturbance. One noteworthy scene in *Wives and Daughters* is heralded by two apposite chapter headings: "Gathering Clouds" (Chapter XLI) and "The Storm Bursts" (Chapter XLII). To illustrate the dysfunctional relationship between Cynthia and Preston, which is characterized by his bullying blackmail and her deception, Gaskell depicts unsettled weather. Molly, sustained by her scruples, has agreed to act as mediator in order to retrieve seven letters in exchange for loaned money so that Preston will not use the letters to compel Cynthia to honor her promise to marry him: "Molly set out on her walk towards the appointed place. It was a cloudy, blustering day, and the noise of the blowing wind among the nearly leafless branches of the great trees filled her ears, as she passed through the park-gates and entered the avenue" (*WD* 503). The noisy tumult of the "blustering, blowing wind" works on several levels. It enables Molly to block out the thought of the hated "errand" (*WD* 503). The atmospheric disturbance symbolizes the human frailty of Cynthia and Preston in their different ways, and is thus a considered emphasis on the power of secrets, deception and human discord to undermine morality in the close-knit community of Hollingford. Standing, buffeted by the wind, their extended dialogue shows Gaskell revealing character and developing plot, with the intensity of feelings which can be interpreted as the human equivalent to the discord of the elements. Given the inclement weather, the reader is left with the sense that nature and human nature are not only co-existent, but, in a sense, unified at such moments.

Unsettled weather may facilitate the action, develop the plot, and highlight character in the same way that fine settled weather may be able to do. In the cases which follow, the inextricable, inescapable and deterministic links between the weather, physiology and the human psyche are apparent. Rain and blustery winds confine characters to their homes and influence their moods. Gaskell realistically evokes the familiar sense of a wet Sunday afternoon causing Squire Hamley to miss church thus making the time seem interminable because of the unrelenting rain:

> They had dined early; they always did on Sundays; and either that, or the sermon, or the hopeless wetness of the day, made the afternoon seem interminably long to the squire … To-day it had rained so unceasingly that he had remitted the afternoon church; but oh, even with the luxury of a nap, how long it had seemed before he saw the Hall servants trudging homewards, along the field-path, a covey of umbrellas! (*WD* 452)

Later that afternoon the squire picks a fight with his eldest son, Osborne, about his marriage intentions and his future, thus causing friction between them. Although, perhaps, the text is equivocal, it is possible to detect that the squire's low spirits and boredom are caused by a combination of dismally wet weather and his anxieties about his son, thus provoking the squabble.

During Roger's absence, on a wet evening, both Mrs. Gibson and Molly are subject to a depression of spirits, which is described thus: "it was a gloomy, rainy evening," Molly and Mrs. Gibson are sitting at "their worsted work, pattering away at small-talk … Molly was … uneasy about many apprehended cares and troubles … and the rain-blurred outer landscape seemed steeped with unpleasant associations" (*WD* 514). The weather perfectly reflects Molly's psychological reality here. Mrs. Gibson then remarks, "To be sure, love, it would be very nice for you and me to go a little journey all by ourselves … If it were not such miserable weather we would have gone off on an little impromptu tour." Molly, in an uncharacteristic response, blames the weather: "Yes! We are very forlorn to-night; but I think it's partly owing to the weather!" (*WD* 515).

Of course, the narrator and reader, like Molly, are aware that the weather is not the only cause of Molly's mood. In part, it is because Cynthia is the recipient of Roger's letters. It is instructive to note that there is a transference of the psychological reality of the character onto the weather outside and an acknowledgment of this by Mrs. Gibson. She also reveals, probably unknowingly, an aspect of her personality as she replies:

> Nonsense, dear. I can't have you giving in to the silly fancy of being affected by weather. Poor dear Mr. Kirkpatrick used to say, "a cheerful heart makes its own sunshine." He would say it to me, in his pretty way, whenever I was a little low – for I am a complete barometer – you may really judge of the state of the weather by my spirits. I have always been such a sensitive creature! (*WD* 515)

This scene slows the narrative as Gaskell, with acute insight and imaginative sensitivity, reveals Molly's mood and feelings and demonstrates that Mrs. Gibson is as capricious as the weather. Throughout the novel Gaskell has created a "silly" woman in Mrs. Gibson. Consequently the reader is aware that she cannot possibly be a reliable barometer of the weather. Cleverly and subtly Gaskell puts the spotlight on her weaknesses. Having admonished Molly for "a silly fancy" she admits to her own causal susceptibility.

Conclusion

As the foregoing discussion has demonstrated, Gaskell's most evocative portrayal of the meteorological landscape features prominently in her last two works. She viewed the atmosphere both visually and sensitively and wanted her readers and her characters to have the same experience. Both dimensions of the atmosphere informed and enriched her writing to engender plot control, narrative drive and character portrayal. Hence, she wrote with "near-scientific" meteorological accuracy and sensitivity which were derived from "lived experience" of her early years in Cheshire. Manchester too, later in her life, emphasized this "weather sensitivity" due to its depressing winter smogs, endlessly short day lengths and the sultry conditions of summer thunderstorms, which, she believed, produced headaches.[17]

Whilst writers from Chaucer onwards throughout the canon of English literature have incorporated the weather into their novels, few, if any, have showcased the *science* of meteorology in such a demonstrable and particularized manner. However, as an aspect of literary criticism the weather has been overlooked. Perhaps it is time to address this oversight. Bonacina's ground-breaking work provided the inspiration for this brief interdisciplinary study linking Gaskell's artistic techniques to the accuracy of her meteorological descriptions. Based on these findings, there seems to be an opportunity for further research to establish the interaction of scientific and will reveal aspects of Gaskell artistic representation of the weather in the imaginative realm of fiction.

The weather continues to play a deterministic role in our lives, despite modern technology, due to the inextricable human link to the envelope of air which surrounds the earth's surface. Consequently, the weather is an inescapable part of both the physical and human environment and is, therefore, an entirely appropriate part of any work of fiction. It is hoped that this close inter-textual reading of "Cousin Phillis" and *Wives and Daughters* will reveal Gaskell as a first-rate innovative writer and a master of fine detail, which enhances her narratives in an unself-conscious understated way whilst at the same time drawing the reader visually and sensitively into her imagined worlds.

Works Cited

Austen, Jane. *Emma*. 1816. Ed. Ronald Blythe. Harmondsworth: Penguin, 1966. Print.

Bentley, P. and J. Ogden. *Haworth of the Brontës*. Suffolk: Terence Dalton, 1977. Print.

Bonacina, L.C.W. "John Constable's Centenary: His position as a painter of weather." *Quarterly Journal of the Royal Meteorological Society* 63 (1937): 485–90. Print.

---

[17]   *Letters*, Ed. Chapple and Pollard, 1966, 606.

———. "Landscape Meteorology and its Reflection in Art and Literature." *Quarterly Journal of the Royal Meteorological Society* 65 (1939): 485–97. Print.

Catalogue of the Art Treasures of the United Kingdom collected at Manchester 1857. 2nd ed. Manchester: Bradbury and Evans, 1857. Print.

Chapple, J.A.V. *Elizabeth Gaskell: The Early Years.* Manchester: Manchester UP, 1997. Print.

———. *Science and Literature in the Nineteenth Century.* London: Macmillan, 1987. Print.

Connelly, Charlie. *Bring Me Sunshine.* London: Little, Brown, 2012. Print.

Forster, Thomas. *Researches about Atmospheric Phaenomena.* 2nd ed. London: Baldwin, Cradock and Joy, 1815. Print.

Gaskell, Elizabeth. *Cousin Phillis and Other Stories.* Ed. Heather Glen. Oxford: Oxford UP, 2010. Print.

———. *The Letters of Mrs Gaskell.* Ed. J.A.V. Chapple and Arthur Pollard. Manchester: Manchester UP, 1966. Print.

———. *Wives and Daughters.* 1865. Ed. Angus Easson. Oxford: Oxford UP, 1987. Print.

Hampstead Scientific Society. *Hampstead Heath: Its Geology and Natural History.* London: T. Fisher Unwin, 1913. Print.

Hill, D. *Constable's Landscape Scenery.* London: Guild, 1985. Print.

Howard, L. "On the Modification of Clouds." *The Philosophical Magazine.* 16 (1803): 97–107. Print.

Larner, A.J. "A Habit of Headaches; The Neurological Case of Elizabeth Gaskell." *Gaskell Society Journal* 25 (2011): 97–103. Print.

Little, W., H.W. Fowler, and H. Coulson. *The Shorter Oxford English Dictionary.* 3rd ed. Oxford; Clarendon, 1933. Print.

Mabey, Richard. *Turned Out Nice Again.* London: Profile Books, 2013. Print.

Mullan, John. *What Matters in Jane Austen?* London: Bloomsbury, 2012. Print.

Nisbet, Euan. "In Retrospect." *Nature* 388 (10 July 1997): 137. Print.

Pretor-Pinney, Gavin. *The Cloud Spotters Guide.* London: Sceptre, 2006. Print.

Reed, A. *Romantic Weather: The Climates of Coleridge and Baudelaire.* London: U of New England P, 1983. Print.

Ruskin, John. *Modern Painters.* 5 vols. 3rd ed. London: George Allen, 1900. Print.

Thornes, John. "Constable's Clouds." *The Burlington Magazine* 121 (November 1979): 679–704. Print.

———. "Constable's Meteorological Understanding and his Painting of Skies." *Constable's Clouds Paintings and Cloud Studies.* Ed. Edward Morris. National Gallery of Scotland and National Museums and Galleries. Merseyside, 2000. 151–9. Print.

———. *John Constable's Skies. A Fusion of Art and Science.* Birmingham: U of Birmingham P, 1999. Print.

———. "Luke Howard's Influence on Art and Literature in the Early 19c." *Weather* 39 (1984): 252–5. Print.

Twinn, Frances Elizabeth. *The Landscapes of Elizabeth Gaskell's Writing.* Unpublished doctoral dissertation. University of Durham. 1999. Print.

Uglow, Jenny. *Elizabeth Gaskell, A Habit of Stories.* London: Faber, 1993. Print.

Virgil. *The Georgics.* Book 1. Trans. L.P. Wilkinson. London: Penguin, 1982. Print.

Waugh, Joanne, Sarah. *Talking about the Weather: Climate and the Victorian Novel.* Unpublished doctoral dissertation. University of York, 2008. Print.

"Weather." *Cornhill Magazine* 2 (1860): 565–79. Print.

Woolf, Virginia. *Moments of Being.* London: Chatto and Windus for Sussex UP, 1976. Print.

Chapter 14
Women's Voices in the Pre-Raphaelite Space of Elizabeth Gaskell's Novels

Sophia Andres

Gaskell's familiarity with the three founders of the Pre-Raphaelite brotherhood, Dante Gabriel Rossetti, William Holman Hunt, and John Everett Millais, is attested in several of her letters. In a letter to Rossetti in 1859, for instance, she profusely apologizes for her error in her address (Back End instead of Bank End) and piquantly justifies the long explanation of her error "as a proof of my very pre-raphaelite love of accuracy," an awareness which is evidenced in her novels, as I will demonstrate. In the same letter she thanks him for the copy of his translation of *Vita Nuova* and suggests that he change a couple of words "which cause the line to strike my ear as unrhythmical" (*Further Letters* 199–200). Later in the same year, in a letter to Charles Norton, she describes her encounters with Rossetti in her characteristically humorous tone:

> I think we got to know Rossetti pretty well. I went three times to his studio, and met him at two evening parties—where I had a good deal of talk with him, always excepting the times when ladies with beautiful hair came in when he was like the cat turned into a lady, who jumped out of bed and ran after a mouse. It did not signify what we were talking about or how agreeable I was; if a particular kind of reddish brown, crêpe wavy hair came in, he was away in a moment struggling for an introduction to the owner of said head of hair. He is not as mad as a March hare, but hair-mad. (*Letters* 444)

In a way this incident wittingly captures Gaskell's love of Pre-Raphaelite accuracy and illustrates the transfiguration of a perceptual moment into different modes of artistic expression: the painter transposing an actual woman into a subject of one of his paintings and the writer transforming the paintings into verbal images. In the same letter Gaskell recounts her emotionally charged response to Rossetti's and William Holman Hunt's paintings: "And then we saw Holman Hunt's picture, & Holman Hunt's self. I am not going to define & shape my feelings & thoughts at seeing either Rossetti's or Hunt's pictures into words; because I *did* feel them deeply, & after all words are coarse things." Referring to Millais's paintings the *Order of Release 1746* (1852–1853) and *The Proscribed Royalist* (1852–1853) in a letter to John Forster in April 1853, she remarks, "Is not Millais' picture this year beautiful" (*Letters* 155). And to her daughter Marianne she writes two years later, "Mrs. Price comes & picks us up, and takes us on in *her* carriage to see Millais's Pictures" (*Letters* 234a). Her letters containing references to Pre-Raphaelite artists, as well as to contemporary newspapers and journals that reviewed Pre-Raphaelite art, are too numerous to mention here. Undoubtedly by 1853, when *Ruth* was published, Gaskell had read reviews of Pre-Raphaelite art, was familiar with their aesthetic principles, and must have eagerly sought their paintings in art exhibits, prints or engravings. Her interest in the Pre-Raphaelites, as her letters attest, continued till the end of her life.

Major Gaskell critics like Linda Hughes, Audrey Jaffe, and Deirdre d'Albertis, have explored Gaskell's unorthodox treatment of the theme of the fallen woman; however, they overlook its Pre-Raphaelite subtext. Gail Marshall, though she refers to representations of female sexuality in Pre-Raphaelite paintings, does not directly relate any of these paintings to Gaskell's novels (44–5). In her chapter in this volume, Divya Athnamathan makes thematic connections between the scene of Margaret's embrace of Thornton during the factory workers' strike *in North and South* (1854) and Millais's popular paintings: *The Order of Release* 1746 (1852–1853), *Huguenot* (1851–1852), and *Peace Concluded* (1856). Racheal Bloom briefly discusses the similarities between Gaskell's writing and Pre-Raphaelite paintings (qtd. in Silkü 104), whereas Jenny Uglow, referring to *Ruth* in particular, remarks, "Gaskell's novel is erotic in the manner of Pre-Raphaelite paintings" (329). By presenting Ruth's beauty as the cause of her victimization, Gaskell, according to Hilary Schor, exposes a woman's precarious existence in a culture that worships feminine beauty:

> For Rossetti and the Pre-Raphaelites, a woman's only story is her beauty made into narrative, that is, when she is seen by a man ... Gaskell, on the other hand, refuses to ignore the possibility that a woman's beauty is a fact not in an abstract oral or aesthetic situation, but in a very real context in a socially determined world. (166)

Though Bloom, Uglow, and Schor recognize the influence of Pre-Raphaelite art on Elizabeth Gaskell's novels, they overlook Gaskell's ekphrasis to specific Pre-Raphaelite paintings and the significance of Gaskell's interweaving the visual with the textual. Here I propose to discuss the Pre-Raphaelite subtextual space in *Ruth* (1853) and *Sylvia's Lovers* (1863) as the site where silenced women, and by extension Gaskell's readers, are empowered to articulate their voices. In her novels, Gaskell emulates Pre-Raphaelite techniques and subjects, but most importantly, she explores the role of Pre-Raphaelite visual art in the endorsement and subversion of gender stereotypes. More specifically, in the subtext of her novels she creates a space where she re-draws popular Pre-Raphaelite paintings, raising questions not only about established gender constructs, but also about Pre-Raphaelite gendered boundaries. Subtly embedded within the subtextual space of *Ruth* and *Sylvia's Lovers*, Gaskell's narrative reconfigurations of Pre-Raphaelite paintings are not merely echoes of these paintings but rather attempts to further extend Pre-Raphaelite gendered boundaries and reveal the constraints imposed on women even in seemingly liberal or untraditional Pre-Raphaelite representations. Gaskell's transformations of Pre-Raphaelite paintings into narrative scenes simultaneously reveal her engagement with contemporary debates on gender issues and disclose her efforts to empower women by redrawing Pre-Raphaelite representations that, even though seemingly unconventional, often perpetuated traditional gender roles.

In her engagement with Pre-Raphaelite art in her novels, Gaskell does not merely make reference to Pre-Raphaelite paintings, but also gives voice to the subjects of these paintings. In the process, as Shuttleworth explains, Gaskell opens up "the silent spaces of history" (256). This impalpable, intangible space of ekphrasis is, as Heffernan reminds us, a space of "speaking out" or "telling in full" (1). The meaning of ekphrasis, he suggests, is bound to its function, for "besides representational friction and the turning of fixed forms into narrative, ekphrasis entails prosopopeia, or the rhetorical technique of envoicing a silent object. Ekphrasis speaks not only *about* works of art but also *to* and *for* them" (6–7). Heffernan's assertion about ekphrasis is directly relevant to Gaskell's fiction, for through the reconfiguration of Pre-Raphaelite pictorial, static representations of women into narrative, dynamic images, Gaskell breaks the silence of stereotypical, passive female figures, giving them, and, by extension her readers, the voice to resist the dominant tradition. Simultaneously, unlike those Pre-Raphaelite artists who inscribe women's limitations in their paintings, Elizabeth Gaskell empowers her female readers by offering possibilities and at times the means by which they may become agents of social change in spite of their dire circumstances.

The Voice of Pre-Raphaelite Subjects in the Subtextual Space of *Ruth*

In a passage pivotal to the novel, yet often overlooked by critics, Gaskell alludes at the very beginning of *Ruth* to the rare possibilities which resistance to the dominant tradition may offer:

> The daily life into which people are born, and into which they are absorbed before they are well aware, form chains which only one in a hundred has moral strength enough to despise, and to break when the right time comes—when an inward necessity for independent individual action arises, which is superior to all outward conventionalities. (4)

In 1851, when the memory of the hostile reception of *Mary Barton* (1848) was still painful, Elizabeth Gaskell undertook the task of breaking the chains of tradition by composing *Ruth*, a daring novel about a teenage woman with an illegitimate child. As in *Mary Barton*, in *Ruth* Gaskell had the moral strength to defy convention, for she felt vindicated by the power of her utterance. In a letter to Lady Kay-Shuttleworth, she begins by relating the adverse and extreme response to the novel, but continues certain of the significance of her achievement, echoing the message she conveys in the beginning of her novel: "[I]t has made them talk and think a little on a subject which is so painful that it requires all one's bravery not to hide one's head like an ostrich and try by doing so to forget that the evil exists (*Letters* 154). No doubt, Gaskell identified with the Pre-Raphaelites who also sought to break the chains of tradition by their courageous rebellion against the Royal Academy. Brushstroke by brushstroke, Gaskell redraws contemporary paintings, not in just one scene but throughout the novel, thus engaging her readers to actively collaborate in the creation of her text, enabling them to see the unseen figures of the past and hear their silenced voices.

When Ruth first encounters Bellingham at the ball, where she mends his partner's dress, he offers her a white camellia in an attempt to attenuate the impact of Miss Duncombe's impertinence. Ruth returns home enraptured by the "exquisite beauty" of the "perfect" and "pure" flower and talks to her friend Jenny about it till she falls asleep. In the early morning, Jenny notices Ruth's happy face as she dreams smiling: "'She is dreaming of last night,' thought Jenny. It was true she was; but one figure flitted more than all the rest through her visions. He presented flower after flower to her in that baseless morning dream which was all too quickly ended" (17). As in the scene of Annunciation in Rossetti's *Ecce Ancilla Domini* (1850), Ruth's dream takes place in the early morning. Inscribed on the frame of this painting, Rossetti's sonnet, "Mary's Girlhood," conveys Mary's psychological state:

> Till one dawn, at home,
> She woke in her white bed, and had no fear
> At all,—yet wept till sunshine, and felt awed;
> Because the fullness of the time was come. (11–14)

Here Rossetti represents a conventional scene in highly unconventional, erotic overtones: "The startling fact that we are witnessing the conception together with the Annunciation is made clear by the stunned expression of the girl" (Smith 87). Gaskell also re-draws this painting with sexual subtlety, adumbrating Ruth's future pregnancy in Ruth's dream of Bellingham. Later in the novel, when she keeps vigil during Bellingham's illness and is startled by the splendid sunrise, we find her in an awkward pose echoing Mary's in Rossetti's painting: "She sat curled up upon the floor, with her head thrown back against the wall, and her hands clasped round her knees" (69). To Mrs. Bellingham, who suddenly opens the door to her sick son's room, Ruth, in her white dress against the wall, appears like a "white apparition" (70). These scenes of Ruth's awkward poses, or her astonished, vulnerable gaze, or her standing in a "long, soft white dressing gown, with all her luxuriant hair hanging disheveled down her figure" (117), strikingly correspond to Christina Rossetti's appearance as the Virgin Mary in *Ecce Ancilla Domini*. By associating Ruth with the Virgin Mary, Gaskell defies and elides the conventional distinction between the polarized Victorian gender oppositions: the Virgin and the fallen woman. Like Rossetti, she subverts female stereotypes entrenched in tradition and invites her readers to identify with individuals and their often extraordinary situations, rather than accepting and perpetuating established stereotypes.

Gaskell's choice of such Pre-Raphaelite paintings as *Ophelia* (1851–1852) and *Mariana* (1851) reveals her determination to undermine feminine passivity and silence endorsed by conventional representations in literature and art. On a walk in

Fig. 14.1   John Everett Millais, "Ophelia," 1851–1852. By permission of
Bridgeman Art Library International, New York.

the woods during their stay in Wales, Bellingham and Ruth come across a "circular pool overshadowed by trees," replete with water lilies. Bellingham, struck by their beauty, gathers a few and proceeds to create his own painting:

> When he came back he took off her bonnet, without speaking, and began to place his flowers in her hair … She stood in her white dress against the trees which grew around; her face was flushed into a brilliancy of colour which resembled that of a rose in June; the great heavy white flowers drooped on either side of her beautiful head, and if her brown hair was a little disordered, the very disorder only seemed to add a grace. (61–2)

Here in her redrawing of *Ophelia*, Gaskell, like Arthur Hughes, through her choice of the crown of flowers, foreshadows Ruth's martyrdom, underscored by her constant sighs to Bellingham's utter irritation. Hughes's painting, depicting Ophelia before her suicide, captures, as Rhodes points out "neither tuberculosis, or even madness, but the wasting diseases of waiting and desire" (51).

The details of this scene also evoke Millais's *Ophelia* (see Figure 14.1). Like Millais's *Ophelia*, Ruth is surrounded by an abundance of plants, trees, and flowers; in this respect, Gaskell's pond resembles more that of Millais than of Hughes. At one point Gaskell evokes the rose floating by Ophelia's figure, in Millais's painting, when she refers to Ruth's face "flushed into a brilliancy of colour which resembled that of a rose in June" (61). It is interesting to note a review of the painting in the *Athenaeum*, which underscores Ophelia's passivity and silence: "There is no pathos, no melancholy, no one brightening up, no last lucid interval. If she dies swan-like with a song there is no sound or melody, no poetry in this strain" ("Royal Academy" 581). The reviewer's description of Ophelia is based primarily on negation: no sound, no melody, no voice. Focusing on silence and absence, the reviewer deprives Ophelia of subjectivity and individuality, relegating her to the stereotype of victimized, passive, silent femininity. Gaskell, however, extricates Ruth from that stereotype by giving Ruth a voice and a subjectivity. Though she does return to the pond soon after Bellingham abandons her with the intention of committing suicide, she is deterred by Benson's cry of pain when he falls over a sharp rock, and she rushes instead to his rescue.

Unlike Ophelia then, Ruth does not yield to a conventional predicament; instead, she adopts a conventionally masculine role by becoming someone's rescuer. When Ruth later loses her job as a governess and decides to become a nurse in the local hospital, she is also instrumental in rescuing her erstwhile lover. Here Gaskell returns to the Ophelia-like scene to emphasize Ruth's growth in subjectivity since her encounter with Bellingham, when she was merely the object of his desire. In his delirium, Bellingham sees her as the beautiful painting he created by the pond that day: "Where are the water-lilies? Where are the lilies in her hair?" he murmurs. Towering over him, Ruth asserts her subjectivity by becoming the subject rather than the object of the gaze: "[H]er looks were riveted on his softly-unclosing eyes, which met hers as they opened languidly ... She was held fast by that gaze of his, in which a faint recognition dawned, and grew in strength" (359). Though Ruth catches Bellingham's typhus and eventually dies, it is important to realize that she does not die as a victim but as a rescuer and a redeemer.

As in Ophelia's case, Gaskell reconstructs the literary Mariana and reframes the pictorial one. Our first encounter with Ruth, for instance, at two o'clock in the morning, occurs when her silent face is framed by "a window (through which the moonlight fell on her with the glory of many colours)" (4). Throughout the novel, Ruth, often framed by a window, gazes outside longing for the freedom the public sphere offers. In the beginning of the novel, for instance, while the other seamstresses admire the ball gown in progress, Ruth "sprang to the large old window, and pressed against it as a bird presses against the bars of its cage" (5). Like Tennyson's eponymous poem, Millais's *Mariana*, in spite of the unconventional touches, such as her sexuality in her tightly fitting strikingly blue dress, depicts a traditionally feminine predicament—the abandoned woman pining for her lover, longing for death rather than experiencing life on her own. Like Ruth, Millais's *Mariana*, as Rosenfeld points out in a recent interpretation of the painting, "is trapped within a space where nature is controlled and rendered artificial ... *caged* by casement and stained glass windows that afford a tantalizing view of an enclosed garden" (my italics 35). When the painting was first exhibited in 1851, the following lines from Tennyson's poem were printed in the catalog:

> She only said, 'My life is dreary,
> He cometh not,' she said:
> She said, 'I am aweary, aweary,
>   I would that I were dead!'

Ruth's despair, soon after she rejects Bellingham's marriage proposal on the beach at Abermouth, is articulated in words strikingly similar to those of Tennyson's "Mariana": "'I am so weary! I am so weary!' she moaned aloud at last. 'I wonder if I might stop here, and just die away'" (247). Gaskell echoes Tennyson's refrain only to underscore the difference between Mariana and Ruth. Unlike Tennyson's Mariana, who subsumes her individuality to a male figure, Ruth asserts her subjectivity in her encounter with Bellingham. Unlike Tennyson's Mariana, who would have rejoiced at her reunion with her lover, Ruth, in a rare moment in the novel, breaks her long held silence and eloquently articulates the repressed suffering she has experienced on her former lover's account:

> I do not love you. I did once. Don't say I did not love you then; but I do not now ... We are very far apart. The time that has pressed down my life like brands of hot iron, and scarred me for ever, has been nothing to you. You have talked of it with no sound of moaning in your voice—no shadow over the brightness of your face; it has left no sense of sin on your conscience, while me it haunts and haunts ... You shall have nothing to do with my boy, by my consent, much less by my agency. I would rather see him working on the roadside than leading such a life—being such a one as you are. (245)

Ruth's fiery assertion of her agency is a surprising repudiation of convention represented by both Tennyson and Millais. Furthermore, unlike her literary and pictorial counterparts, Ruth is not self-contained, enclosed in a cocoon of solipsistic despair. Her expansive personality is revealed in the scene when looking out the window she reiterates Mariana's wailing but is suddenly struck by the splendor of the sunset framed by her window, forgetting herself in the "sense of God's infinity," thus liberating herself from the constraints of self-pity, thus expanding outward rather than turning inward:

> Ruth forgot herself in looking at the gorgeous sight. She sat up gazing and, as she gazed, the tears dried on her cheeks and, somehow, all human care and sorrow were swallowed up in the unconscious sense of God's infinity. The sunset calmed her more than any words, however wise and tender, could have done. It even seemed to give her strength and courage. (247)

Thus Gaskell redraws her heroine in portraits similar to conventional literary and Pre-Raphaelite women, only to emphasize her difference and in the process offer possibilities to women who are "chained" by convention. It is as if she commended the Pre-Raphaelites for their efforts to represent literary heroines in unorthodox ways, but undermined them at the same time for promoting the restrictive boundaries of tradition.

If only for moments, Gaskell liberates Ruth from the chains of tradition. Even after the disclosure of the secret of her past, when Bradshaw ruthlessly turns her out of his house and she loses her job as a governess, Ruth does not wallow in despair or psychologically disintegrate, but channels her energy into her work at the local hospital. Thus Gaskell demonstrates that even a woman in Ruth's ostracized position can be empowered and become a social agent of change. Her work is finally recognized at Eccleston even by those who rejected her for her "sinful" past. One evening, walking by the hospital, her son Leonard, hitherto stigmatized and traumatized by his mother's transgression, overhears an old man's words celebrating Ruth's work: "Such a one as her has never been a great sinner; nor does she do her work as a penance, but for the love of God, and of the blessed Jesus. She will be in the light of God's countenance when you and I will be standing afar off" (346). His comments resonate in the crowd and generate more laudatory remarks by others who have also been moved by Ruth's selfless caring. As Katherine Inglis remarks in "Unimagined Communities and Disease in *Ruth*," "here Gaskell reveals the invisible network Ruth has circulated within, the scale and extent of her movements unknown until this moment, when typhus draws the community together" (79). Furthermore, by associating Ruth with "the light of God's countenance" in this scene and having Ruth utter "I see the Light coming" on her death bed the narrator transforms her into the light of the Eccleston world, possibly an implicit allusion to Hunt's celebrated *Light of the World* (1853–1854).

The Past in the Pre-Raphaelite Present Space of *Sylvia's Lovers*

Like *Ruth*, *Sylvia's Lovers* takes place in the temporally remote space of past historical events which shaped the lives of individuals excluded from traditional historiography. Gaskell's historical fiction, set in the Napoleonic wars, seeks significance in everyday experience, particularly in occasions of dissension and resistance to tradition; it records a multiplicity of voices traditionally excluded from monolithic histories. Yet various contemporaneous and modern critics have regarded the lag between the present and the past as one of the flaws of the novel that distances readers from identification with the fictional characters and events in the novel. *The Observer* on 1 March 1863, for instance, remarked: "A story of a country town in England, at the end of the last century, is like the story of a foreign place, so dissimilar is it to anything within our present knowledge." Referring to the atrocities of the press-gangs, the critic points out (missing entirely Gaskell's point about the cyclical rather than progressive nature of history): "we have so far improved since those days that we can read of such doings now as if they applied to Mexico and Tahiti" (Easson 440). Agreeing with this Victorian critic, Pettitt recently observes in a similar tone: "Gaskell's story is set at the uncomfortable semi-distance of two generations, making it difficult for her first readers to gauge the distance from the action of the novel; it was both near and far … The novel negotiates distances oddly and unevenly" (616–17).

Yet if we consider Gaskell's reconfigurations of Pre-Raphaelite paintings subtly embedded in the subtext of the novel, we become aware that she had foreseen such objections. As she interweaves the textual and the visual, Gaskell also bridges the fictional and the real, the past and the present. By alluding to works of Pre-Raphaelite art, Gaskell establishes "an imaginative space where the fictional world and the real world come together" (Byerly 121). Like Victorian readers, twenty-first-century ones may see in galleries the paintings which she reconfigures in this novel and thus experience the past in the present moment. Invested with the reader's own emotional response to the paintings, the present and the past are indelibly etched on the reader's imagination. Such readings are not merely aesthetic but rather sociopolitical experiences too, for they reveal Gaskell's subtle criticism of the disastrous consequences that restrictive gender boundaries may entail not only in the past but in the present as well. Gaskell's major theme in the novel, training her readers in new modes of perception, dovetails with one of the goals of Pre-Raphaelite art which made new demands on spectators, compelling them to see hitherto overlooked details, disturbing and subverting established gender and class constructs.

An early image of Sylvia at her cottage spinning with her mother calls attention not only to her "graceful figure," but also sets up a contextual interplay:

> the pretty sound of the buzzing, whirring motion, the attitude of the spinner, foot and hand alike engaged into the business … all make it into a picturesque piece of domestic business that may rival harp-playing any day for the amount of softness and grace which it calls out … The blue ribbon with which she had thought it necessary to tie back her hair before putting on her hat to go to market had got rather loose, and allowed her disarranged curls to stray in a manner which would have annoyed her extremely, if she had been upstairs to look at herself in the glass; but although they were not set in the exact fashion which Sylvia esteemed as correct, they looked very pretty and luxuriant. (42)

Depicted within the walls of domesticity, her luxuriant hair flowing freely, the image of Sylvia echoes the moment when the Lady of Shalott strays from her work, allows her gaze to enter the public sphere, and seeks freedom and death over the restraints of conventional gender boundaries which relegate her to the domestic sphere. But unlike the Lady of Shalott, who initiates an erotically visual interplay with Lancelot, Sylvia averts Philip's fixated gaze: "All this Philip could see; the greater part of her face was lost to him as she half averted it, with a shy dislike to the way in which she knew from past experience that cousin Philip always stared at her" (42). Sylvia's averted gaze in this scene strikingly resembles that of Elizabeth Siddall's drawing *The Lady of Shalott* (1853) (Figure 14.2), which art historians recognize as a distinct representation of the lady's legend from other numerous versions. As Cherry points out, "Siddall's image seems at odds with a central icon of nineteenth-century femininity … Siddall refutes the poem's narrative drive, providing instead a vision of artistic activity" (188). Unlike William Holman Hunt's famous picture (which began as an illustration of the poem in Moxon's edition of Tennyson's poetry) representing her entangled in the skein of her unraveling tapestry, Siddall's representation captures "the most significant moment … the one in which the Lady defies whatever authority is mysteriously controlling her actions" (Prettejohn 227). At this point in her young life, Sylvia, believing she is in control of her destiny, defies patriarchal authority, that is, the traditional expectation that she marry her cousin—"the curse." Even when she

Fig. 14.2   Elizabeth Siddall, "The Lady of Shalott," 1853. By permission of
               Bridgeman Art Library International, New York.

marries Philip later on, due to the horrendous events in her life—her father's
hanging and Kinraid's presumed death through Philip's lie—Sylvia desperately
fights "the curse" with her silent resistance to Philip's loving. When he reprimands
her for yet another walk by the seashore, sensing the intangible connection Sylvia
desperately tries to create with Kinraid, Sylvia calmly responds:

> "Philip, mother hadn't many more years to live; dunnot grieve her, and set
> her again' me by finding fault wi' me afore her. Our being wed were a great
> mistake" ... He almost shook her: she was half frightened by his vehemence of
> behaviour, which she took for pure anger, while it was the outburst of agonized
> and unrequited love. (367)

It is Philip then, not Sylvia (unlike the Lady of Shalott), who suffers from unrequited
love, though the loss of Kinraid destroys her emotional and psychological life, just
as Lancelot's indifference to the Lady of Shalott causes her demise.

Longing for escape from the smothering boundaries of domesticity, Sylvia
experiences momentary relief by the sea:

> she would sit down on a broken piece of rock, and fall to gazing on the advancing
> waves catching the sunlight on their crests, advancing receding, for ever and for
> ever, as they had done all her life long—as they did when she had walked with
> them that once by the side of Kinraid; those cruel waves that, forgetful of the

happy lovers' talk by the side of their waters, had carried one away, and drowned
him deep till he was dead. (359–60)

This scene is just but one of a series of seascapes with women waiting for the
return of those who may be lost at sea. Sylvia and Molly's carefree walk to the
market in the beginning of the novel, for instance, is interrupted by the sight of the
approaching *Resolution*, returning from Greenland with the whalers. Having been
gone for six months, the members of the crew are as apprehensive and impatient
to meet their families as their relatives on the shore: "no one knew what might
have happened. The crowd on shore grew silent and solemn before the dread of
the possible news of death that might toll in upon their hearts and this uprushing
tide" (19). Here the narrator focuses on the expectant and anxious crowd rather
than on the crew, just as Elizabeth Siddall focuses in *Ladies Lament* (1857) on
the women awaiting Spens and the Scottish King, who would be lost at sea. As
Rosenfeld, recently commenting on this watercolor, points out, "the amorphous
and imagined east coast of Scotland reflects their internal anguish" (75). Indeed, the
landscape in Siddall's watercolor resembles an early description of Monkshaven:
"high above the level of the sea towered the purple crags, whose summits were
crowned with greensward that stole down the sides of the scaur a little way in
grassy veins" (3). Huddled by a crag, the women in Siddall's watercolor await their
men in anguished expectation. Behind the crag, two other women are watching the
scene as Molly and Sylvia are watching the crowd waiting for the sailors' arrival.
In a letter to Rossetti in 1861, Gaskell is solicitous about Siddall's health (*Further
Letters* 221). And in April of the same year she writes to Charles Norton: "We
went to see Rossetti though; so prettily full of his wife [—] that Miss Syddall who
was partly his pupil & partly Mr. Ruskin's" (*Letters* 485). No doubt her visits to
Rossetti's studio would have given her the opportunity to view Siddall's works.

Rather than remaining passive spectators of the approaching ships, like the
women in Siddall's watercolor, Gaskell's women on the shore unite to bring in
a troubled ship which, in an attempt to save time on its journey, had taken the
inner channel and was caught in a raging storm. Sylvia joins the crowd and "in
an instant … it seemed as though she was holding fire in her bare palms … One
more great push and mighty strain and the danger was past; the vessel … was
in the harbour, among the lights and cheerful sounds of safety" (370–71). In her
reconfiguration of *Ladies Lament* then, Gaskell's empowers Siddall's helpless
women. Unbeknownst to Sylvia, Kinraid is aboard that ship; thus, in an interesting
gender role reversal, Sylvia becomes Kinraid's rescuer, reminiscent of such Pre-
Raphaelite women rescuing men as in Millais's *The Order of Release* or the
Proscribed Royalist. In an extraordinary, emotionally charged scene, no doubt one
of the most intensely poignant scenes in a Victorian novel, Sylvia sees Kinraid
the next day when she goes to her old home to gather tea leaves to soothe her
ailing mother:

"Sylvia!" He said, in a voice tremulous with joy and passionate love. "Sylvia!"
She looked round; he had turned a little, so that the light fell straight on his face.
It was bronzed, and the lines were strengthened; but it was the same face she

had last seen in Haytersbank gully three long years ago, and had never thought to see in life again. He was close to her and held out his fond arms; she went fluttering towards their embrace, as if drawn by the old fascination; but when she felt them close round her, she started away, and cried out with a great pitiful shriek, and put her hands up to her forehead as if trying to clear away some bewildering mist. (377)

Gaskell intensifies the following scenes by re-drawing one Pre-Raphaelite painting after another in a very short space. Stunned by the awareness of Philip's lie and the impossibility of an escape from her marriage, Sylvia runs away from Kinraid "and a mad notion flashed across her brain that she would go to the wide full river, and end the hopeless misery she felt enshrouding her" (378). By referring to Ophelia, once again Gaskell underscores her heroine's ability to reject a stereotypically feminine predicament. Instead, Sylvia breaks her long-held silence and articulates her fierce anger:

> "Philip," she said, "this is Kinraid come back again to wed me. He is alive; he has niver been dead, only taken by t' press-gang. And he says yo' saw it, and knew it all t' time. Speak, was it so?" … "Would God I were dead!" moaned forth the unhappy guilty man. (380–81)

Reminiscent of yet another Sylvia in *Valentine Rescuing Sylvia from Proteus* (Figure 14.3), Gaskell's redrawing of the painting represents Philip, like Proteus, as a "fallen man" (Prettejohn 211). Ruskin's description of the painting could also be that of Gaskell's scene, especially if we consider Sylvia's posture "on the ground, huddled up in a heap": "The action of Valentine, his arm thrown round Sylvia, and his hand clasping hers at the same instant as she falls at his feet, is most faithful and beautiful" (12: 324–5). Unlike Hunt's Sylvia, however, Gaskell's heroine does not remain passive but confronts the wrongdoer. And, in spite of her rage at the recognition of Philip's treachery, when Kinraid attempts to strike him, she prevents him, once again becoming a man's rescuer.

At the sound of her child's cry, Sylvia becomes conscious of her responsibility as a mother; at that moment she renounces Philip but simultaneously her chance at happiness: "I'll make my vow now, lest I lose mysel' again. I'll never forgive yon man, nor live with him as his wife again … I'm bound and tied, but I've sworn my oath to him as well as yo'" (383). Though Gaskell eventually draws our sympathy for Philip and has Sylvia forgive him by the end of the novel, it is Sylvia's harrowing victimization by Philip's lie that remains. It seems as if only for women in future generations does Gaskell foresee the possibility for escape from the restrictive, smothering social and cultural boundaries. Though her mother's life has been destroyed, Bella is given a chance at happiness through her emigration to the new world.

In her interpretation of Gaskell's fiction, Camus commends Gaskell on "her refusal of stereotypes … her ability to listen to and to sympathize with all the voices of womankind" (280). Sylvia is representative of Gaskell's other female

Fig. 14.3   William Holman Hunt, "Valentine Rescuing Sylvia from Proteus,"
1851. By permission of Bridgeman Art Library International, New
York.

characters who are not determined by "one event in their lives ... [but] are able
to change and grow" (100). The collision between silence and articulation,
poignantly expressed in *Ruth* and *Sylvia's Lovers*, remained a problem in Gaskell's
own private life as her letters, particularly those responding to hostile reviewers,
attest. Yet Gaskell's multivalent rhetoric invites us to explore the space that the
pictorial nuances of her discourse create, evoking the articulation of women's
subjectivity, the voice silenced in Pre-Raphaelite paintings and often stifled in
Victorian culture.

Works Cited

Camus, Marianne. *Women's Voices in the Fiction of Elizabeth Gaskell (1810–1865)*.
    Lewiston, NY: Edwin Mellen P, 2002. Print.
Cherry, Deborah. "Elizabeth Eleanor Siddall (1829–1862)." *The Cambridge
    Companion to the Pre-Raphaelites*. Ed. Elizabeth Prettejohn. New York:
    Cambridge UP, 2012. 183–95. Print.
d'Albertis, Deirdre. *Dissembling Fictions: Elizabeth Gaskell and the Victorian
    Social Text*. New York: St. Martin's P, 1997. Print.

Easson, Angus, Ed. *Elizabeth Gaskell: The Critical Heritage*. London: Routledge, 1991. Print.

Gaskell, Elizabeth. *The Letters of Mrs. Gaskell*. Ed. J.A.V. Chapple and Arthur Pollard. Manchester: Manchester UP, 1997. Print.

———. *Further Letters of Mrs Gaskell*. Ed. John Chapple and Alan Shelton. Manchester and New York: Manchester UP, 2000. Print.

———. *Ruth*. 1853. Ed. Tim Dolin. New York: Oxford UP, 2011. Print.

———. *Sylvia's Lovers*. 1863. Ed. Andrew Sanders. New York: Oxford UP, 1999. Print.

Heffernan, James. *Museum of Words: The Poetics of Ekphrasis from Homer to Ashbery*. Chicago, IL: U of Chicago P, 1994. Print.

Hughes, Linda and Michael Lund. *Victorian Publishing and Mrs. Gaskell's Work*. London: UP of Virginia, 1999. Print.

Inglis, Katherine. "Unimagined Community and Disease in *Ruth*." *Place and Progress in the Works of Elizabeth Gaskell*. Ed. Lesa Scholl, Emily Morris, and Sarina Gruver Moore. Burlington, VT: Ashgate, 2015. 67–82. Print.

Jaffe, Audrey. "*Cranford* and *Ruth*." *The Cambridge Companion to Elizabeth Gaskell*. Ed. Jill L. Matus. New York: Cambridge UP, 2007. 46–58. Print.

Marshall, Gail. *Victorian Fiction*. London: Arnold, 2002. Print.

Pettitt, Clare. "Time Lag and Elizabeth Gaskell's Transatlantic Imagination." *Victorian Studies* 54.4 (2012): 599–623. Print.

Prettejohn, Elizabeth. *The Art of the Pre-Raphaelites*. Princeton, NJ: Princeton UP, 2000. Print.

Rhodes, Kimberly. "Desperate Detail: John Everett Millais and Ophelia's 'Muddy Death.'" *John Everett Millais Beyond the Pre-Raphaelite Brotherhood*. Ed. Debra N. Mancoff. Studies in British Art 7. New Haven, CT: Yale UP, 2001. 43–68. Print.

Rosenfeld, Jason. "Elizabeth Siddall." *Pre-Raphaelites: Victorian Avant-Garde*. Ed. Tim Barringer, Jason Rosenfeld, and Alison Smith. Catalogue. London: Tate, 2012. 73–5. Print.

———. "John Everett Millais 1829–96. *Mariana*." *Pre-Raphaelites: Victorian Avant Garde*. 58. Print.

Rossetti, Dante Gabriel. *Collected Writings*. Ed. Jan Marsh. Chicago, IL: New Amsterdam Books, 2000. Print.

"Royal Academy." *Athenaeum* (7 May 1853): 581–3. Print.

Ruskin, John. *The Works of John Ruskin*. Ed. E.T. Cook and Alexander Wedderburn. Vol. 12. London: George Allen, 1903–1912. Print.

Schor, Hilary M. "The Plot of the Beautiful Ignoramus: *Ruth* and the Tradition of the Fallen Woman." *Sex and Death in Victorian Literature*. Ed. Regina Barreca. Bloomington, IN: Indiana UP, 1990. 158–77. Print.

Shuttleworth, Sally. "Natural History: The Retro-Victorian Novel." *The Third Culture: Literature and Science*. Ed. Elinor S. Schaffer. New York: De Gruyter, 1998. 253–68. Print.

Silkü, Rezzan Kocaöner. "Deviant Femininity as a Metaphor for Female Liberation in Elizabeth Gaskell's *Ruth*." *Elizabeth Gaskell: Victorian Culture and the Art of Fiction. Essays for the Bicentenary.* Ed. Sandro Jung. Lebanon, NH: UP of New England, 2010. 99–111. Print.

Smith, Alison. "Dante Gabriel Rossetti 1828–82." *Ecce Ancilla Domini (The Annunciation)* 1849–1850. *Pre-Raphaelites: Victorian Avant Garde.* Ed. Tim Barringer, Jason Rosenfeld, and Alison Smith. Catalogue. London: Tate, 2012. 89. Print.

Uglow, Jenny. *Elizabeth Gaskell: A Habit of Stories.* New York: Farrar Strauss, 1993. Print.

Chapter 15
"Look Back at Me":
The Material Re-Performance of the
Victorian in *North and South* (2004)[1]

Amy L. Montz

There is something intensely appealing about Elizabeth Gaskell for a twenty-first-century audience. Unlike Jane Austen's intra-social conflicts or the Brontë sisters' gothic interior struggles, Gaskell's characters develop through socioeconomic and geographic prejudice to arrive at an understanding of the world at large, and their place in it. *North and South* (1854–1855), perhaps the most traditionally romantic of her novels—with its quiet and strong-willed woman and its Byronic, quietly passionate man divided not only by situation, family, prejudice, and miscommunication but also by geographical misunderstandings themselves—offers the traditional happy ending that her other novels such as *Ruth* (1853) and even *Mary Barton* (1848) do not. Margaret Hale sacrifices little of herself, and John Thornton is a better person because of her. The couple seem to "get" each other in a way that comments on their success as a couple, and ultimately, the success of uniting North with South. They—and here, I am purposely ambiguous—have gone through trial and tribulation to arrive not only at happiness, but also at contentment and understanding. Happy endings, it seems, are what make *North and South* so popular.

Gaskell herself has become enormously popular over the last 10 years, in no small part thanks to BBC mini-series adaptations of her works. Typing "Elizabeth Gaskell" into YouTube, for example, yields over 5,000 hits, ranging from video clips from *Wives and Daughters* (1999), *Cranford* (2007), and *North and South* (2004) to tribute videos comparing the heroes of Austen to those of Gaskell, as well as musical videos of the characters in the television dramas created by what seem to be a large female teenage fan base. A survey of websites such as CafePress and Etsy reveals a wealth of fan-made material for purchase; one such CafePress store, "Swoonable Knits," offers shirts, coffee cups, and mouse pads declaring "I found my thrill at Marlborough Mills," "Thornton's Marlborough Mills: Quality English Soft Cotton," "The Helstone-Milton Line: fast travel, free biscuit,

---

[1]   This chapter was first presented at the Interdisciplinary Nineteenth-Century Studies Conference in Lexington, KY, in March 2012 on the panel (Re)Performing the Victorian. I am grateful to the comments from my panelists and the audience attendees who helped to shape the paper into this chapter. I will use *North and South* when referring to the novel, and *North and South* (2004) when referring to the BBC drama.

true love" (which, I must confess, I own in coffee mug form), and the ultimate challenge, "THORNTON > DARCY." Gaskell does not have the household name recognition of Charlotte Brontë or Jane Austen—two other writers whose works are broken down into consumable bites of popular culture—but if this growing market of consumable goods is any sign, she is well on her way.

One sign that Gaskell is becoming more popular to twenty-first-century audiences is the 2004 BBC mini-series *North and South*. As Gaskell's 1854–1855 novel is preoccupied with the differences between Northern and Southern England—the fictionalized Milton (Manchester) and Helstone (an idyllic Southern village)—so, too, is the 2004 mini-series obsessed with the differences between the nineteenth century and the subtext of the twenty-first. It is in this unseen twenty-first century and its understanding of the Victorian era that I argue true adaptation transpires. To fully create accessibility for a modern audience, this mini-series must create recognizable and familiar historical spaces. Significant scenes in *North and South* occur in areas visually recognizable as Victorian; the mill, the slums, the parlor, and the Great Exhibition allow for a recreation of the concerns of Gaskell's novel that do not alter a twenty-first-century audience's expectations. The televised mini-series therefore becomes not adaptation but rather recreation, striving to present the Victorian era through an attention to its accoutrements. Contemporary viewers understand the Victorian specifically through these material re-performances, which offer them a chance to "look back" at the Victorian era through the objects they themselves wish and expect to see. Focusing on the rewriting of three of the major thematic structures of Gaskell's novel—the consumption of Empire, the industrialization of England, and the romance between working-middle-class John Thornton and upper-middle-class Margaret Hale—I argue that the 2004 televised production of *North and South* re-performs the Victorian not through the characters and their lives, but rather through the proliferation of the material items that surround them. It therefore is Victorian not because of its source, but because of the materiality it exhibits, discusses, and, in the end, fetishizes.

The nineteenth century and the Victorian novel are no strangers to film, television, or even literary adaption. The growing field of Neo-Victorian studies examines not only how, but also why the Victorian era has appealed to contemporary audiences, and, more importantly, where the audiences insert themselves into the scene. Alexia L. Bowler and Jessica Cox argue that "film adaptations of Victorian fiction are nearly as old as cinema itself" (6), while critics such as Sharon Aronofsky Weltman, Katherine Byrne, and Chris Louttit discuss the proliferation of Victorian adaptation present in contemporary theater and television. Rachel Carroll's introduction to *Adaptation in Contemporary Culture: Textual Infidelities*, begins with the argument that "[a]ll adaptations express or address a desire to return to an 'original' textual encounter; as such, adaptations are perhaps symptomatic of a cultural compulsion to repeat" (14). She further argues that "[a] film or television adaptation of a prior cultural text—no matter how 'faithful' in intention or aesthetic—is inevitably an *interpretation* of that text: to this extent, every adaptation is an instance of textual *in*fidelity" (14).

Patsy Stoneman notes this same concern and begins her argument about the televised production of Gaskell's *Wives and Daughters* with the age-old question, "Was it faithful to the book?" and reminds us that "[s]uch discussions, however, quickly reveal widely different concepts of what 'faithfulness' entails" (85). We can ask ourselves the same question, but ultimately, we love period dramas because we love the period. The popularity of the Victorian is in no small part due to the drama we associate with the period's materiality. Fans cannot help but love presentations of rigid social customs highlighted by correspondingly rigid clothing; the corsets, crinolines, and cravats—the dreaded three C's of Victorian fashion—all present an understanding of a culture deeply repressed and confined by its own materiality. Yet recent work on Victorian textiles and fashion attempts to show that Victorian clothing was, in fact, just that: clothing.[2] One cannot ascribe will to a pair of pantyhose, for example, more than to a corset, yet modern society often insists on the corset's evils because it was an instrumental part of Victorian women's lives, those same women who were seemingly enslaved by their era and by their clothing. There is, ultimately, no way to separate gender politics from textile and fashion history, and we should not strive to do so. However, we must endeavor to understand how gender politics influenced and shaped textile and fashion history—and vice versa—and, most importantly, how our contemporary understanding of gender, fashion, and production shapes our understanding of the nineteenth century. Scripting these aspects of materiality for contemporary expectations rather than historical fact falls to the directors, designers, and actors.

Few signals of Victorian materiality are more epic than the Great Exhibition in 1851, itself a signal of Britain's might and strength in industry and commodity. Christoph Lindner notes that "[t]hough uncomfortably, the commodity sits at the very center of Gaskell's account of the industrial condition" (386), and, as Anne Longmuir argues, *North and South* itself is in no small part both about production *and* consumption. Longmuir notes that "[u]nderstanding the role of consumption in *North and South* therefore allows us to offer a more complex picture of female engagement with the public sphere in this novel. Importantly, Margaret Hale's relationship to the public sphere is riven [sic] by these two competing and contradictory understandings of the female shopper" (239). Nowhere is Gaskell's engagement with consumption seen more clearly than in Episode Three of the mini-series, when Margaret returns to London to visit with her aunt and cousin; accompanied by Henry Lennox, Margaret's would-be lover, the party visits the Great Exhibition to see the delights of the Empire laid before them. The first scene of the Exhibition is one of height, focusing on the glass-arched ceilings of the Crystal Palace, framed by exotic palm trees and more traditional black columns. As the camera pans down, people and the goods of the Empire become visible, and everyone and everything is lit by natural sunlight. No darkened mornings or sooty streets here, this is the pinnacle of Victorian achievement. A glass-top

---

[2] An interview with Valerie Steele conducted by *Collectors Weekly* goes far in revealing how normal and everyday corsets were for women of the nineteenth century. My 2011 article in *Neo-Victorian Studies* also discusses Steampunk and Neo-Victorian novels' reconstruction of Victorian women's clothing for contemporary audiences.

table reflects Aunt Shaw and Margaret just before the two women come into view. While Aunt Shaw complains of the exotic nature of the Exhibition, Margaret's smile and words declare it "wonderful" (Episode 3, Chapter 3) instead. When Margaret suggests, "It seems as though all the world is here for us to see," Henry's brother notes, "I was impressed by the machinery … I never realized the power and the money to be made from cotton" (Episode 3, Chapter 3). This revelation to the average Londoner—accused later of "dabbling" (Episode 3, Chapter 3) in cotton by John Thornton, who claims to be unable to think thus—suggests that perhaps there is more to domestic industry than first believed. Of course, Henry Lennox is keenly aware of Margaret's departure from the south of England and tells his brother, "We don't need heavy machinery to make money in London. Nor do we need to suffer the Northern climate" (Episode 3, Chapter 3). This pointed comment to Margaret forces her to admit, "It's true. The air is not so clean in Milton" (Episode 3, Chapter 3).

The contrast between North and South often is played through materiality in Gaskell's novel not only in the clothing the working class wears, but also through the goods offered in Milton. While the seat of industry, it cannot offer its middle-class citizens the same comforts they experience back in London. In Gaskell's novel, these trappings of Empire are best seen in Margaret's displaying and wearing of Indian shawls, both in the famous opening scene of the novel when she models cousin Edith's trousseau, and even in those scenes where she meets with Thornton, who upon first sight of Margaret notes that her dress "was very plain; a close straw bonnet of the best material and shape, trimmed with white ribbon; a dark silk gown, without any trimming or flounce; a large Indian shawl, which hung about her in long heavy folds, and which she wore as an empress wears her drapery" (62). While the Great Exhibition scene in the mini-series speaks of the goods of Empire, it emphasizes the manufacture of home, as John Thornton prophesizes, "If only there was a mechanism to enable us all to live together" (Episode 3, Chapter 3), North and South would live in harmony. Since there is not, he tells Henry Lennox, "You may enjoy the machinery like an exhibit in a zoo. I have to go and live with it" (Episode 3, Chapter 3). This scene is immediately followed by one of the reality of the production of those very goods on display—complete with men carrying plain wrapped packages of fabric to waiting platforms, ready to be distributed, and Mrs. Thornton walking through the dirty mill yard—which emphasizes how much the North must live with the machinery the South depends on for goods.

Set against the backdrop of Marlborough Mill, a fictionalized yet representative industrial center of England's cotton production, Gaskell's *North and South* is fully invested in production and consumption. It is no accident, then, that the popularity of the BBC mini-series would spark the production and consumption not only of Gaskell, but also of the materiality of the Victorian era itself.[3] David Kelly and

---

[3]   The televised mini-series of Elizabeth Gaskell's novels *North and South*, *Wives and Daughters*, and *Cranford* were wildly popular in the US and the UK, and several articles on Gaskell and adaptation have been written in which the books' translations into mini-series are discussed at great length. Katherine Byrne's article "'Such a fine, close weave':

Margaret Harris look specifically at *North and South* (2004), from a cinematic and a literary scholarly perspective respectively, and Harris in particular examines how the mini-series helps viewers understand the Victorian era. She argues that the Great Exhibition scene of *North and South* was "an inspiration" on the part of the screenwriter, as it is "invoking significant Victorian iconography. It provides an opportunity for the characters from the South to experience manufactures at first hand—and to modify their perceptions in light of what they see" (75–6). The novel—and subsequently, its mini-series adaptation—is obsessed with the presentation of difference, particularly how that difference is articulated through materiality. At the heart of *North and South* is a dichotomy that Margaret Harris notes, "whether on screen or between covers, [*North and South*] is driven by the dialogue of two cultures and two ways of life" (68), as well as a larger purpose of materiality.

Industry, of course, remains the center of that production, and whether in the novel or in the mini-series, few if any of Margaret's encounters with Marlborough Mills end well. At the end of the first episode of the mini-series, Margaret writes a letter to Cousin Edith in which she tries to explain her discomfort and loneliness. As she rests at a desk, quill in hand and cheek pressed against paper, the words of her letter are spoken over the subsequent scenes. Margaret writes, "How lonely I am. How cold and harsh it is here" (Episode 1, Chapter 8). But when she notes that "everywhere there is conflict and unkindness" (Episode 1, Chapter 8), the scene changes from an exhausted Margaret to the mill, men and women working the looms while puffs of white cotton float in the air, like snow, a suggestive threat of the material that causes Bessy Higgins's death. The faces of the workers are nearly obscured by the flying cotton, and the uniformity with which they work the machinery contrasts sharply with the sunlit gardens and lazy afternoons Margaret experiences at the beginning of the series, back at home. "I think God has forsaken this place" (Episode 1, Chapter 8), Margaret says as the camera closes in to detail the size of the cotton fragments, emphasizing the inability of any living thing inside the mill to escape them. "I believe I've seen hell. It's white. It's snow white" (Episode 1, Chapter 8). At this moment, the music swells and John Thornton appears in the background, a sinister but brooding Lucifer overseeing his human hell. He is in profile, dark suit made darker by the white of the cotton in the air and comprising his stark shirt and collar. Shadows darken his profile and the camera follows him until the screen goes black.

This presentation of Marlborough Mills directly contrasts with twenty-first-century expectations for nineteenth-century industry, as contemporary audiences expect William Blake's "dark satanic mills" rather than a "snow white" hell. Sarah Wootton notes that in this moment, "Thornton now resembles a devil presiding over his satanic mill" (32). Even Margaret's first glimpse of mills in

---

Gender, Community and the Body in *Cranford*' (2007) argues that these mini-series have "established, or [are] perhaps still establishing, Gaskell as a canonical author" even though they "still seem to be critically neglected by adaptation scholars" (44–5). Of particular import to Byrne is the translation of the concerns of age and community, two major themes in Gaskell's novel.

the novel show them darkening the landscape: "Here and there a great oblong many-windowed factory stood up, like a hen among her chickens, puffing out black 'unparliamentary' smoke, and sufficiently accounting for the cloud which Margaret had taken to foretell rain" (59). The Thorntons' home, so close to the factory, was itself "blackened, to be sure, by the smoke" (111). The expected darkness is in this moment seen instead in the human industry, the laboring workers who are endangered by the work they perform and the conditions of the mill. The danger for the average middle-class Victorian may be the smoke and soot of the nearby working mills, but for the working-class citizen, the dangers are irrevocably the cotton fragments floating everywhere, breathed into lungs. The workers in the scene wear un-dyed cotton, rough woven and simple, when compared to Thornton's impeccable middle-class suit. The loudness of the mill itself, in Gaskell's novel, can be heard by Margaret even outside the "immense, many-windowed mill, whence proceeded the continual clank of machinery and the long groaning roar of the steam-engine, enough to deafen those who lived within the enclosure" (111). In the "snow white hell" scene of the mini-series, however, the clank of the mill is hidden instead by the swelling music, entreating pathos in the viewer as we watch the young, poor workers overseen by their rich employer who, as Margaret Harris argues, is played by Richard Armitage as "Thornton as Heathcliff"; she notes, "there is something Brontë-esque in Armitage's brooding expressions and projection of barely controlled violence" (72). This addition of a Byronic tone to Thornton lends to the overall dangerousness and sexiness of his presentation, overall, leading even more, perhaps, to the attractiveness of the mini-series to a contemporary fan base.[4] Lesa Scholl's chapter "Moving Between North and South: Cultural Signs and the Progress of Modernity in Elizabeth Gaskell's Novel," in this collection, notes another "sexy" moment in Gaskell's original novel in which Margaret shakes Thornton's hand. Scholl notes that "[a]lthough Margaret is oblivious to the significance of the moment, Thornton is very aware that this is the first time their hands have touched" (102). This awareness of bodies, of bodies moving in spaces coded as untouchable, becomes for the *North and South* 2004 adaptation essential to its portrayal of the nineteenth century.

Three scenes from the 2004 mini-series rewrite major themes of Gaskell's 1855 novel for visual effect and contemporary understanding: the Great Exhibition for Gaskell's discussion of the consumption of Empire, the mill for Gaskell's presentation of the increasing industrialization of England, and Margaret's taking leave of Milton for the seemingly desperate, unrequited love Thornton feels for Margaret. These three scenes have no actual corresponding scene in Gaskell's novel, and they approach the thematic structure abstractly rather than concretely. However, we can see these parallels within key scenes in Gaskell's

---

[4]   Sarah Wootton argues, "[y]et although Thornton's lack of pretension and absence of guilt mark significant departures from the customary Byronic traits, there are many significant parallels. His physical prowess, dark hair and pale, marble features are directly descended from portraits of Byron and illustrations of his protagonists" (31).

novel: Margaret's modeling of the Indian shawls in Chapter 1, the discussion of Milton's soot and dirt in Chapters 10 and 15, and Margaret's departure from Milton in Chapter 18. For the purposes of the final part of this chapter, I wish to focus specifically on Margaret's departure, as it is both the inspiration for this chapter and is a scene lovingly reposted on popular video blogs. This scene, with its intensity of emotion, the dark, smoldering eyes of Richard Armitage, and—it is fair to say—its sexiness, is the scene most distributed by amateur fans.

After the deaths of her mother and her father, Margaret is collected from Milton by her Aunt Shaw to return to southern England: to home. Brooding over his love for Margaret, her rejection of his marriage proposal, and the identity of the mysterious man he saw Margaret with at the train station, Thornton watches as she leaves, seemingly for the last time. The majority of the scene focuses not on Thornton's emotions but rather on the details surrounding him: Milton's sooty streets, the dangerous cotton mill, and Margaret's sweeping skirts. The scene begins with funereal music, a dirge to reflect Margaret's departure as well as the loss of her father. Margaret's face is framed with white lace around the black mourning bonnet and veil, and when she steps into the carriage, we see Thornton through the carriage door and window, as if framed. This framing continues as the carriage door closes on Margaret and the camera moves behind Thornton's shoulder. He, too, is framed, not by the material trappings of Victorian social mourning customs and the intense fashion restrictions that come with it—Margaret's veil, while somber, is fashionable and frames her face beautifully—but rather by the trappings of industry that produces the very materiality worn by Victorian female bodies. He stands overlooking the Mill yard, positioned above Margaret so that he looks down upon her. He is to the left of the frame, the carriage and rider in the middle, and the large Mill door to the right. The swirling snow coats everything in white, hearkening back to Margaret's initial definition of England's industry as a hell that is "snow white." This hell, which has kept Thornton and Margaret apart again and again, is what takes her away from him once more. When the carriage begins to move, we hear but do not see Thornton demand that Margaret "look back" (Episode 4, Chapter 5). When Thornton demands "look back at me" (Episode 4, Chapter 5), the camera frames him again, his face expressing the seriousness of his plea as it is contrasted against his dark yet fashionable cravat and the whiteness of his shirt. Margaret, of course, does not "look back" at him, but the audience cannot do anything but, as the camera remains on Thornton's face for the duration of the scene.

This demand—"look back at me"—becomes with the camera's new focus an audience imperative that connects the historical with the material; while the audience sees the historical divisions keeping the couple apart, it is all framed within a material context beginning and ending, always, with the mill. But it also represents the demand of the audience, as we desire the Victorian era to "look back" at us with familiar and desiring eyes. Our concerns were its concerns; our loves were its loves. If Victorian novels do not reflect that which we most desire to see, then we can recreate them in our own image. Yet it is not that simple—if, indeed, such a demand could be seen as "simple"—in a mini-series that allows for if not historical *accuracy* then at least historical *familiarity*. *North and South* (2004) is not a costume drama with twenty-first-century heroines inserted. Never does Margaret wear pants, argue for the vote, smoke cigarettes, or any other dastardly deed associated with New Women of the nineteenth- and twenty-first-century varieties. In fact, Margaret and Thornton behave much as their literary originals do: as characters, caught in desperate and undesirable circumstances, falling in love despite themselves, their classes, their societies, and their families. England would separate them by region; renewed finances and idealism bring them together in the novel, and the modern technological marvel, the train, brings them back together in the mini-series.

But the materiality associated with the novel, re-performed by the mini-series, and re-created again by fans argues for a deeper material connection to the Victorian era than perhaps we are willing to believe, in our corset-, crinoline-, and cravat-less age. The revival of Victorian garments seen in the Steampunk subculture and in Neo-Victorian novels, or suggested in haute couture's nouveau-bustles and that damning phrase, the "New Victorians," is matched only by our contemporary concerns of industrialized cities, diminishing resources, and persons separated by creed, by geography, by socioeconomic distinction. The scene most contemporary in our eyes is the final scene, when Thornton and Margaret meet by chance at the train station and mutually declare their love. Margaret Harris notes that "[t]he closing sequence is Welch's most radical and most disconcerting change. It makes sense in terms of the adaptation but violated my sense of Victorian propriety" (77). My sense of Victorian propriety, too, was for a moment violated by this very non-Victorian recreation of the Victorian novel. As Thornton kisses Margaret, in public, those familiar with the Victorian era might gasp our gasp of scandal, until we remember how Gaskell ends her novel:

> "You must give them to me," she said, trying to take [the roses] out of his hand with gentle violence.
>
> "Very well. Only you must pay me for them!"
>
> "How shall I ever tell Aunt Shaw?" she whispered, after *some time of delicious silence.* (436, emphasis added)

That delicious silence is perhaps not as visibly sexy as Thornton's smoldering eyes or casual kisses on a train platform, but it is in and of itself full of tangible reality: the "delicious silence" slyly tells us how the two lovers did manage to pass that lengthy period of "some time" while alone, together, at last. For this reason, we see material tributes not only to the 2004 *North and South* adaptation in contemporary materiality, but also to Elizabeth Gaskell herself. While we cannot help but acknowledge the attraction of materiality in bringing audiences to adaptations of Victorian novels, we also cannot help but acknowledge the attraction of the novels themselves in maintaining the audiences, and offering further performances—and re-performances—of the Victorian era.

Works Cited

Blake, William. "Milton." Copy A, Object 2, 1811 (British Museum). *Blakearchive.org.* 2008. Web. 4 March 2012.

Bowler, Alexia K. and Jessica Cox. "Introduction to Adapting the Nineteenth Century: Revisiting, Revising and Rewriting the Past." *Neo-Victorian Studies* 2.2 (2009/2010): 1–17. Print.

Byrne, Katherine. "'Such a fine, close weave': Gender, Community and the Body in *Cranford* (2007)." *Neo-Victorian Studies* 2.2 (2009/2010): 43–64. Print.

Carroll, Rachel. "Introduction: Textual Infidelities." *Adaptation in Contemporary Culture: Textual Infidelities.* Ed. Rachel Carroll. London: Continuum, 2009. 1–7. Print.

Gaskell, Elizabeth. *North and South.* 1855. Ed. Angus Easson. Oxford: Oxford UP, 2008. Print.

Harris, Margaret. "Taking Bearings: Elizabeth Gaskell's *North and South* Televised." *Sydney Studies in English* 32 (2006): 65–82. Print.

Hix, Lisa. "Everything You Know About Corsets Is False." *Collectors Weekly.* Market Street Media, LLC. Web. 17 January 2012.

Kelly, David. "In Its Own Light: A View of *North and South.*" *Sydney Studies in English* 32 (2006): 83–96. Print.

Lindner, Christoph. "Outside Looking In: Material Culture in Gaskell's Industrial Novels." *Orbis Litterarum* 55 (2000): 379–96. Print.

Longmuir, Anne. "Consuming Subjects: Women and the Market in Elizabeth Gaskell's *North and South.*" *Nineteenth-Century Contexts* 34.3 (2012): 237–52. Print.

Louttit, Chris. "*Cranford,* Popular Culture, and the Politics of Adapting the Victorian Novel for Television." *Adaptation: The Journal of Literature on Screen Studies* 2.1 (2009): 34–48. Print.

Montz, Amy L. "'In Which Parasols Prove Useful': Neo-Victorian Rewriting of Victorian Materiality." *Neo-Victorian Studies* 4.1 (2011): 100–18. Print.

North and South. Dir. Brian Percival. Perf. Daniela Denby-Ashe, Richard Armitage, Sinead Cusack. Warner Brothers, BBC Video, 2004. Film.

Scholl, Lesa. "Moving Between *North and South*: Cultural Signs and the Progress of Modernity in Elizabeth Gaskell's Novel." *Place and Progress in the Works of Elizabeth Gaskell.* Ed. Lesa Scholl, Emily Morris, and Sarina Gruver Moore. Burlington, VT: Ashgate, 2015. 95–106. Print.

Stoneman, Patsy. "*Wives and Daughters* on Television." *The Gaskell Society Journal* 14.1 (2000): 85–100. Print.

"Swoonable Knits." CafePress.com. Café Press. n.d. Web. 19 February 2012.

Weltman, Sharon Aronofsky. "Victorians on the Contemporary Stage." *Journal of Victorian Culture* 13.2 (2008): 303–9. Print.

Wootton, Sarah. "The Changing Faces of the Byronic Hero in *Middlemarch* and *North and South.*" *Romanticism* 14.1 (2008): 25–35. Print.

Conclusion
Gaskellian Prospects

Emily Morris, Sarina Gruver Moore, and Lesa Scholl

In an early letter composed while visiting her maternal relatives, Gaskell writes to her sister-in-law: "I wish I could paint my present situation to you" (*Letters of Mrs. Gaskell* 4). She describes her location with all the evocative power of the future novelist:

> Fancy me sitting in an old fashioned parlour, "doors & windows opened wide", with casement windows opening into a sunny court all filled with flowers which scent the air with their fragrance—in the very depth of the country—5 miles from the least approach to a town—the song of birds, the hum of insects the lowing of cattle the only sounds—and such pretty fields & woods all round. (4)

If her dashes and italics and exclamation points are here tumbling over themselves in an excess of interjectory pleasure, it is because all of her life Gaskell will feel at home in the country: a place of welcoming woods, thick cream, baby pigs, and fields "gay with bright spring flowers—daisies, primroses, wild anemones, & the 'lesser celandine,' & with lambs all around" (4). At the end of the letter, 26-year-old Elizabeth, young mother and unpublished writer, speculates for a moment: "Oh! That Life would make a stand-still in this happy place?" (4). But the interrogatory nature of that speculation implies the inevitable answer: neither people nor places stand still in time. Gaskell will return to spend most of her life in "misty foggy Manchester, which gives [her] a perpetual headache very hard to bear" (*Letters* 453), but she will continue throughout her life, letters, and literary works to negotiate and investigate the equation of pleasure, health, and happiness with place.

Gaskell's dream of rural simplicity as happiness is repeated throughout her letters, but a more complicated narrative of the relationship between place and person finds voice in her analysis of another woman writer's life. In *Writing A Woman's Life*, Carolyn Heilbrun argues that "women have been deprived of the narratives, or the texts, plots, or examples, by which they might assume power over—take control of—their own lives" (17), and she demonstrates the means by which biography-writing becomes a new geography of the female authorial soul. In *The Life of Charlotte Brontë* (1857), Gaskell portrays Haworth village, moors, and parsonage as bleak, rough, and uncivilized—necessarily formative of the sometimes violent, always Romantic fictional world of the Brontës. Gaskell's argument has been thoroughly critiqued by writers such as Lucasta Miller and

Juliet Barker, among others,[1] who argue that Gaskell uses place as a convenient way to *displace* the unladylike passions in the Brontës' works in order to reclaim Charlotte's reputation as a woman as well as a writer. Heilbrun similarly suggests that "Gaskell restored Brontë to the safety of womanliness," her inner geography remapped, as it were, in the biographical landscape (22). But in Gaskell's role as biographer, she also uses the connections between health, happiness, and physical location to claim freedoms and privileges. Place might be a convenient excuse for unwomanly writing—"the heath made me do it!"—but an emphasis on place also allows for the re-feminization of human and historical geography, a re-scripting of women into the landscape, women who, in turn, script new modes of literary and professional being.

An example of Gaskell's use of geography as a conspicuous factor in health and well-being can be found in her account of Charlotte's resignation from teaching at her friend Miss Wooler's school, which becomes a physical threat to her health:

> Miss Wooler removed her school from the fine, open, breezy situation of Roe Head, to Dewsbury Moor, only two or three miles distant. Her new residence was a much lower site, and the air much less pure and exhilarating to one bred at the wild hill-village of Haworth. Charlotte felt the change extremely. (165)

Charlotte gives up her job at Dewsbury, and Gaskell insists it is a necessary change because Charlotte's physical surroundings have a deleterious effect on both her physical and mental state. Calling her "Brave heart, ready to die in harness," Gaskell notes that it is only "through Miss Wooler's entreaty" that a doctor's advice is sought, and that his prescription is that "the soft summer air, blowing round her home, the sweet company of those she loved, the release, the freedom of life in her own family, were needed, to save either reason or life" (182). Charlotte is excused for putting down the burden of teaching, because, as Gaskell builds up to phrasing it, "One higher than she had over-ruled that for a time she might relax her strain" (182). The physical location of Dewsbury, its low site and impure air, is crucially presented as a site-specific cause of Charlotte's illness—this is place as adversary. By contrast, the (perceived) purer, cleaner windy hilltop of Haworth provides a place of possibility—of renewed health; of divinely sanctioned rest; of a fuller, richer personhood. The Doctor's advice is presented as a similar mixture of causes and cures—Charlotte needs both the emotional familiarity and comfort of her family and also the breezes that blow in the place where she was raised in order to save her sanity, or perhaps even her life. In the letter from which Gaskell draws this information, however, Charlotte puts the case thus: "My health and spirits had utterly failed me, and the medical man whom I consulted enjoined me, as I valued my life, to go home" (183). Charlotte's own account does not

---

[1]   See Miller's *The Brontë Myth* and Barker's "The Haworth Context." Both point out how very different Gaskell's presentation of the place is both from reality and from Brontë's own perceptions of it, although others have noted that what Brontë perceived and what she shared with Gaskell may have been quite different. See for example Frances Twinn's "The Portrait of Haworth in *The Life of Charlotte Brontë*."

create the same emphasis on the importance of the physical locations of Haworth and Dewsbury as does Gaskell's. But for the bifocalized Gaskell (to use Julia McCord Chavez's conceit)—country girl and urban minster's wife; homemaker of ordinary, daily tasks and world-builder of imaginative texts; international traveler and "provincial" novelist—physical location as an irrefutable rationale for a change in lifestyle, a change that might otherwise be interpreted as unnecessary, whimsical, or a shirking of duty, is compelling logic.

While Gaskell did not write her own biography, she did leave a further sense of the importance of choosing, even embracing a place in her final letters and actions. At the peak of her career, after her daughters were grown and right before her own unexpectedly early death, Gaskell managed what she calls "a terribly grand thing" (*Letters* 774); she bought a house in the "middle of a pretty rural village" (775). Her plan was that she and her husband would retire there, and that the house would be a home for the two daughters who were not married and did not seem likely to be. One can imagine, as Gaskell contemplated the rural home she was able to gain through her own means, her satisfaction in achieving that pastoral dream that she wrote about to her sister-in-law so many years before. The Gaskells had spent many years in Manchester because of William Gaskell's work as a minister there, work that Elizabeth speaks of as important, especially in terms of social duty. However, her decision to buy the Holybourne house once she had the financial means to do so suggests that she always held on to that ideal of the happy rural home. Gaskell's representation of the inextricability of health and happiness from place in Bronte's life is perhaps reflective of her own sometime frustration with sooty Manchester, a place in which she stayed in deference to William's pastoral (in a very different sense) work and calling. Throughout *The Life*, Gaskell repeatedly sets up the same division between duty and staying, versus health and leaving. In the tensions manifested in Gaskell's own life and in her perspective on Brontë's domestic and professional duties, the ability to leave one place in exchange for another, either temporarily or permanently, is invaluable to the "architecture of identity" (Tange 3). Where one is and where one wants to be plays an important role in who one is and who one can be.

As the sesquicentennial of Gaskell's death approaches; as the Gaskells' Manchester home, Plymouth Grove, is renovated and reopened to the public; as Elizabeth Gaskell's presence in popular culture and in digital environments continues to grow, we might ask what Gaskellian prospects are yet on the horizon. The essays in this collection, through engaging Gaskell's complex understanding and representation of the intersections between place and progress, each suggest the relevance of that voice 150 years after her death, as we seek new kinds of freedoms, identities, and homes in the new technological and imaginative landscapes of online places and in the increasingly globalized notions of who and where we are. Susan Hamilton's assessment that "Gaskell now 'holds her own' in new places, for new audiences, and in different ways" is surely right (190), and there is no way to predict what "new Gaskells" will emerge as new generations encounter her voice.

Works Cited

Barker, Juliet. "The Haworth Context." *The Cambridge Companion to the Brontës.* Ed. Heather Glen. Cambridge: Cambridge UP, 2002. 13–33. Print.

Gaskell, Elizabeth. *The Letters of Mrs Gaskell.* Ed. J.A.V. Chapple and Arthur Pollard. Manchester: Manchester UP, 1966. Print.

———. *The Life of Charlotte Brontë.* Ed. Alan Shelston. Markham Ontario: Penguin, 1975. Print.

Hamilton, Susan. "Gaskell Then and Now." *The Cambridge Companion to Elizabeth Gaskell.* Ed. Jill L. Matus. Cambridge: Cambridge UP, 2007. Print.

Heilbrun, Carolyn. *Writing A Woman's Life.* New York: Ballantine, 1988. Print.

Miller, Lucasta. *The Brontë Myth.* London: Jonathan Cape, 2001. Print.

Tange, Andrea Kaston. *Architectural Identities: Domesticity, Literature, and the Victorian Middle Class.* Toronto: U of Toronto P, 2010. Print.

Twinn, Frances. "The Portrait of Haworth in *The Life of Charlotte Brontë.*" *Brontë Studies* 30.2 (2005): 151–61. Print.

Index